THE
ISIAH THOMAS
STORY

THE
ISIAH THOMAS
STORY

FROM THE BACK COURT
TO THE FRONT OFFICE

PAUL CHALLEN

ECW Press

Published by ECW Press
2120 Queen Street East, Suite 200, Toronto, Ontario, Canada M4E 1E2

NATIONAL LIBRARY OF CANADA CATALOGUING IN PUBLICATION DATA

Challen, Paul, 1967–
From the back court to the front office : The Isiah Thomas story.

Previously published under the title: The book of Isiah.
ISBN 1-55022-662-2

1. Thomas, Isiah, 1961- 2. Basketball players—United States—
Biography. I. Challen, Paul, 1967– . II. Title.

GV.884.T47C42 2004   796.323'092   C2004-902549-X

Cover and Text Design: Tania Craan
Cover Photo: © Mike Segar/Reuters Newmedia Inc/Corbis/MAGMA
Typesetting: Wiesia Kolasinska
Printing: St. Joseph's Print Group

This book is set in Minion and Eurostile.

DISTRIBUTION
CANADA: Jaguar Book Group, 100 Armstrong Ave., Georgetown, ON L7G 5S4
USA: Independent Publishers Group, 814 North Franklin Street,
Chicago, IL 60610

PRINTED AND BOUND IN CANADA

ECW PRESS
ecwpress.com

The author would like to thank the following people: Jack David and Bob Pipe of ECW PRESS; John Kernaghan of the *Hamilton Spectator*; Chris Young of the *Toronto Star*; Bradley D. Cook of the Indiana University Archives; Jon Churchill and Kim Pickett of the Serials Department, Mills Memorial Library, McMaster University; Rose Ann McKean of the *Detroit Free Press* Photo Reprint Sales Department; the staff of the Media Relations Office, Department of Intercollegiate Athletics, Indiana University; Mrs. J. Bradshaw of the *Toronto Star* Photo Syndicate; Tor Lukasik-Foss for his advice; the Challen and Belzak families for their support; and most of all, my wife Janine Belzak and our son Sam for their patience and guidance.

In the photo section, top photo on p. 1 by K. Berty, courtesy of the *Toronto Star*; Indiana University photos on pp. 1–2 courtesy of Hoosier Basketball; Detroit Piston photos on p. 3 by William Archie, courtesy of the *Detroit Free Press*; photo of Magic Johnson and Isiah Thomas on p. 4 by Ron Brenne, courtesy of The Bettmann Archive; bottom photo on p. 4 by D. Lock, courtesy of the *Toronto Star*; top photo on p. 5 by B. Spremo, courtesy of the *Toronto Star*; bottom photo on p. 5 by M. Stuparyk, courtesy of the *Toronto Star*; top photo on p. 6 by R. Eglinton, courtesy of the *Toronto Star*; bottom photo on p. 6 by T. Bock, courtesy of the *Toronto Star*; top photo on p. 7 by Veronica Henri, courtesy of Canada Wide Feature Services; bottom photo on p. 7 by Craig Robertson, courtesy of Canada Wide Feature Services; top photo on p. 8 by R. Lautens, courtesy of the *Toronto Star*; bottom photo on p. 8 by Veronica Henri, courtesy of Canada Wide Feature Services.

TABLE OF CONTENTS

CHAPTER ONE

The Floor General

Wednesday June 26, 1996, had been a pretty good day in the life of Isiah Lord Thomas III. As Executive Vice-President of Basketball Operations (better known as General Manager, or simply "GM") of the fledgling Toronto Raptors, Thomas was working the third floor of Wayne Gretzky's restaurant in  downtown Toronto, just blocks away from SkyDome where the Raptors play their home games. Isiah, along with a bevy of Raptors' personnel and the usual flock of press, radio, and TV people, had converged on Gretzky's to watch live coverage of the NBA Draft from the Continental Airlines Arena at the Meadowlands in East Rutherford, New Jersey. The Raptors, preparing for their second NBA season in 1996–97, had lucked out by obtaining the second pick overall in this yearly selection of the cream of the U.S. college basketball crop. In fact, since a league rule prohibited the Raptors and the Vancouver

Grizzlies (the two NBA expansion franchises that entered the league in 1995–96) from selecting first, the second pick was the best possible draft position. It essentially meant that Toronto would be able to select and sign a bona fide college superstar — the kind of player that can go along way toward turning a young franchise around immediately. Just picture the Bulls before Michael Jordan. What about the Orlando Magic without Shaq? Heck, even the Cavaliers before LeBron James? Exactly. That kind of player was now about to become a Raptor.

Draft day 1996 was something of a triumphal homecoming for Thomas. At the previous year's draft, he had made what was the first major move to directly affect the Raptors' on-court presence. Isiah had selected Damon Stoudamire from the University of Arizona in the first round. Stoudamire, a super-quick point guard, is now listed at 5–10 in the Raptors' program, but he's almost certainly smaller than that (he's admitted to being 5–9). There was in fact nothing wrong with Stoudamire as a player. His stats as a Wildcat had been impressive, and his ability to dish out assists, run the offense, score, and play defence, had definitely been proven at the college level, where he led Arizona in the tough PAC 10 Conference. But what was Thomas thinking? Why waste a draft pick on a point guard, especially when Toronto had already chosen two men at the position — veteran B.J. Armstrong and the younger but talented B.J. Tyler — in the expansion draft? A first-year club being led by a diminutive, unproven rookie? Didn't Thomas remember how tough it had been to play point guard with the big boys, especially for a player unaccustomed to the bigger, faster, and meaner world of big time hoops? After all, Thomas' 13 years as a point guard in the NBA with the Detroit Pistons must have taught him something about the position, and about playing the part of floor general. Hadn't the guy been an All-Star guard himself, twelve years in a row?

The NBA had cleverly awarded the actual draft-day proceedings to Toronto in 1995, in a move designed to stir up fan interest in one of the league's new Canadian cities. This move certainly seemed to have succeeded as far as excitement went. Over 20,000 people showed up at SkyDome on June 28 to watch the proceedings, but the hype that the NBA had been hoping to generate was quickly turning into the wrong kind. Fans who had chanted "We Want Ed" in favor of the Raptors picking UCLA superstar Ed O'Bannon, a whippet-quick leaper who had carried the Bruins to the previous season's NCAA title, suddenly erupted in raucous boos when the Stoudamire pick was announced. Stoudamire met the catcalls with class, smiling and saying all the right things: how he would try to do his best to lead the Raptors in the upcoming season, and how he "hoped to get a lot of advice from Isiah" about being a point guard in the NBA. "By the time I'm finished playing ball," he promised, "they'll know who Damon Stoudamire is." For his part, Thomas would only flash his characteristic grin, and punctuate his comments about how he believed Stoudamire would contribute to the team right away with a sly smile that seemed to say, "Wait and see, wait and see . . ."

That was the 1995 draft. Isiah's hoops judgment had been proven infallible regarding his selection of Stoudamire during the 1995–96 season, just as it had so many times on the court during his playing career. Damon repaid his gm's confidence in him by completely running away with NBA Rookie of the Year honors. He earned the award after putting together an amazing season in which he recorded 37 double-doubles, 37 20-point games, and 36 10-assist games. In addition, Damon set an NBA record for rookies with 133 3-point shots made, and was the MVP of the All-Star Rookie Game. At many times during the Raptors' first campaign, it looked as though Stoudamire was single-handedly carrying the team — exactly what an NBA point guard is supposed to do. Now, when it came time for the 1996 Draft, there would be no questioning Isiah Thomas' ability to look at a player fresh out of college and say, "This is a guy who is going to succeed when the going gets tough and the bodies start banging. This is the player we want!"

In fact, people around the league did start treating Thomas' pronouncements on matters draft-related like sacred gems of wisdom. In the months preceding Draft Day, Toronto basketball writers, needing to fill the void created by the end of the Raptors' first year and the near-boredom produced by the Chicago Bulls' unchallenged romp through the playoffs, began to write "Isiah speculates" and "Isiah might pick so-and-so" articles to drum up interest in the upcoming draft. At first, Thomas had fun with the whole process, earnestly telling reporters that "I'm not married to the second pick. If there's a deal that makes sense to us, we'll pursue that deal," and similar snippets to contribute to the sense of mystery about who was going to be the newest Raptor. For his part, Damon Stoudamire joined in the creation of the smoke screen, telling media five weeks before the draft, "You guys won't know until the last minute. Isiah might have an idea right now what he wants to do." What was Thomas planning? fans wondered.

Throughout the 1995–96 season many experts and newly-converted, Raptors-inspired NBA fans agreed that what the

Toronto Raptors lacked was a big man, either a true center or a strong power forward who could clog up the middle, haul down his fair share of rebounds, intimidate people by blocking some shots, and maybe score a few points in the paint as well. Conventional wisdom has always been that you don't win in the NBA without a dominating big man in the middle. Of course, the Chicago Bulls were putting this theory to a pretty stern test, but then again, how many teams have had players like Michael Jordan and Scottie Pippen on their side, not to mention a rebounding fiend like Dennis Rodman, to take some pressure off their big men? As one expert put it, in reference to Chicago's fast-improving but still not All-Star-caliber center, "No offence to Luc Longley, but the Bulls could have won the [1995–96] championship with my grandmother in the middle."

The Bulls notwithstanding, though, teams made up of mere NBA mortals need strong big men, and the Raptors were no exception. It wasn't as though Toronto didn't have any tall trees up front. Throughout the team's 21-win first season, high-flying 6–11 forward Carlos Rogers had his moments, especially late in the year, both as a scorer and as a shotblocker. But the ex-Golden State Warrior seemed to need some help. Chubby 6–9 ex-Piston Oliver Miller had been erratic in his play and then ultimately declared himself a free agent at the end of the season instead of deciding to remain with the Raptors. This decision was roundly deemed unwise by the press, who noted that as one of Isiah's "project" signings, Miller had actually had a pretty decent season as a Raptor in 1995–96. Given his reputation for a bad attitude and his problems with weight control, it seemed unlikely that Miller would ever be able to find a better situation than the one he had in Toronto.

Then there was the seven-foot Croatian Olympian Zan Tabak, who had exceeded most people's expectations after coming over from the Houston Rockets, where he had seen little playing time as Hakeem Olajuwon's backup. But no matter how much he had improved, the slow-footed Tabak's lack of quickness did not exactly make him the kind of big man you could build a franchise around. NBA vets John Salley and Ed Pinckney started the year as Raptors, but were traded. Acie Earl had shown flashes of brilliance, but the 6–10 center was considered too quirky (he liked to consume large quantities of coffee and Coca-Cola before games and favored strange hairstyles), too weak defensively, and too unpolished. And Sharone Wright arrived late, and then was injured for much of the time, only appearing in 11 games.

Everyone in the Raptors organization was talking about how the club needed a truly effective big man. "We need some help at both ends of the floor," said Stoudamire after talking with Isiah, "and our biggest need is tighter defence, players to block shots, and rebound." There was no question about it — Toronto needed a strong presence up front if they were going to progress beyond the "expansion-team-with-promise" stage in the NBA.

Given this glaring requirement, then, it came as no surprise when the Raptors began to express strong interest in a 6–11 junior from the University of Massachusetts named Marcus Camby. Camby had won the John R. Wooden Award as College Player of the Year at UMass, and had led the Minutemen throughout his career as a powerful rebounder and inside scorer. Best of all, he also had a nice touch from the outside, ran the court well, and could pass and play outstanding, shot-blocking defence. Camby decided to forego his senior year at

UMass and take a shot at the pros. Isiah was obviously impressed, saying that Camby "can play more than one position; he runs the floor well, he's going to be a good one." A good one, the gm hoped, in a Raptors' uniform.

While there was no question about Camby's toughness and mental abilities on the court, there had been some uncertainty about him as a physical specimen. Marcus had collapsed during the pre-game warm-up before a contest with St. Bonaventure's on January 14, 1995. Camby had quickly declared himself fine after the collapse, and his subsequent play during the rest of the college season certainly seemed to bear out his contention that he was fully fit.

But another, more burning concern of the NBA talent scouts prior to the draft, centered on Camby's size. At almost seven feet, he was plenty tall enough for the pros. But what made people skeptical was Marcus' build. Sometimes his 223-lb. frame — some reports listed him at 210 lb., which looked more accurate — just seemed too skinny for the NBA. In the bigs, you had to have some bulk to go with your height if you wanted to take the pounding that goes along with trying to establish position inside. Was Camby wide-bodied enough to handle it?

Some sportswriters had speculated that perhaps Toronto might use their high pick to select another guard to complement Stoudamire. Their reasoning was that perhaps Isiah was attempting to rebuild his Raptors in the image of the hugely successful Pistons, a team that had won back-to-back NBA titles under Isiah's leadership in 1989 and 1990. On that squad, Thomas was the leader of a three-guard rotation that also included Joe Dumars and Vinnie "The Microwave" Johnson. Maybe Toronto would pick 6–5 junior shooting ace Ray Allen from the University of Connecticut, who made headlines in the weeks leading up to the draft by outspokenly criticizing NCAA rules that prohibit players from earning pocket money and signing shoe contracts during their college years. (Allen also distinguished himself later as one of the NBA's few superstars not to have an agent.) Also bandied about were the names of two point guards, sophomore Allen Iverson of Georgetown and freshman Stephon Marbury of Georgia Tech. Would Isiah consider picking one of these two in a move toward a three-guard offense?

Pre-draft speculation also ran high as to the Raptors' interest in 6–9 freshman forward Shareef Abdur-Rahim of the University of California. An all-around player adept at just about every aspect of the game, Abdur-Rahim was at the center of some strange events concerning his decision to go pro. After only one year at Cal, in which he was named PAC–10 player of the year, PAC–10 freshman of the year, and Basketball Freshman of the Year by at least one major U.S. magazine, the nineteen-year-old declared his eligibility for the NBA draft in early May. Soon after that, though, Abdur-Rahim changed his mind. He claimed to have sent the NBA a letter to the effect that he would be staying at Cal, but the league claimed it never received the written withdrawal. Amidst reports that the Cal program might be the target of an NCAA investigation into illegal recruiting practices, Abdur-Rahim decided once and for all to go pro in 1996–97. It seemed as though the Vancouver Grizzlies, picking third, would be the first team to get a crack at the youngster, but sportswriters were speculating that Abdur-Rahim might run well with Damon Stoudamire. Isiah admitted that he'd been considering Abdur-Rahim all along, even with the youngster's back-and-forth indecision about his pro intentions. "He's very impressive," said Thomas. "He's one of those guys it's [going to be] tough to pass on. We've got some tough decisions to make."

The 1996 draft was loaded with some amazing talent at every position. But it was also notable for another reason. Just about every player projected as a top draft pick was coming out of college in advance of his allotted four years of varsity ball. Freshmen Abdur-Rahim and Marbury, sophomores Iverson and 6–11 Lorenzen Wright of Memphis, and juniors Allen, Camby, and forward Antoine Walker of Kentucky led the list of underclassmen deciding to go pro early. Only John Wallace of Syracuse, Kerry Kittles of Villanova, and Canadian Steve Nash of Santa Clara were mentioned by the basketball press as top draft picks who also happened to be seniors. In all, almost 40 non-seniors finally declared for the draft, a number way up from the 12 who did so the year before. One of the senior states-men of basketball writers, Jack McCallum of *Sports Illustrated*, had come down hard against college players declaring early for the draft (or like the Minnesota Timberwolves' Kevin Garnett in 1995, skipping college entirely and going straight to the pros after high school). In McCallum's opinion, "The growing exodus of star underclassmen to the NBA is ripping the heart out of the college game." Citing falling television ratings and an increasing lack of classic matchups like the Larry Bird–Magic Johnson duel in the 1979 NCAA Championships, McCallum contended that by going pro early, college superstars were destroying "the charm of the college game . . . watching players and teams develop over the course of three or four years." What was just as bad as this, he claimed, was that the early departures weren't even improving the quality of the pro game.

Isiah Thomas himself provided another perspective. In an article written especially for the *New York Times* on May 19, 1996, entitled "Early Entry, Tough Calls: In Defence of the Players," Thomas maintained that "the idea that young basketball players have been overcome by greed or simply do not appreciate the value of education is misguided." According to Isiah, what drives the underclassman's decision to turn pro early is "the fact that these young men have the opportunity to play a game they love and earn the type of money that most people only dream of." For Isiah, there wasn't anything necessarily wrong or immoral about declaring early.

Indeed, Thomas had some first-hand experience of the situation in which these players found themselves, and was speaking from a vantage point very different from that enjoyed by the typical NBA exec. Thomas had himself gone pro after his sophomore season at Indiana University in which he led the Hoosiers to the 1981 NCAA title. The reason for his decision, said Isiah, was simple. "I wanted to help my family. . . . Playing professional basketball would provide me with the opportunity to insure financial security for the Thomas family. Based on this fact alone, there was no other decision to make."

It was need, and not greed, said Isiah that was leading most NCAA underclassmen into the NBA. In addition, he made two other valid points in the *Times* article. The first was that leaving college to go pro did not necessarily mean you had to forget about your education. Isiah was himself living proof of that, having gone back to school in the off-season to complete his degree.

In the *Times* article Thomas also declared that a double-standard exists in the media and the popular sports mentality when evaluating a non-senior's decision to go pro. For just about everybody else, it is considered socially acceptable — or at least not contemptible — to leave school early if a once-in-a-lifetime business opportunity comes along before you've graduated. So why castigate basketball players, many of whom come from backgrounds like Isiah's, where hoops is the only realistic form of social mobility? The argument that it is "dishonorable" for student-athletes to renege on scholarships and abandon schools that invest vast amounts of time and money on them is also laughable. Given the cost of a four-year scholarship to the typical school, plus "sweeteners" like cash, watches, cars, and whatever else notorious "boosters" might wish to pass along to their favorite young men, and you still don't come close to the profits realized by college basketball teams. After all is said and done, colleges need these players to put fans in the seats, put points on the scoreboard, and put checks from supportive alumni into the bank account. It was within this context that players like Isiah Thomas, Ray Allen, and later Marcus Camby were contending that bonuses given to players while still in college weren't such a bad idea.

With all of the speculation and contentious issues, draft day approached. And as it did, Thomas appeared to have made up his mind to go with Marcus Camby. The UMass star was brought to Toronto for a workout, went to lunch with Damon Stoudamire, and spent time talking about the future with Isiah. The controversy that erupted when Camby went public with the admission that he had received cash payments and jewelry while in college didn't seem to bother the Raptor front office. In an interview with Elliotte Friedman on Toronto's all-sports radio station, "The Fan," and later in an article in the *Toronto*

Sun, Thomas went on record as saying that Camby was the man the Raptors wanted. This commitment was further strengthened by Isiah's comments at half-time of the sixth and final game of the Bulls-Sonics NBA final on June 16, when the normally close-to-the-vest Thomas surprised the media by revealing that the Raptors would take Camby if he was available, or try to trade for him if he was picked before them. But would the Raptors really take Camby, or was Isiah simply trying to be tricky by making it look like he knew what he was going to do? What made things even more confusing was the Abdur-Rahim flip-flop that kept everyone guessing.

Draft day finally dawned. The Philadelphia 76ers, who had suffered through an awful season in '95–'96, had won the right to pick first. The one bright spot of the previous year for the 'Sixers had been Jerry Stackhouse, who likely would have won Rookie of the Year honors if it hadn't been for Stoudamire. Other than that, Philadelphia had played badly, and it was obvious that their one glaring weakness was the lack of an effective point guard to quarterback their offense. Perhaps keeping in mind Isiah's move of the year before and the subsequent stellar play of Damon Stoudamire in leading the Raptors, Philly chose Georgetown's Allen Iverson. Next, it was Toronto's turn to pick. Did Isiah have any surprises in store? Nobody gathered at the Meadowlands or at Wayne Gretzky's had to hold their breath for very long. Commissioner David Stern, after a short celebratory pause by Iverson and some 'Sixers officials, announced that "The Toronto Raptors pick Marcus Camby."

And so the Raptors had their big man. In a draft where the top seven picks were all underclassmen, the Raptors got exactly the player they needed. "Camby can step in and play 30 to 35 minutes [a game]," said Isiah after the draft, "and he's got a big upside." The "upside" according to Isiah, was that while the other big-man possibilities in the draft — like the enigmatic Abdur-Rahim, who was selected by Vancouver — might take a few years to develop, "This guy is now."

June 26, 1996, was indeed a success for Isiah Thomas, and one not based solely on a smart draft pick. While it must have been satisfying to leave his mark on another NBA draft, this too did not comprise the full measure of success he now enjoyed via the 1996 NBA Draft. No, it was something deeper, and it didn't take a basketball genius or a sports sociologist to figure out what it was.

Strip away all of the hype surrounding professional basketball. Take away the countless articles written about who is going to draft whom, the TV commercials about what shoes so-and-so wears, and who drinks what brand of soft drink. Forget all of the stats, the points-per-game, the assist-to-turnover ratios, and the arguments about who's the greatest shotblocker of all time. Eliminate the fancy uniforms, the tattoos and the big shorts. Get rid of the marketing, the licensing, and the stadium deals. Tune out the trash talking, the cheap shots under the basket, the no-easy-layups-during-the-playoffs rule, the 24-second clock. What's left? What's the single most important thing about the NBA, the thing to which all of the other facets of the sport are only partially relevant?

Winning. That's it. Winning. When you take away everything else, NBA basketball is big — even huge — business, and the best way to succeed in that particular business climate is to win. Win basketball games, win NBA championships. Although it sounds ridiculous now in light of the success of the Chicago Bulls in the past few years, it wasn't too long ago that people in bars and backyards across North America would end arguments in favor of Michael Jordan being the greatest player of all time by contending, "Yeah, but the Bulls have never won a championship."

But if winning is all-important, it follows that the process of just how you win becomes an important skill to learn. Those who possess this skill come to be admired for it. As a team game, basketball is all about finding the right combination of players who, when they work together doing the things they do best as individuals, mesh in such a way as to prove unstoppable to their opponents.

Looking at hoops as a team game, though, only illuminates a small part of the truth about the way it's really played, and about those who are truly great at playing it. For at every level of the game, whether it's a bunch of kids playing three-on-three with a rubber ball on asphalt, or Game Seven of the NBA Finals, you begin to see something happening. On the schoolyard, it's the one guy who, when the call of "next basket wins" is sounded, starts yelling for the ball from his winded teammates, who for their part would just as soon call it a night and head for ice cream. It's the kid crashing the boards, calling out picks, wanting, demanding the ball so he can take his man to the hole as his buddies only watch, knocking down the last layup or jumper so that when they do call it a night, he can go home with a little something extra until next time.

In the pros, it isn't much different. Around the time when the guys with bad haircuts up in the broadcast booth start crowing about the "go-to guys," the crowd in the stands and the fans at home have already felt it. There's always one player who, for whatever reason, just decides that he's got no other choice than to take the game over all by himself. Some do it by going on a scoring tear, others by blocking every shot that comes anywhere near their basket, and others by concluding that everything that comes off the rim is their own exclusive property. Some take control of the ball, making tired teammates look like all-stars with passes for wide-open layups, or dribbling through arms and legs, daring opponents to foul them and then calmly draining free throws amidst a sea of crowd noise and "miss" banners. Some great players have even been able to win games using several of these approaches in the same contest. Whatever the chosen route, a select few have always seemed to make these choices a part of a regular winning routine.

When all is said and done, Isiah Thomas understands winning. He's done it at every level of the game of basketball — playground, high school, college, pro — and knows how to win, better perhaps than anyone else involved in the sport.

Really, it's ultimately about control. Controlling the game, your opponents, your teammates, the crowd, even your coach. Taking control and not letting go. Orchestrating something, anything so that your guys come out on top. And whether it's for champagne, a trophy, and a microphone thrust in your face in the locker room, or for the right to yell "Game!" and make the losers sit while you get to stay on the playground court, those who win are those who control in the world of basketball.

Isiah Thomas is a man of control. As a player, he could manipulate a full court game of some of the finest athletes in the world as if it was laid out on a point-and-click computer screen in front of him and he had the only mouse. Whatever the situation required, the man they called "Zeke" could bring it on. Scoring: inside and out. Three pointers, or taking it to the rack. Defense: steals, in-your-face, let's see what you got. Assists: drive and dish, the no-look pass through the double team, and there's the man, open down low for the jam. For thirteen years, whenever the Pistons needed a go-to guy, even the limo drivers outside the Palace listening to the game on the radio knew they were going with Isiah. Sure, it might be Vinnie or A.D. or Dumars or even Laimbeer who'd actually hit the shots to win it, but one way or another, Isiah would be involved.

So how surprising was it that the one man who really controlled the Toronto Raptors (and went on to call the shots for the Continental Basketball Association, the Indiana Pacers, and now the New York Knicks) was this same take-charge artist from the tough part of Chicago? Lots of other people were part of the Raptors organization, of course, but when Toronto sportswriters started to call the Raptors "Isiah's Team" they were being completely accurate. To begin with, Thomas was a part owner of the team. As General Manager, he achieved a level of day-to-day involvement with the team that's unprecedented. Prior to the team's first NBA campaign, Isiah had hand-picked the head coach, and then, when the season ended, ultimately fired him and chosen his successor. He selected the remaining coaching staff, and signed the team's players, including a number of successful "projects." It's hard for a gm to be much more involved than that, but add to this list the orchestration of several important trades, determining the team's overall image, both on the court and as a marketing/merchandising commodity, and a willingness to express via the media a high-profile opinion on everything from the stadium to the play of a certain forward or off-guard, and you had a picture that looks a lot like the one Isiah Thomas painted as a player in Detroit. Sure, events were unfolding just on the other side of the border, and the old red, white, and blue number eleven uniform has been replaced with executive garb more in keeping with front office expectations. But the images of winning, and the desire to win, to be successful, to take control and to lead — were still all there. It really was the same old Isiah.

Many people were stunned by the speed with which Isiah moved from being a player to an executive, although it is true that speed was one of his main attributes as a player. But they shouldn't have been, because for Isiah, the process was simply a matter of transferring his vast competitiveness from one arena into another. "You gotta have that type of intensity, that type of fire, type of passion about what you do," he has said about life in general and basketball in particular. "It's a game you either love or hate. You're a person who's really on the edge. There's a fine line when you channel all that and you put it out on the court, you know, you're playing with a blind type of madness. The emotions that drove me were love and hate and fear — fear of losing, fear of losing the game."

In part, Isiah Thomas' move to create "his" Toronto Raptors in his own image was the logical outgrowth of his experiences as an athlete. For one thing, he had got several success models in his own background to use as templates in Toronto. His high school team was an Illinois state powerhouse, his college won the NCAA's, and his pro squad took the NBA crown twice, back to back. You don't have this kind of winning record as an athlete and not learn something about how successful organizations operate, how to put the right people in the right positions. For another, his involvement in several lucrative business ventures — including a printing company, a bank, and an event management company — taught Isiah a thing or two about business on a grand scale before the Raptors started calling. Wisely, he had been exploring the competitive world outside the stadiums of the NBA before he retired. And finally, from the start, beginning with boyhood games on the playground in K-Town and moving all the way through to the pros, Isiah Thomas had played the one position on a basketball court that absolutely demands leadership qualities of those who occupy it. If a point guard doesn't want to lead, there's really no reason to play there. And for a little man in a game of giants, a reluctance to play the point usually means only being able to get off your jump shots as an off-guard with the help of a lot of picks, or seeing if maybe the baseball team needs a shortstop.

By now, Isiah's rise from poverty in Chicago is well-known. A movie has even been made about the way in which his mother raised nine children and kept them, for the most part, off the mean streets. But what seems to emerge from this rags-to-riches story more than anything else is the extremely intense calculation, the careful planning, and the precise orchestration that makes up Isiah's life. It would seem almost improbable if it weren't true. It's almost as if Isiah had said, at an age when most kids are struggling to overcome their anxiety over beginning high school, "I have to do this, and then that, this and this, and one day, I'll end up a success." And what's doubly incredible is that he's actually done it.

Another possible explanation for the Isiah-as-Raptors' unquestioned-leader phenomenon is the fact that as a completely new spectacle in Canada, an NBA basketball franchise would need to present a fairly unified front to its fans. Keep in mind that as a direct result of a Raptor/NBA marketing campaign, many of these new fans were young and were attracted to games more by the hype and the shoe commercials and the look of the NBA than by such details as the pick-and-roll and the 20-second time-out. Given this approach, it might have been best for the team's ownership to put the team's image — how it functioned on the court and the message it brought to fans off it — in the hands of one person. This idea makes even more sense when one considers that the person who ultimately took charge of the team also owned some of it. Part of Thomas' deal in becoming GM was ownership of a 9 per cent slice of the team, which puts him in a unique position among NBA General Managers. Some fans even wondered if he wrote his own paychecks.

But why Isiah? Why not, say, his pal Magic Johnson, who after all was initially interested in bringing pro hoops into Toronto until his group lost out in the bidding wars? What exactly was — and indeed is — there about Isiah Lord Thomas III that has enabled him to make that seamless transition from the hardwood to the boardroom, all the while keeping up the intensity, drive, and above all, the control that has characterized his life? It's a long story — and not always a rosy one — that reveals as much about fame and success in North American professional sports as it does about Isiah.

CHAPTER TWO

Growing Up on the West Side

In the Bible's Old Testament, the Book of the Prophet Isaiah contains a passage that has proven to possess considerable predictive power, at least as far as those who follow the sport of professional basketball are concerned. In the seventh century B.C., the Biblical Isaiah warned his people of the  coming Judgment Day, and told them to trust God for their ultimate restoration.

But for basketball fans almost 3,000 years later, the Prophet's words take on a different significance. Many sportswriters have noted that the Old Testament's Book of Isaiah contains the passage "And a little child shall lead them," and have connected this prophecy with the on-court leadership of a different Isaiah — one who spells his name without that extra "a." In a game dominated by giants, Isiah Lord Thomas III has indeed led successful basketball teams at all levels of the sport despite being a comparative "little child" in physical stature.

But Thomas' leadership has a different component to it than just the marshalling of forces on the hardwood floor. It is also written in the Old Testament Book that God promises to "give children over to be . . . princes, and babes shall rule." This passage mirrors a part of Isiah Thomas' life that is far more significant than knowing how to orchestrate a fast break or when to take a jump shot. As the ninth of nine children, Isiah was indeed the "babe" of the Thomas family, and over time, he would be called upon to deliver those closest to him from difficult surroundings to a better life. Fans of pro hoops who possessed a familiarity with Biblical prophecy would come to realize that this particular Isiah was a man who, if not exactly a worker of miracles, would certainly overcome incredible odds in support of his closest kin.

The story of the Thomas family takes place in Chicago, Illinois, U.S.A. The tourist-brochure Chicago is a huge, inspiring place that boasts, among other things, baseball's Wrigley Field, the towering John Hancock Center, and a steel sculpture by Pablo Picasso in Civic Center Plaza. Movie buffs have become familiar with the city's affluent suburbs like Lake Forest and Winnetka as the setting for such films as *Ferris Bueller's Day Off* and *Risky Business.*

Those are the some of the highlights of Chicago, and any visitor to the Windy City on the shores of Lake Michigan would be well advised to visit them. Sightseers, however, usually avoid the city's West Side. In 1995, *Toronto Life* magazine sent writer Sarah Hampson to the neighborhood in an attempt to present its readers with a first-hand look at the environment that had spawned the Raptors' new General Manager. Hampson called it "the 'hood to which Federal Express drivers often refuse to deliver," and described the setting thus:

Flat, square tenement buildings, curtainless windows, few stores, church spires pointed like fingers at the motionless sky. Rows of grey-brown skinny houses — some boarded up, others torn down — leaving gaps like holes in a set of badly decayed teeth. No greenery, except for a few sad trees and, in cracks of the asphalt desert, tufts of grass leaking defiantly through the sealed landscape.

It was here that the perennial All-Star — born Isiah Lord Thomas III on April 30, 1961 — grew up, learned the lessons that would guide him for the rest of his life, and perhaps most importantly, began playing basketball. The Thomas clan moved a lot, and Isiah's mother, Mary, remembered years later that "I was always running with my kids," away from gangs and ghetto violence. "I was like a gypsy. When things started getting bad, I started moving."

Just a stone's throw from one of his childhood homes on Congress Street, Isiah learned how to play pickup ball at Gladys Park. The park held a near-magical significance for many of the young men in the neighborhood because it was there that they could act out their fantasies of NBA stardom. Later, Gladys Park became an even more hallowed Mecca of West Side Playground hoops, as The Place Where Isiah Thomas Learned His Game. "Go anywhere on the West Side and say, 'Meet me at the court,'" he would recall later, as an established pro player with the Detroit Pistons, "and they'd know what you were talking about. That's where I really learned to play."

There's something about hoopsters who have cut their basketball teeth on the playground game. Others, schooled in the fundamentals at YMCA camps or by clipboard-wielding high school coaches, never seem to acquire that hustler's knack, those tricky edges to their game that countless hours on the asphalt build into a graduate of Streetball U. Later, when he'd go on to star at Indiana University and with the Pistons, observers would note that Isiah's style had a freelance quality to it, an approach that was often described in complimentary tones as "playground." The sneaky steals, the speed-dribbling, the nifty layups that left defenders flat-footed and pawing at air — these are Isiah Thomas trademarks that were developed in Gladys Park among some pretty stiff competition. "There were some basketball players there," he recalls. "I mean some basketball players. You could always get a game there. Any time of day, any time of night. Me and my brothers used to go over there with snow shovels in the winter so we could play."

The nine children in the Thomas family consisted of Isiah, his six brothers — Ronnie, Larry, Preston, Mark, Gregory, and Lord Henry — and two sisters, Ruby and Dolores. It was Isiah's brothers who gave him his initial instruction in the game of basketball, and the playground clinics they put on developed the basis for an array of skills that would one day propel the littlest Thomas out of the ghetto they all inhabited. While all of Isiah's elder brothers were solid players, the oldest, Lord Henry, was especially impressive, and his moves on the court made him Isiah's first basketball role model. "All of them were really good," Isiah revealed when he had made it to college and people wanted to know how he had developed his talents. "They never had the chance that I've had. . . . Lord Henry . . . I've never seen anybody like him. The things people are doing now [in basketball] he was doing then. Had he had the chance, I think he could have changed the whole complexion of basketball."

Lord Henry was known around Windy City high school hoops circles as "Rat" because of his tricky play on the court, and he came to be regarded as a minor legend. The displays he put on against high school rivals were watched intently by Isiah, who'd try to mimic his brother. "Every move that Lord Henry made on the court, we'd try to duplicate it," admits Isiah. "The excitement he created in the gym is something I will never forget. Oh, he was sweet! He was everything."

In sort of a reverse-George Orwell scenario, seven-year-old Isiah started watching Big Brother constantly as he played his home games at St. Phillip's High School. And even though he couldn't go to the away matches in person, Isiah wouldn't be prevented from experiencing them on a mental plane. "Everyone would come back afterward and sit around telling stories of what Lord Henry had done that night," he recalled, "and I could see it in my mind, how it was happening." This ability to visualize the choreographic intricacies of a basketball game in his head would stand Isiah in good stead throughout his career.

The fact that Lord Henry Thomas didn't get a chance to play big-time college and pro ball like his little brother eventually did, points up a significant detail of life that all of the Thomas kids had to confront. The West Side of Chicago, and the family's K-Town neighborhood, was an incredibly tough place where drugs, prostitution, and gangs were commonplace. The lure of these powerful elements of street life can easily prove too much for young kids, whether they are talented basketball players or not. While Isiah managed to escape them, his older brothers didn't. Paradoxically, it was only because of the watchful guidance of the older Thomas boys, combined with that of his mother, that Isiah managed to stay out of trouble. "I think all of them could have played professional basketball," he said of his brothers. "I think they all wanted to go to college. It's just that they met the wrong people at the wrong time and started hanging around with gangs and stuff. They protected me. Everything that I've done . . . it's all because of them. They made the sacrifices and they took the lumps and bad times for me."

While the contribution of Isiah's brothers to his basketball career — and by extension, his entire life — cannot be emphasized enough, an equal part of the credit must go to his mother. Mary Thomas, who all of the kids called "Dear" (in turn, the family refers to Isiah as "Junior") was the glue that held the family together under stresses that likely would have torn most kin groups apart. Now the subject of a movie called *A Mother's Courage: The Mary Thomas Story* which features actress Alfre Woodard in the role of Isiah's mom, Mary provided for her kids, fought off the encroachment of rival gangs eager to recruit them, and stressed the value of education as the one thing that would allow the youngsters to rise out of the West Side — despite the fact that she herself had failed to make it past the third grade.

In one celebrated incident — a happening that's almost as legendary on the West Side as Isiah's playground exploits — members of a notorious gang called the Vice Lords arrived at the family house on Congress Street, hard by the city's

Eisenhower Expressway. The Vice Lords figured that having found a house that contained 6 able-bodied young men, they had come upon an excellent source of potential gang members.

One of the Vice Lords' leaders asked Mary to speak to her boys, but was met with a firm maternal rebuke as little six-year-old Isiah cringed in the background. "There ain't but one gang in this family," she told the assembled hoods, "The Thomas gang." When the Vice Lords' spokesman informed her that he intended to pluck her sons off the street if necessary, Mary disappeared, only to return seconds later brandishing a sawed-off shotgun. Aiming at each of the gang members, she told them, "If you don't get off my porch, I'll blow you across the expressway."

"They didn't come back anymore," Mary Thomas remembered later.

The streets, though, did get to some of the Thomas gang in the end. Lord Henry experimented with heroin and became an addict; Gregory developed a drinking problem. Both men later went through rehabilitation programs. Larry, who had also been a stellar high school player, had gone on to compete for Wright Junior College, but his career was ended by an ankle injury before a tryout with the Chicago Bulls and he turned to street hustling. Preston, Ronnie, and Mark hadn't made it as players, either.

Fortunately for hoop aficionados the world over, it was Larry's plunge into street life that turned Isiah away from a dangerous career as a hustler. When Larry came back from college, he had assumed the position of role model for Isiah. "Larry was my idol at the time," he said. "I'd go in and try on his clothes. I'd walk like him, talk like him."

So while he used to mimic the antics of one brother on the basketball court, Isiah was now copying the actions of another on the street, and this particular brother was involved in something a lot more serious than cross-over dribbling and the occasional foul for elbowing. Larry Thomas had turned to pimping and dealing heroin. "The street was the game, the con, shooting dice," said Isiah, describing the way of life that prevailed on his home turf. "I knew how to hustle at an early age. Every con artist, every hustler, was trying to beat the game. In order to get money, you had to hustle."

It looked as though Isiah was headed for trouble through his emulation of brother Larry. But he took the copying routine a step too far, and that was what eventually saved him. One day, Larry was driving his 1971 powder-blue Cadillac through the streets when he saw someone dressed a lot like him. In fact, it was Isiah, who, in the best tradition of little brothers everywhere, had swiped one of Larry's suits and hats and had hit the pavement. Larry didn't have to be convinced any more that he'd set a bad example for Isiah. Holding up a bag of heroin, Larry told his kid brother that "this stuff will kill you," and that on the streets, "the best way to win that game is don't play. Don't play and you can't lose."

Begging Isiah not to walk in his footsteps, Larry admitted that he was not a person who should be followed. "I hate the way I chose," he confessed. "I chose the easy way. I hate myself. Don't look up to me. Don't do what I'm doing. You're throwing it all away." And if by then Isiah Lord Thomas III hadn't realized that he had become, by the process of elimination, the standard-bearer for a family struggling to beat the "con" of the street, Larry drove the point home. "Somebody has got to get the NBA paycheck," he told Isiah. "Lord Henry failed. Gregory failed. I was that close to it, and I failed. We owe it to ourselves. Somebody has got to get that money!"

Apparently the lesson sunk in, as did the countless hours that Larry started spending with his little brother on the court, helping him hone his game and teaching him what he knew about pursuing success. "Of all my brothers, he was the one who really saved my life," Isiah would declare later. "At that time in my life, I was lost. He started to spend a lot of time with me." While this time spent together would strengthen the bonds of brotherhood and provide Isiah with some much-needed guidance, it also did wonders for the youngster's game. Soon, he would be ready for high school, and would be testing his mettle against the toughest competition yet.

The number of building-blocks that must come together to produce a first-rate athlete is considerable. There are the obvious factors, the physical skills that a person competing in any sport must possess or be unable to keep pace, regardless of how tenacious and determined he or she is. In basketball, a certain degree of competence at running and jumping, as well as basic hand-eye co-ordination are required. Beyond these minimum standards, though, lie a myriad of other factors like persistence, the ability to work hard, a love of the game, and a certain, hard-to-define mental stamina that refuses to give up when the going gets tough. While many of the needed physical tools are in place at birth and simply develop naturally over time, the more nebulous psychological attributes are often a product of a player's upbringing and background. For Isiah, a number of elements combined in the very early stages of his playing career to give him an edge in the area of what sports observers often refer to as "the intangibles."

As well as the inspiration and encouragement he received from his brothers, the central inspiration in Isiah's youth was his mother. Mary had come up to Chicago from Mississippi at the age of 16, part of a World War II-era migration of Southern Blacks to the North and Midwest of the U.S. Actually, as Mary Thomas tells it, her arrival in Chicago was precipitated by slightly-less sociologically quantifiable factors. "I was going in the ten-cent store," she recalled, "just as a white woman was coming out of one of those swinging doors. Well, I bumped her and she slapped me. I grabbed her by her hair, threw her down on the ground, and was beating the living mess out of her. Needless to say, at that time, I was on the next thing smoking, coming to Chicago to stay with my father's brother." Fans of her son's on-court exploits, especially during his pro career in Detroit, could easily recognize the same pluck in his mother!

It was in Chicago that Mary met her future husband, a fellow Mississippian named Isiah Thomas II. An Army veteran, Isiah II was the first black supervisor at the International Harvester plant in Chicago. He was a keen reader, and insisted that his kids could only watch educational TV. One of the father's main messages concerned the importance of family teamwork. "He would gather seven sticks together and put them in a bunch and tell us, 'It's a lot harder to break seven sticks together than one at a time,'" says Preston Thomas.

But despite his sons' love of the game, Isiah II was never a hoops fan, stressing academic achievement over sports success. "My father never liked basketball," Isiah recounted when he was in college. "He was the type — you get your grades, you be the doctor, you be the lawyer."

Isiah II was eventually let go from International Harvester, and even though he possessed considerable mechanical and drafting skills, could only find employment as a janitor. He and Mary separated when Isiah was very young. "My dad left home when I was three years old," says Isiah. "After seeing eight of us come along before me I guess he'd had enough. It was my mother that raised us all." Isiah has also said that his father — intensely frustrated at not being able to find appropriate work and being prevented from using his talents — had become so angry at the world that it might well have been a good thing he left home when he did, as opposed to physically venting his anger on his family.

So Mary Thomas was in charge of the bunch, and she governed in the mode of a benevolent disciplinarian. When Isiah was growing up, Mary Thomas insisted that her kids behave with class, no matter what the family's financial situation was at any given period. "I showed them how to carry themselves, and how to behave properly in school and out," she claims. "And when I had to, I got the message across with an ironing cord. I loved my children. I cared for them. I looked after them, but they had to abide by my rules." Isiah's mom had regulations for her kids, like a strict adherence to curfew, but she also followed a few basic ones herself. One was that the family should always have a safe — or at least safe by West Side standards — place to live. "As poor as I was, I always found the best living situation possible," she says. "I wouldn't live in a courtway building with my family, or anything over two stories tall. And I certainly wouldn't live in the housing projects."

Once, a welfare official informed her that unless she'd agree to move into one of the government-supported projects, her assistance check would be withheld. Mary was furious, "because I didn't think anybody had the right to tell me where to go and live, just because they were giving me a check." Her solution was a study in take-it-to-the-top directness: she hopped a bus straight to the office of Chicago Mayor Richard J. Daley, to tell him of her pique. She got past the Mayor's secretary, and informed the Boss himself of her situation. Shortly thereafter, Mary got a call from the welfare case worker, who in turn presented her with her deserved check. "I had willpower," she said. "If I wanted something, I figured I could get it if I went about it in the right way. I was kind of a strong willed person."

Another self-imposed regulation that Mary Thomas followed in the solo administration of her West Side family concerned food. Although she had been raised a Baptist, Mary had swung towards Catholicism when Isiah was born, and presently took a job in the family's church, Our Lady of Sorrows, cooking in the cafeteria of the school that accompanied it and running its youth center. In her own home, meals were often hard to come by, but Mary insisted on always trying to have something to eat, even if it meant sometimes relying on unusual products donated by the church.

Her youngest child remembers: "We got food from the church one time that was all Hamburger Helper. Boxes and boxes of Hamburger Helper. No hamburger, just the helper. We ate that, like, forever." Isiah also recounts another case of how a repetitive diet turned out to be better than no diet at all. "When Quaker Oats came out with their granola, they gave a lot of it away," he says. "My mother used to get all of that granola and bring it home. We never had any milk or anything. We'd just eat granola until we got full. Get hungry again? Eat some more granola."

While Isiah does not remember the days when he and his siblings went hungry with fondness, he at least does so with a sense of humor, as his re-telling of the Hamburger Helper and Quaker granola incidents illustrate. Mary Thomas likes to relate another anecdote along the same lines. After Isiah had achieved his — and his family's — dream of making it to the pros, he used some of the money the Detroit Pistons were paying him to buy Mary a house in the Chicago suburb of Clarendon Hills. Once, for a family meal there, the mother remembers, "I made a big breakfast of biscuits, eggs, grits, bacon, and sausage." Brothers and sisters were together, "all seated around the table," says Mary, "and Isiah started laughing. I asked him what was so funny, and he said, 'There are too many things on this plate; there isn't supposed to be anything but the grits.' And we all fell out [laughing]."

For Isiah, purchasing the house for his mother represented a major achievement, not only because of the way in which it enabled her to attain a physical distance away from the ghetto, but also for what it represented in the bigger picture of material security and the knowledge that she and her family did not have to scrape by on Helper without the Hamburger any longer. "Seeing her in that house when she moved in — that probably is the most happiness, the most pleasure, I've had in all my life," he admits. "Watching her going from having nothing to having something. When I go home, I can walk to the refrigerator, and it's got food in it! That's happiness. We've got food in the house,

and bills are being paid!" Although Isiah called these achievements the fulfillment of "just the simple things," they were, for
a family that never had them, the realization of a major goal.

Materially, it would be an understatement of vast proportions to claim that the Thomas family "had it tough." But in the
same way that Mary had taken what she was able to get in the
way of food for her family, smallest son Isiah had become rather
resourceful in his pursuit of every young basketball player's
most cherished commodities — hoop sneakers. Many years
after his childhood, Isiah was in New York City to accept the
award as the Most Valuable Player in the 1990 NBA playoffs. "I
never told this story," admitted Isiah at the awards ceremony, as
he recounted the way he would stand outside Chicago Stadium
after Bulls' home games and pester players for used equipment.
One night, after the Bulls had taken on the New York Knicks,
Isiah saw New York's legendary guard, Walt "Clyde" Frazier, a
player as famous for his flashy style of dress off the court as for
his excellent playmaking and scoring on it. "I used to ask for
gym shoes and autographs," Isiah continued. "I was standing
outside the Stadium, it was wintertime, and Clyde had his big
white fur coat. I asked him for his autograph, and he said no."
Was it a disappointment, someone asked, that one of the game's
all-time greats had passed him by without signing? "No, 'cause I
got gym shoes," Isiah responded. "I was standing there with
about five pairs of gym shoes from the Knicks and the Bulls. I
think [Frazier] had to catch a bus or something."

Before Isiah would be able to sign pro contracts that would
enable him to buy houses for his family and pro-style shoes for
his feet, however, he still had a few giant steps to take. The tutelage of Larry, Lord Henry, and the other Thomas brothers had

started to take hold, and Isiah was starting to figure out his way around the playground court pretty nicely. In fact, the youngest Thomas had been a promising chunk of basketball raw material for quite a while before he was ready to enter high school. Actually, Isiah had begun displaying his roundball talents to a public audience as a three-year-old!

At Our Lady of Sorrows, the miniature version of the man who would later wow audiences in pro arenas throughout the NBA was a tiny halftime show stopper. The team's coach, Brother Alexis, gave Isiah a basketball jersey that was oversized in the extreme, and Isiah, thus costumed, would perform for the crowd. "It hung to his ankles," said Brother Alexis. "At age three, he could shoot the eyes out of the basket."

Many years later, Larry remembered what it was like having a three-year-old hoops prodigy around the Thomas household. Occasionally, it even meant transporting the little guy to games without the assistance of a motorized vehicle. On a walk through K-Town, Larry would recall that "this is where I carried him all the way from the house to the gym. Momma didn't want him to go, because it was the worst snowstorm in Chicago, but I said I'd look after him. We were slipping and sliding. Junior was heavy." Once they made it to the game, though, little Isiah would make his presence felt. "He would lead our team out on the floor," Larry recalls. "The first time he did that, I tell you, a star was born."

From these early beginnings, Isiah kept on improving. "Later, we got him in the summer leagues," continues Larry. "He was eight years old and he was playing as a point guard against thirteen- and fourteen-year-olds. Ooo-eee, he was on their asses!" Even at that young an age, Isiah knew what a point guard's job was — to distribute the ball to his teammates in a position where they can score. In this case, several of those teammates happened to have the same last name as he did. "We'd tell Junior, 'Just get the ball up the court, get the ball up the court,'" Larry reminisces, "because you know it just needs to touch your hands and it was gone, baby!" Putting the ball into the hands of teammates was a lesson that Isiah would learn early, and exploit for the rest of his playing career.

For Isiah, things had developed on the basketball court to the point where he and his brothers had begun to think seriously about the possibility of his playing big-time college basketball. But to do that, Isiah would have to get out of the inner city, and into a first-rate high school program that stressed both basketball and academic achievement. That's why a delegation of Thomas boys, led by Larry, trekked out to St. Joseph's High School, a Catholic, Christian Brothers-sponsored school located in Westchester, an affluent, mostly-white suburb of the Windy City.

Geographically, St. Joe's was about 10 miles from the Thomas home on the West Side. Culturally, it might as well have been on Mars. Here was a well-appointed gym, expert coaching, and a student body comprised of many kids who actually expected to go on to college. The Thomas brothers showed up at St. Joseph's in an attempt to persuade the school's coach, a man named Gene Pingatore, to give their youngest member a scholarship to play there. "Coach Ping" was more than willing to give Isiah a shot. After all, he'd seen him play before!

"He had an aura about him," Pingatore remembers. Any basketball fan who has seen the excellent film *Hoop Dreams* has seen Coach Ping in action, and knows of the success of the St.

Joseph's program, both athletically and academically. Movie buffs who have seen the documentary will also know that while at the Westchester school, Isiah blossomed into an Illinois state legend. His success is today held up as an example to all young players who attend St. Joe's.

Life for an inner-city kid going to high school in the suburbs is not easy, especially considering that for most of them, owning a car is not a reality. So it was public transit for Isiah, and that meant getting out of bed every morning at 5:30 a.m. and leaving for school 30 minutes later. Mary later admitted that she used to watch him leave the house with tears in her eyes. After an hour and a half on buses, Isiah would walk it over the last one-and-a-half miles, and in the winter, this meant enduring weather that was, by his own account, "cold as a bitch. . . . I'd get on the bus and it would be dark and get off the bus and it would be daylight."

Even though the big, two-way commute was difficult, Isiah started to thrive at St. Joe's. In the classroom, he qualified for the Honor Roll, thereby making him all the more attractive to college recruiters who wouldn't have to worry about offering a scholarship to a student who couldn't use it because of academic ineligibility. In his freshman year of high school, however, Isiah almost messed up his chances by slipping to a D average. "There's no question you'll get a Division I [college] scholarship," Pingatore predicted, "but if you don't get the grades, it's going to go down the drain."

The adjustment to a white, suburban school also had its rough spots for Isiah as far as his self-discipline was concerned. At times, it seemed as though the standards there were simply too tough to follow. But in the end, the support he received from his family pulled him through. During his first year at St. Joseph's, Isiah was disciplined for being late to class, and he telephoned Mary at work at Our Lady of Sorrows to tell her what he thought of the situation. "I'm quitting this school," he insisted. "Now, Junior," Mary answered calmly, "you do what you think is right. But tell me again what you're going to do, and say it slowly." "I'm quitting this school," was again Isiah's response. "Say it slower," responded Mary. Then there was silence on the telephone line. "I'm," answered Isiah, pausing, "staying."

After he'd been at St. Joe's for a while, the other Thomas kids started chiding Isiah for "talking white," or unconsciously slipping out of ghetto dialect into the patterns of the suburban kids he was hanging out with in Westchester. His emergence from K-Town was starting to change him a little.

For Gene Pingatore, Isiah was the kind of once-in-a-lifetime athlete that coaches dream of working with, a disciplined worker possessing the inner motivation to succeed, and with a strong family backing him up. "Isiah has intelligence, mental toughness, the determination to win, plus charisma," he says. "There was only one time when his mother and I had to set him straight. He had come to the school with the idea that he was there simply to play basketball. We told him that if he didn't change his attitude, he wouldn't get a scholarship to university. That was the last time we had a problem."

Isiah was catching on at St. Joe's, and his family, which had been so supportive, so hopeful right from the very start, was loving it. "It was so much fun to watch him play," says Ruby, Isiah's sister who became a schoolteacher. "That was our entertainment on the weekends. Wherever he was playing, that's where we went. After those games, my brothers would bring him home, and they would gather around and critique him, tell him all the mistakes that he had made that night. This would sometimes go on till one, two o'clock in the morning. This was after every game."

These late-night skull sessions, featuring budding star Isiah and his in-house team of coaches and color commentators, laid the foundation for the youngest Thomas' intelligent, cunning approach to playing the point guard position. With his every move coming under the family microscope, Isiah knew that he'd have to make every millisecond count out there on the court or he'd certainly hear about it back home.

"By the time I got to high school I felt that I had to succeed," admitted Isiah. "If I didn't, in terms of my family, our life on earth was kind of meaningless. It didn't have to be basketball because my success model was not built on sports or celebrity." Certainly, Isiah was beginning to put things together in the classroom to such an extent that he could afford to think about succeeding in realms outside the confines of the hardwood. But basketball was what he did best, and given his progress at St. Joseph's under Coach Pingatore, it was starting to look as though a wide, accommodating world of hoops might open up to him.

As a high school sophomore, Isiah still had to work a bit of the playground magic out of his system before he could adjust to the more regimented, team-oriented world of the organized indoor game. "As talented as he was, he didn't know how to play," remembers Coach Ping. "He was out of control as a sophomore, his first year on the varsity. He'd take the ball out of bounds, and I knew he was going all the way. Then he'd run over somebody, and I'd pull him out of the game."

In his junior year, however, Isiah learned to play with more refinement, and led his school to a 31 and 2 record and a runner-up finish in the Illinois state Class AA tournament. He was also named to the all-state team that year. As a senior, Isiah took St. Joe's to another superb campaign, this time a 26–3 season in which they missed getting into the "Sweet 16" of the state tourney by one game.

"He was a natural-born leader," asserts Pingatore. "He is special. I'll never forget the game in his senior year when Isiah and I walked through this massive crowd of [college] coaches and scouts. Isiah pulled me aside and said, 'Let me know if I change.' I have seen kids come from circumstances similar to Isiah's and they may have as much talent, but for one reason or other they don't make it. There will never be another Isiah."

It's likely that one of the central reasons for Isiah Thomas' having "made it" is a straightforward one, a factor from which all of his other attributes flow naturally. By virtue of the support he received from his family — mother, sisters and brothers, all working together — Isiah was able to leave the West Side, succeed at St. Joseph's, and to go beyond it, into college and the pros. Perhaps it isn't so surprising that the Thomas Gang would get behind their youngest member like they did. After all, their future was at stake, too. A pro contract, and the paychecks that would come with it, meant not only personal success for Isiah, but a kind of deliverance for the family as well. In practical terms, Isiah was an investment, sort of a fund into which the other members deposited love, encouragement, discipline, and dreams, in the hopes that this capital would one day reach maturity.

"I was the last stop," confesses the future NBA star. "After me, there were no more kids. There was enormous pressure for me to succeed because I wanted to make a difference for me and my family." Isiah Thomas simply wanted to pay back his family's investment in him, and in order for him to do so, he'd have to remember something his mother had told him when he was a kid. "Junior, life isn't fair," Isiah remembers Mary telling him. "When you start from that premise, you can accept anything. If you're sitting there, waiting for something to be made right, to equal out, well, life is not that way. It's just not that way. Whatever problems, whatever comes your way, it's easier for you to deal with it if you just move on." It would be a lesson he'd remember many times in the years ahead, on occasions when life was going well, and at times when it wasn't.

After his superb junior and senior campaigns at St. Joseph's, college scouts had become interested in Isiah's plans for post-secondary education. As Coach Ping mentioned, games toward the end of his young star's high school career were becoming a little more crowded than usual, what with the hordes of NCAA Division I talent scouts who had started showing up in Westchester. In April 1979, Isiah had narrowed his choices of college down to the University of Iowa, Indiana University, and DePaul University. Immediately, there was pressure to attend DePaul, which is located in Chicago.

Mary Thomas believed that Bloomington, where Indiana University is located, was too far away from the West Side — about 5 hours by car — and its big-time, Big Ten basketball program would be too much for her son. Many of Isiah's brothers were angling for DePaul too, and an argument between Gregory and Indiana Coach Bobby Knight almost erupted into fisticuffs during a recruiting visit to the Thomas home. In addition, Isiah's friend Mark Aguirre had committed to DePaul and Coach Ray Meyer's program, and would be staying in Chicago for college.

Remaining in the city in which he grew up was exactly what Isiah wanted to avoid. It wasn't that he wanted to leave his family behind; far from it. For Isiah, getting out of the Windy City and K-Town meant starting college with a clean slate. Not only did Indiana have a top-flight basketball team that had won national championships under Coach Knight, but its location, in the eyes of one budding young point guard, was a plus. "I could come here without all the chaos of the city and really concentrate on things that I had to do," he asserted once he'd made up his mind to sign with Knight and attend Indiana. "If I had stayed in the city, I was taking a chance something might happen. I might have gotten involved in something."

The fact that IU had a great coach and a strong team influenced Isiah as well, but ultimately it was a decision based more on a desire to alter his surroundings, and not his jump shot, that propelled Isiah to Bloomington. "I've been in the city all my life, and I've been in the ghetto all my life," he said once he had arrived at IU. "Now I had a chance to go someplace outside the ghetto where I could see something new, where I could see how other people lived."

Isiah had seen how his half of the world lived; now was the time to experience something different. For those who'd put their faith in him, this new experience would determine whether or not the effort to leave his native city had been worth it.

CHAPTER THREE

Hoosier!

Once Isiah had decided that Bloomington, Indiana, was the place where he wanted to play his college basketball, it didn't take long for him to establish himself as a major presence in the tough Big Ten conference. This legendary athletic grouping of schools was comprised of Indiana, the University of  Michigan, Michigan State, Wisconsin, Iowa, Northwestern University, Purdue, Illinois, and Minnesota, and had long been regarded as an important testing-ground for future NBA talent. It was at Indiana that Isiah's impact on the basketball court began to be felt on a nation-wide level. Soon he would come to be regarded as one of the most deadly players — at any position — throughout the entire National Collegiate Athletic Association.

Big Ten competition was tough during the years Isiah attended IU. Kevin McHale, later a star with the Boston Celtics, attended Minnesota, and future NBA players Clark Kellogg, Joe Barry Carroll, and Derek Harper wore the jerseys at Ohio State, Purdue, and Illinois, respectively.

The kid from Chicago was now being watched by many more hoop fans than just those who followed the game at the high school level in the Windy City. By displaying his abilities as a member of the powerful Indiana Hoosiers, Isiah started to garner headlines throughout the country as a prolific scorer, passer, and team leader. His picture began appearing in national publications. Viewers nationwide got to know the ins and outs of his game through the larger-than-life medium of television. But perhaps more importantly, Isiah's time at IU would lay the groundwork for even bigger things both on and off the court, and would establish a foundation for his life beyond the collegiate milieu.

College freshmen who have been stars in high schools often find themselves the victims of tremendous pressure to succeed. Nobody wants to go back to the old neighborhood on summer break and have to tell his old playground running-mates that life on the big campus was just too tough, that he was simply unable to raise his performance to a higher level. But this is often what happens to many high school hot-shots after a season or two in college.

Many high school heroes discover all too often that the game they were once able to dominate so easily is now controlled by more talented and more experienced foes. Added to these athletic pressures are the increased demands of the college classroom. Course work is invariably tougher than ever before, and homework, which might never even have been an issue in the past, is now plentiful. Combining sports and academics is tough, and if a young student-athlete wants even the barest semblance of a regular social life, well, that's just another beanbag that has to be added to the complex juggling act that comprises the life of a scholarship-winner in the U.S. college system. And there's a price to pay for not keeping up.

Failure in the classroom, under NCAA regulations, means being ineligible to compete in varsity sports. Lack of success on the court might well mean that the juicy scholarship a smiling coach had dangled as the major enticement for attending *his* school back in the glory days of high school will be cut back or even taken away in subsequent years. After all, there are lots of other talented youngsters playing in tiny gyms across the country who would just love a shot in a big-time college program.

As he's done at every transitional stage in his basketball life, though, Isiah rose to the challenge of elevating his skills — and his aspirations — once at IU. Wearing a number 11 Hoosier uniform, Thomas made the tough jump from high school to college look almost easy. In his freshman year, he led Indiana to the 1980 Big Ten championships. Isiah shot 51 per cent from the field in his first collegiate campaign at Indiana, and scored 14.2 points per game against conference rivals, and 13.9 over the entire season.

What's more, the young man from the West Side of Chicago silenced any critics who might have doubted his ability to be the leader of a major college team like he'd done at the high school level. Thomas finished his freshman year as the number-one Hoosier on the individual stats list in assists, total points, and steals, and was second on the team in rebounds (no mean feat for a 6–1 point guard!). He was the only first-year player ever to be named to the All-Big Ten team up to that point, and was the only Indiana player to start every game during the season.

Isiah's stellar play in his freshman year won him a spot on the U.S. Olympic team. In the days before "Dream Teams," the U.S. selected its Olympic squad from the best amateur — read, college — players in the nation, and Thomas was the hands-down choice for the point guard position. Unfortunately for Isiah, his basketball teammates, and for the rest of the U.S. Olympic team athletes in all sports, the country decided to boycott the 1980 Games in Moscow. President Jimmy Carter had urged the stay-at-home action to protest the Soviet Union's invasion of Afghanistan. Many countries followed Carter's lead and boycotted Moscow; in retaliation, the Soviet Union and its supporters were no-shows at the 1984 Games in Los Angeles.

More than two decades later, Thomas had a chance to advise others about missed Olympic opportunities, as several prospective members of Team USA debated whether or not to attend the 2004 Games in Athens in the face of a possible terrorist threat that many felt was sure to disrupt the game somehow. In fact, point guard Stephon Marbury, a member of Isiah's New York Knicks, was one of the American players that Thomas had in mind when he urged them to journey to Athens. "I would definitely encourage players to go," he said. "Sports has always had a great role in our society, in terms of bringing people together. Sports has been the catalyst for a lot of social change in our culture and throughout the world. . . . I remember being at the White House when President Carter told us [the U.S. team would not be going to Moscow], and watching swimmers and track and field athletes just fall apart . . . for many of them, it was their one shot."

In the U.S., most sports still selected their nominal "Olympic teams," despite not going to Moscow. Basketball was no exception. Instead of a Russian vacation, Isiah and his fellow American hoopsters — including such future pro stars as Sam Bowie, Mark Aguirre, Rolando Blackman, Buck Williams, and Danny Vranes — had to be content with a five-game series of exhibition games against NBA competition. It actually wasn't bad practice for a young man with pro aspirations some day!

Isiah's smooth move to college basketball was the product of a few factors, some based partially on luck and most based on the wise choice he had made in coming to IU. For one thing, Indiana University was indeed an excellent — and perhaps the best — place Thomas could have selected to play college basketball, and thus further his career as an athlete. As anyone who has seen the Gene Hackman film *Hoosiers* can attest, Indiana is a basketball-mad state, and Bloomington was, and is, a basketball-mad college town within it. Because of this state-wide passion, the head coach of the Indiana University varsity basketball team has been elevated to near-God status among young and old fans alike.

Throughout his long career at the helm of the IU program, the name Bobby Knight has been synonymous with Hoosier basketball. But while Knight achieved tremendous success in the Big Ten and at the NCAA level, his renown as a varsity mentor stemmed as much from his philosophical approach to coaching as it did from the success of his teams.

For Knight, there is only one way to play basketball — his way — and all other factors are subsumed to this one, over-riding proviso: if you played ball for him at IU, you played it the way Coach Knight wanted you to play, or you got the hell out of Bloomington! Knight stressed what are commonly referred to as the "fundamentals" of the game: accurate passing, tough but sound team defence, boxing out for rebounds, taking high percentage shots, and above all, no hotdogging. With this constant emphasis on fundamental basketball, it's no surprise that many men who have served as assistant coaches under Knight during his long career at both Army and IU have gone on to achieve tremendous success on their own as head coaches, like NCAA title winner Mike Krzyzewski of Duke University.

Along with sound roundball practice, Bobby Knight stressed classroom performance and a team approach to the game on the court. Over the years he was at IU, Knight came in for much criticism from those who believe — perhaps correctly, to some degree — that no one coach should, in effect, be bigger than the game he's coaching. In other words, opponents of Knight's system maintained that there should be some allowance within his "system" for individual differences and special abilities.

Indeed, those who decried what they felt is Knight's overly-fixed hoops mentality point to the case of a young star who emerged from the obscure and bizarrely-named Indiana town of French Lick in the 1970s. The kid had been a high school god in a state that idolizes such deities, and his ascension to Bloomington had been heartily praised by roundball cognoscenti in Hoosier country. But the kid couldn't handle Knight's stern discipline, and rumors out of Bloomington had it that he'd come under special fire from Knight. As quickly as he'd come, the kid hightailed it away from IU and allegedly started drinking a lot more than was good for him.

In a short while, though, he was back at cross-state rival Indiana State, with his head back together, and perhaps more importantly for his future, his jump shot back to the near-automatic level. The kid eventually led the ISU Sycamores into the 1979 NCAA championships against Michigan State and Magic Johnson, and although his team lost that one, he would go on to become nothing short of one of the greatest NBA stars of all time. That kid was Larry Bird.

The fact that Knight could reject someone like a Larry Bird, the pundits said, was proof that his near-dictatorial approach to college ball was highly suspect. What's more, critics loved to point out Knight's character oddities. This after all was a coach not exactly known for controlling his temper or for his displays of tact. In 1979, exasperated at what he believed was an almost total lack of competence on the part of the organizers of the Pan Am Games in Puerto Rico — a competition in which Isiah represented the U.S. — Knight assaulted a police officer in San Juan. Several years later, his hurl-a-chair-across-the-court episode was widely discussed by college basketball fans and replayed on television highlight shows, almost as though it had been a spectacular dunk or miracle three-pointer.

Whether his approach was intrinsically correct or not is far less important than the central dynamic governing Knight's coaching career at IU: in Bloomington, Knight was given almost unlimited authority to do what he wanted with the Hoosiers' basketball program. It was his show to run, as he saw fit, without particular concern for outsiders or critics. And that's why Isiah Thomas' choice of Indiana as the college to which he would devote the most crucial years of his basketball development was so intriguing. Up to the time of his first practice as a

Hoosier, Isiah had always been "The Man," and that privileged status was about to undergo a serious revision.

On the playground in K-Town and at St. Joseph's, Thomas had developed his freelance style to the level of artistry. No one, least of all him, knew exactly what he was going to do with the ball once it was in his hands. Because of his amazing skills, superior speed, and uncanny court sense, Isiah could create as he went along. Once a defender committed himself one way or another, why, then was the time to decide on whether it was better to shoot or to give it up for the assist. When you're that much quicker than anyone else, your accelerated sense of timing enables you to do pretty much whatever you want in an instant, without the need for plans made up in advance.

Coach Pingatore had seen this ability at a very early age in Isiah and, once he'd taught his young star how to bring it under control, had allowed it to flourish, building a successful team around him. For many coaches, this approach is not all that unusual and in fact prevails at all levels of the game. Look, for example, at the classic Lakers teams of the late-1980s or the Chicago Bulls of modern times. In those instances, Magic and Michael have clearly been given the freedom to create as they go along; their teammates, happy to win championships, have chipped in with supporting roles that complement the improvisations of their star leaders. But there was to be none of this marquee-player stuff within the Isiah-plus-Knight-plus-Hoosiers-equals-success equation.

Even before he enrolled at Indiana, Isiah had received an earful from Knight about his style of play, and about how he would have to change things once in a red-and-white Hoosiers' uniform. At the 1979 Pan Am Games, Knight threatened to kick

Isiah off the squad for his lack of control. "You ought to go to DePaul, Isiah," Knight remembered yelling, in reference to the youngster's runner-up choice of college, "because you sure as hell aren't going to be an Indiana player playing like that!"

In the early stages of Isiah's career at IU, Knight was clear in stating his views that this was one high school graduate who would have to improve on the fundamental aspects of his all-around game if he was to be a success in the red-and-white of the Hoosiers. In the same vein, however, the coach believed that his prize recruit had the ability and the drive to be one of the best young point guards in the country. "He can truly be a great player," said Knight, while cautioning that, "he's not there yet. He's not as fundamentally sound as he has to be to be a great player, and I think that is the thing he is working the hardest on."

In hindsight, it would have been easy to imagine Isiah ignoring the necessity of working on the basics of his game and deciding on a college program that would have allowed him to hog the spotlight like he'd done at every prior stage of his young career. After all, there were certainly schools that would have been more than happy to have him run the show on the court. This approach — "Come here and you'll be the star right from the beginning; go somewhere else and you'll be forced to play team ball" — is often used as a powerful incentive in the recruiting of top high school athletes in all sports. In addition, college coaches know that elite players have an eye on the pros in the not-too-distant future, and many intend to use the college game as a showcase for their talents, in order to impress NBA scouts. In turn, this prima donna situation is fine by the college coach, as long as his team wins. A good example of this environment involved Isiah's old buddy Mark Aguirre, whose talents were pretty well given free rein under coach Ray Meyer at DePaul.

But for Isiah, college represented more than just an opportunity to impress the NBA hawks. He realized that while he was a good, maybe even fantastic, basketball player, he wouldn't be able to get away with his magician's routine for very long. It might even work in college, but never in the pros, where everybody was a playground and high school legend! Remembering his family's urgings, and mindful of the crucial need for him to succeed, both as a way of fulfilling his personal dreams of going pro and his close kin's need for "that NBA paycheck," Isiah suppressed whatever longings for immediate personal glory he might have had and went to IU in the hopes of developing a sound, fundamental skill base under the stern discipline of Bobby Knight.

Lessons learned about defence, about playing under control and, above all, about playing as a team would be ones that would, depending on how successfully they were learned, make him or break him down the line. As it turns out, going to Indiana was a move that was to pay off handsomely for the rest of his life.

With Isiah committed to working on — and improving — the nuts and bolts of his game, and with Knight dedicated to helping him do it, IU took the aforementioned 1980 Big Ten Title behind Isiah's big individual numbers. The Hoosiers made it as far as the Mideast Regional Semi-finals of the NCAA tournament before being knocked out by Big Ten rivals, Purdue. After all, given Isiah's talent and ambition, it was virtually impossible for him not to put up fantastic stats once he had adjusted to the college game. But the important thing to remember is that he was doing it within a bigger, team-first context. Given Coach Knight's insistence on co-operative play, no one who watched the Hoosiers in 1979–80 was surprised that the squad was much more than an all-Thomas show. Isiah was joined by such college standouts as Mike Woodson, Ray Tolbert, Landon Turner, and Butch Carter, and their combined talents were meshed into a cohesive and powerful whole by Knight.

As proof that Knight's sound, stress-the-fundamentals philosophy was taking hold of Isiah's basketball psyche, he was beginning to talk in such a way as to convince people that he'd really benefited from an exposure to the world of IU hoops. "The main reason[s] why we win here at Indiana," said Thomas, were not difficult to understand. "For one, we play harder than any other team. And, two, the game's just simple here. We go out, we pass, we screen and whoever has the shot takes the shot. Then we come down and we play defence." It was compact, fundamentally-sound basketball, the Bobby Knight way.

The Hoosiers coach — who had taken to calling Isiah "Pee Wee" — must have beamed when he heard his young point guard talking about life on the hardwood in such Knightian terms. "It's just like a foot specialist. He just specializes in one thing," continued Isiah. "If he starts going up there and messing with your brain or arm, he's gonna screw up. His thing is best with your foot. Our thing here is just playing defence and scoring points."

Once each player's role was defined within Knight's system, the Hoosier team could congeal as a cohesive unit. For Knight, the critical mass of a team as a whole was decidedly greater than the sum of all of its parts. And in the manner of accomplished drill sergeants, math teachers, and Zen Buddhist masters, whose lessons have a way of affecting the very patterns of their disciples' lives, the teachings of praeceptor Knight were beginning to creep into the very subconscious of a particular young basketball player from Chicago. "I love him [Knight] and I love the players on this team," intoned Isiah. "I think coach Knight keeps everything so simple. And he makes the drills so simple that you specialize. That's something you do every day, every night you dream about it. It's just a part of you. I think that's where he brings out the potential in the individual."

With all of this emphasis on discipline, drills, and the team-first approach, it's still clear that Isiah did not mind shouldering his new role of the Hoosiers' floor general in the least, even though college freshmen are rarely expected to deliver such leadership until later in their careers. Conventional wisdom holds that the transition from high school to college is too tough for a young player to be expected to step in immediately and run a big-time program's offence. But following convention has never been one of Thomas' strong suits — leadership has. "I think the reason the guard is the leader most of the time is because he always has the ball," he observed. "If you've got the ball everybody's got to listen to you." Emphasizing his own particular specialty within the Hoosier framework, Isiah admitted that distributing the basketball was priority number-one for him, a part of his game that would be his trademark for the rest of his career. "My job is to get other people open, to get the ball in position where they can go up [and score]," he declared. Coach Knight apparently trusted Isiah to do this crucial part of the point guard's job, because during his freshman year, Isiah was the only Hoosier to start every game.

While playing basketball was a huge part of Thomas' collegiate life, it wasn't the only thing that occupied his time in Bloomington. Far from it, in fact, and for a young man as driven to succeed as Isiah, getting into a rigorous daily routine was difficult but necessary. Remember, though, that this was a person who'd wake up at 5:30 a.m. for that 2-hour, bus-and-walk commute to high school! In college, then, it was just a matter of establishing priorities and keeping focused.

"You're up late, a lot of times," he admitted. Anyone who's engaged in an athlete's ravenous, post-workout meals followed by the inevitable drowsiness that follows — a stupor caused as much by the digestion of the feast as by the prior exertion — knows the feeling. "You come home from practice dead tired and all you want to do is sleep," he asserted. "So you sleep three, four, five hours and then you wake up and try to study. People say you're supposed to get eight hours of sleep. I know a basketball player doesn't." At least, not a college basketball player with some interest in his schoolwork. "I know I don't," he maintained.

With a course-load equivalent to that of the typical student and the responsibility of several hours a day of practice, plus travel to and from games and time spent watching film and discussing strategy with the coaching staff, Isiah Thomas' life as a conscientious IU student was not easy. Adding to the strain was the fact that by his sophomore year he was struggling to raise his Grade Point Average from 2.9 to the 3.0 he'd need to get into law school (in the GPA system used in U.S. colleges and high schools, a 4.0 represents an "A" grading, a 3.0 is a "B" and so on down).

Classes usually started at 8 or 8:30 a.m. for Isiah, and by 2:30 p.m. during the basketball season, he'd be on the hardwood practising with his IU teammates until 5:30. After a training-table dinner, the study part of the day began at around 7:30, with some varied amount of sleep to follow. Within all of this tightly-scheduled activity, Isiah started to notice that there wasn't a lot of time for much else. "It's hard to have any friends. Nobody tells you you can't go see him or her, but you know if you do you'll lose the time for study," he lamented.

In all fairness, though, it should be remembered that most student-athletes, given the passage of time, reflect as alumni that the closest friendships made during their collegiate years were in fact the very people engaged in identical endeavors; in other words, their teammates. There is something about this shared effort that builds bonds that seem to last forever. This fact is borne out in Isiah's life by the presence of ex-Hoosier teammate Jim Thomas (no relation) many years later within the Toronto Raptors organization.

Besides, most time-management specialists would agree that having a set block of time taken up every day by an athletic-team practice simply forces the youthful student-athlete — a specimen invariably imbued with boundless energy anyway — to budget his or her time more wisely. Such skills usually prove invaluable later in life. Given Isiah's tremendous capacity for involvement in many different things like business, community activity, and of course playing basketball as a pro athlete and beyond, it looks as though he learned something through this baptism-by-fire as a busy undergrad. It was hard not to feel sorry for the young Thomas, though, when he was unable to enjoy many of the social activities that comprise the existence of the typical college student. "Your life is so isolated," he complained.

The grinding schedule needed to mix basketball and school-work was tough, but Isiah had come to IU with some pretty definite ideas about what he wanted to study, and what he wanted from a college education. During his youth on the tough streets of West Chicago, Thomas had seen countless peers — some friends, others he knew by name or reputation only — run into major trouble with the law through drugs, violence, and gang warfare. He was aware that within the criminal justice system, it was difficult for inner-city blacks to escape jail sentences after committing even relatively minor crimes, or at least offences that within the context of the ghetto were not serious ones. Because of this inescapable fact about the place in which he grew up, Isiah had high hopes of moving into the field of criminal law. "I know people who got a lot of [jail] time, six, seven years, for doing crimes, even though they were petty theft," he remembered. "I think that's too much time to take out of a person's life. I'd just like to help people like that."

Providing assistance to the kind of people he grew up around was a major goal for Thomas, one he believed could be attained through becoming a lawyer. His exposure to the court-room came early at IU, but it wasn't through a pre-law field trip or anything of the sort. Instead, he was involved in a much-publicized case before the Monroe County Misdemeanor and Small Claims Court, a case stemming from an assault against him by a fellow student in an IU dormitory.

Isiah received a wound on his right eyebrow that needed eight stitches to close, but it didn't prevent him from playing basketball. The other student was charged with battery, and the trial gave Isiah his first real exposure to the world of jurisprudence. "There was no way they were going to win that case," he said. "But they tried. I learned a lot about being a lawyer. I told my attorney to tell his attorney — it was like a plea bargain thing — if he'd stay away from me, doesn't cause me any more trouble, then I'd just let it go."

Having had this first-hand look at both the courtroom and the tough circumstances faced every day by inhabitants of the inner city, Isiah was committed to the idea of becoming a lawyer. "I don't think people really understand the circumstances or obstacles that are put in front of a person's life if he's living in the neighborhood," he said as a way of explaining his chosen field of study. "In my neighborhood, you had to be with the gang or get beat up every day. That was the only way you could make it."

With his family depending on their youngest member, "making it" became the crucial element in Isiah's life. But for a youngster from the streets, it was often difficult to relate the terms of his struggle to those more privileged than he in the ivory-tower surroundings of a college campus. "People on the outside can look in and say, 'you could have done this and you could have done that,'" he says of those who would judge people who hadn't managed to emerge from the ghetto like he had. "But when you're living there, it's a totally different story."

Isiah knew that his time at Indiana represented more to him — and by extension, to his family — than simply the chance to improve his basketball skills. Sociologists can analyse the concept of "mobility" through college and professional sports endlessly, but for Isiah, the facts surrounding his life and how it could be improved by college were as simple as one of coach Knight's practice drills. "I look at myself this way. Basketball is the best thing I can do," he asserted self-critically. "I'm not a better student than I am a basketball player. And when I go on the court, I just try to do my best. I'm not not gonna feel nervous or anything like that because this is the best thing I can do."

This attitude might have simply been a way of taking the pressure off, sort of a don't-put-all-your-eggs-in-one-basket defence mechanism, but it was a canny one nevertheless. Paradoxically, many top athletes have reported that their performance has improved when they've been able to admit to themselves that failing in sports is really OK because in the end they've got something to fall back on to pay the rent if the sports part of their life doesn't work out exactly as planned. For Isiah, this was one of the big reasons for acquiring a college education.

"If the opportunity is there, yes, I'd like to play [on a professional team] because basketball has been my life," he declared. "But I don't want basketball to be the main point in my life. I want it to be that I can play and I can go on and do something else." The hard fact of the matter, though, was that if a young man like Isiah wanted to escape his surroundings — attain some mobility — sports was the only way he was ever going to gain access to the training, education, and coaching that would enable him to do the "something else," and to prepare for the fall-back career.

Thomas had a pretty good sense about the way in which the "haves" and the "have-nots" went about taking advantage of opportunities in his native country, and had made up his mind about how he'd get ahead. "If you play basketball or football, it's the only way out," he admitted. "If you're smart and a straight-A student, that doesn't mean anything. Colleges give out academic scholarships, but they only give out one or two and usually some rich doctor's son or daughter gets that. So what does that guy do who's really smart but can't go anywhere, his parents can't send him to school?"

Isiah was answering that question himself at IU. Given his amazingly hard-nosed and realistic attitude, and given the equally stunning contrast between his approach and the lack of responsibility and foresight shown by far too many "me-first" college basketball superstars in recent memory, it would have been a near miracle if Isiah had not succeeded at IU. But the way in which the pace of his college career picked up in the 1980–81 season couldn't have been depicted better by a professional screenwriter trying to create a different version of the Hoosiers movie.

By Isiah's sophomore year, Indiana was being touted as a first-rank contender for both the Big Ten title and for the NCAA crown. Opposing teams were beginning to zero in on Thomas as the key to the Hoosiers offence, and this often meant his being the brunt of some rough handling in the paint. In February, he was ejected — for the first time in his career — from a game against the University of Iowa Hawkeyes for a flagrant foul against an Iowa player, Steve Krafcisin. Isiah later called the foul "just dumb" and remembered that "I was cutting down the middle and I don't know if he grabbed my shirt or placed his arm in my way." Despite the fact that it's highly unlikely that anyone has ever just "placed" an arm, or any other limb in front of a player driving the lane in a Big Ten game during the last, say, 30 years of the rough-and-tumble conference, Isiah maintained that he was just protecting himself. "I went to knock away his hand with my arm and it went into his face. I'm not a fighter," he told reporters, smiling in his best pre-law rhetoric. "I'll fight if I have to. But I'd rather talk my way out of a situation."

Years later, Isiah would instruct a Detroit Pistons rookie named Michael Williams about the necessity of a small man protecting himself on the drive to the hole amidst a swarm of giants "placing" their arms in his path. Williams had been completely laid out by Detroit veteran Bill Laimbeer in a preseason scrimmage at the Pistons' camp in Windsor, Ontario. After the session, as Williams struggled to regain his reeling senses, Isiah told him, "You know, if you're going in on a big guy like that, you got to know how to protect yourself. In college, you just go. You jump over them, and you dunk on them. But at this level, everybody's so much stronger and so much taller that you got to find ways to protect your body while you get your shot off."

Unfortunately for Isiah, fans who booed him after his altercation with Krafcisin didn't completely buy the "protection" alibi, especially since he had been involved in another tussle a few weeks earlier in a game against Purdue. Isiah had allegedly slugged Boilermaker guard Roosevelt Barnes, but game films shown by Bobby Knight demonstrated that Barnes had unmistakably thrown the first punch. For his part, Isiah was nonplussed about the whole Barnes incident, saying only that, "It's not worth the time to comment."

The adverse press that came out of the Barnes first incident certainly didn't help Isiah's reputation when it came time to explain his part in the Krafcisin altercation, but both served to teach him something about how fickle the perception of fans can be. "I was booed and I knew the fans were remembering Purdue and Roosevelt," he said. "That hurt me personally. I don't want them to think of me that way." In fact, credentials as an accomplished scrapper were the last thing Isiah wanted listed on his roundball résumé. Certainly, he had learned to defend himself on the playgrounds, but any reputation that was beginning to grow as a brawler was unwelcome. "I don't want people to think that 'Hey, there's the guy who punched so and so.' I want them to think of me as the guy who helped so and so."

As is the case with just about every other athlete in the world of high-profile American sports, Isiah had to deal with controversies like the ones that surrounded his on-court scraps with Krafcisin and Barnes. Typically, though, he was beginning to gain a name for himself as a very poised and controlled young man when it came to facing the media. This grace under fire held him in good stead when his play, and by extension his decision-making abilities, came up for criticism at the hands of Al McGuire, one of the most respected men in the college game. McGuire, who had been a longtime coach at Marquette University and had led the school to an NCAA championship, was a color commentator for NBC during the 1980–81 collegiate season.

After the Hoosiers had lost 63–56 to the University of North Carolina (who were shortly to acquire the services of a youngster named Michael Jordan), before a national television audience, McGuire went on record as saying that Isiah's game was being slowed down by fatigue accumulated by playing through two summers without a break. Isiah had been a member of the 1979 Pan Am team (the one coached by Knight the Cop Slugger of San Juan) and a part of the 1980 non-Olympic team that took on NBA talent in exhibition games. McGuire's argument was that instead of using the summers to rest and recharge for the upcoming seasons — usually the prescribed approach for collegians — Isiah had been barn-storming with the national teams, and this had in turn wiped him out at a point where his Hoosiers needed him.

Having his on-court play and his off-court decisions ripped by such a hoops authority as McGuire, however, fazed Isiah not one iota. "That's his opinion," he commented tersely, adding, "I don't think I'm tired." Later, he would tell a local reporter that playing internationally was an honor for him. "The most important thing about it was that I was representing my family, my friends, and my country." Not surprisingly, Thomas maintained that neither the fights nor McGuire's comments would budge him from his principal goals: playing good, team-oriented basketball and leading IU to an NCAA championship. "The only thing that distracts me is when we lose," he insisted. "Sometimes when we lose, though, I feel like I'm the cause."

Causation, at least insofar as sports is concerned, goes both ways. And although Isiah was prepared to internalize IU's losses as his own fault, there were many more people around the country who were equally ready to give him lots of the credit for the Hoosiers' victories. Happily for basketball fans in Bloomington, those wins were coming fast and furious during Isiah's sophomore year, and kept on coming well into the NCAA tournament.

Along with team wins, though, Isiah began racking up individual awards. In March of 1981, he was chosen as a first-team All-American by the Associated Press and The Sporting News, and was named to the UPI's All-Big Ten first team. In typical fashion, Isiah put these solo awards on the back shelf, choosing instead to focus on the larger, and for him vastly more important, realm of team success. "No biggie," he responded after hearing about his All-Big Ten appointment. "To be honest, I don't care about that stuff." When told of the All-American selection, Thomas was similarly unmoved: "It's nice, but there's nothing I can do with it. I just want to win the NCAAs, and if I can do that, everything has been accomplished."

To everyone who had been watching the team during 1980–81, it looked like the Hoosiers were beginning to gel at just the right time for a big run at the NCAAs and the hype and fanfare of "March Madness." Of the team chemistry that had developed, Isiah had nothing but praise. "We all get along well," he said. "We're all like a family." This was a good sign for IU fans, who Isiah also described as having "more class" and being "more friendly" than other crowds he'd played in front of.

At the beginning of the season it appeared that Isiah and Knight still had some philosophical differences to work out, as Bobby kicked Thomas out of a practice. But Isiah's joking reaction to this ejection — "It was my turn, I guess" — indicated that things weren't critical. In addition, observers began to notice that while Knight was unerring in his insistence that the game be played according to his dictates, he had started to loosen up a bit in his attitude to Isiah. In December, Knight had made the sophomore point guard team captain and had told him in no uncertain terms that the team was his to run — at least insofar as on-court inspiration and playmaking went — as he wanted.

Indiana won its second Big Ten title under Isiah's leadership in 1980–81, a campaign in which he averaged 16.3 points and 5 assists per game in conference play. In the NCAA tournament, two efficient wins prefaced a victory over St. Joseph's University of Pennsylvania in the Mideast Regional in Bloomington, setting the stage for the tourney's Final Four. Against the

Louisiana State Tigers, he took charge. In 26 minutes on the floor, Isiah poured in 14 points on 6-for-8 shooting from the field, while distributing four assists in the Hoosier victory. After downing LSU, there was only one obstacle standing in the way of an NCAA title for IU and Isiah, and that was the powerhouse University of North Carolina team that had beaten them earlier in the game that inspired Al McGuire's criticism of Isiah. The Tar Heels, under the guidance of Dean Smith, a coach revered as a member of the same upper echelon as Bobby Knight, had pummeled the University of Virginia and their giant but erratic 7–4 center, Ralph Sampson, to make it into the final.

The 1981 NCAA final in Philadelphia's Spectrum was classic Bobby Knight, classic Hoosier basketball, and classic Isiah Thomas. Though playing sluggishly and trailing the Tar Heels 16–8 midway through the first half, IU woke up and thrashed UNC, 63–50 to capture the school's third national crown. Curry Kirkpatrick of *Sports Illustrated* called it an "unrelenting team performance that couldn't be upstaged by individual heroics." But this didn't prevent *SI* from adorning their front cover with a full-body shot of Isiah cutting down the net after the game, and entitling the feature story on the Hoosier win "And a Little Child Led Them," a reference to a quotation from the Bible's Book of Isaiah.

The victory surge came about when Knight sent Jim Thomas into the game to join Isiah in the back court, and moved Randy Wittman into the swingman's spot. Jim Thomas responded by hounding the Tar Heel's main offensive threat, Al Wood, and essentially shutting him down. On the wing, Wittman "took what I could get" and hit four long-range jumpers that put IU ahead 27–26 at the half. With Landon

Turner all over the 'Heels big Sam Perkins, the Hoosiers began turning the screws that would eventually tighten to the point of a UNC submission.

At the start of the second half, Isiah, who had bricked his way to a sorry 1-for-7 performance in the first 20 minutes, started to turn it on. A series of steals by the player Kirkpatrick called "the little prophet with the balloon cheeks" led to easy Hoosier baskets and a 39–30 lead. Isiah would finish with a game-high 23 points in addition to his 5 assists, but it was his tenacious defence, and that of his teammates, that turned things around for the Hoosiers. As can so often happen in college ball, one big defensive turn-around of 4 or 5 minutes can make all the difference. Dejected Tar Heel Al Wood confessed after the game that "the way they jumped on us there broke our backs." For his part, Isiah was modest, claiming that the reason for his game-altering steals, many off passes intended for Perkins, was that "the ball was slippery."

When the ink had dried on the sportswriters' reports, the extent to which IU had dominated the 1981 NCAAS was revealed. Five years previous, the Hoosiers had defeated the five teams they faced in the tournament by a total of 66 points. This time, the margin was a whopping 113!

True to form, Bobby Knight had made headlines during the tournament by dealing with a critical fan in a New Jersey hotel room by shoving him into a waste basket. After the defeat of UNC, somebody asked Isiah if he'd ever received that particular form of treatment from coach Knight. "Not yet," he kidded. But Isiah had himself relegated IU's foes to the trash heap on the court, and had achieved, for himself, his family, his teammates, and for Coach Knight, the ultimate success in college basketball.

The newspapers and the glossy magazines were full of pictures of the sophomore in the number-eleven jersey, grinning cheerfully in the aftermath of victory. The Hoosier faithful were ecstatic, and hoop fans across the country were left wondering what the young dynamo would do for an encore. After all, Tar Heel Coach Dean Smith, gracious as always in defeat, had described Isiah as "one of the best point guards in college history" after the iu star had run rings around his best players. Perhaps another NCAA win in 1982 would do the trick?

Isiah Thomas did have quite a surprise in store. But for Indiana University basketball fans, it wasn't quite what they'd been hoping for . . .

CHAPTER FOUR

Now a Pro

Shortly after the victory celebration had
died down in Bloomington, Isiah dropped a
bombshell on his Hoosiers supporters.
Following two great collegiate campaigns,
and with two more remaining, Thomas
decided that it was time to go pro.

The wise observer might well have seen it
coming. Before the big NCAA win over North Carolina, Isiah
had told *Sports Illustrated* that "If I have opportunity" to turn
professional early, "I probably will look at it." But *Sports
Illustrated* also reported that after IU had defeated St. Joseph's in
the Mideast Regional in the NCAA tournament, Isiah told a
couple of potential Hoosier recruits to practise hard over the
summer holidays "so we can do it again next year," suggesting
that he'd be back to join them.

Those who knew of Isiah's home life realized that going pro
early — what was often called taking the "hardship" option in

those days — might be the best thing Isiah could do to help the Thomas family. Still others, though, mindful of Isiah's often-stated desire to get an education so as to have something to fall back on when he was done with hoops, believed that he'd stay at IU for all four years to complete his degree and thus be ready for law school one day. "You can only play basketball so long," he asserted, "and then you have 35 or 40 more years to do something with your life." (Of course, those who would follow Thomas' career for the subsequent 25 years would note that he managed to stick pretty close to the game.)

Indeed, a Bloomington newspaper had reported shortly before the Final Four that Isiah was adamant about his plans to remain at Indiana to finish his degree, and that if he was offered a spot on an NBA squad, he wouldn't take it. Isiah was quoted as saying that "After I finish at IU, if I have a chance to play professional ball, I'll take it; but I would like to have a career of my own when I'm finished."

As late as three weeks after the Hoosiers' NCAA victory, Isiah was still claiming he'd be staying at IU, but the headlines were beginning to change a bit. They suggested now that there was some indecision creeping in about whether staying at Indiana was really in the best interests of everyone involved. "It's kind of tough," said Isiah in reference to the vast number of issues he'd been forced to think about while making his decision to stay in college or declare himself eligible for the hardship draft. "You have to consider a lot of things. I have to consider myself. Financially, I could be set for life." Typically, though, Isiah was thinking about how his choice would affect more people than just himself. "I could provide my family with a lot of opportunities, and my mother would never have to work again," he noted.

Heart of Darkness writer Joseph Conrad once wrote that as human beings, "we live as we dream: alone." In Isiah Thomas' case, the process of weighing his long-held dreams of one day supporting his family with an NBA paycheck against his desire to stay in school was also conducted on his own. While other top pro possibilities like Mark Aguirre and Ralph Sampson had availed themselves of the opportunity to discuss their NBA futures with several team officials, Isiah did not seek out any such advice, nor had he been made a formal offer by any pro team. "I haven't talked to anybody about this," he admitted, in a style that would have made Conrad proud. "It's my decision. I have to live with it. It would be unfair to bring anyone else into it. Anyone else would be prejudiced about the decision."

With all of this solo tough-guy rhetoric, though, Isiah was still prepared to admit that in the event that he did leave IU, he'd be making an emotion-laden decision. "It's hard to make the choice. I have a lot of friends here, especially on the basketball team," he confessed. "I don't really know what I'm going to do." But with the Detroit Pistons and the Dallas Mavericks dangling over $1 million a year in front of the University of Virginia's Sampson, and the Pistons offering $1.28 million to Dominique Wilkins of the University of Georgia, it was hard for Isiah to resist the lure of big-league cash, especially considering what it would mean for his family. But no matter what his choice, Thomas insisted in keeping the whole thing as low-key — and as honest — as possible. "I'm not big enough to have press conferences yet," he declared. "I'll probably tell Coach [Knight] what I've decided. He's the one who really matters."

By the end of April, 1981, less than a month after leading the Hoosiers to the NCAA title, Isiah declared himself eligible for the

NBA draft. In a statement published in the Indiana University school newspaper, Isiah laid out clearly his reasons for deciding to pass up his final two years at Indiana:

> *I wish to announce that I have requested that my name be placed on the eligibility list for the 1981 National Basketball Association collegiate draft.*
>
> *In so doing, I wish to acknowledge the obligation I have to those who provided me an opportunity to obtain a fine education at Indiana University and the privilege of playing for a great American basketball tradition, the Indiana Hoosiers, and for a great coach, Coach Knight.*
>
> *While I can never fully repay these obligations, I hope that whatever contribution I may have made to the success of our team will, in some way, partially redeem my indebtedness.*
>
> *I have, however, a greater obligation to myself and my family, and while the decision was difficult, the choice was clear.*
>
> *I wish at this time to thank Coach Knight and the coaching staff for their great interest and help in my behalf and in my development as a person and as a basketball player.*
>
> *I need also to thank my teammates, whom I will miss greatly.*
>
> *I owe a great deal to the loyal Indiana fans, who encourage and inspire the Indiana tradition, which will continue long after I leave.*
>
> *Finally, to my fellow students — it may take me a little longer, but I'll be coming back to Indiana until I graduate.*
>
> *— Isiah Thomas*

Within Isiah's published statement, one that shows some pretty clear signs that he had already learned a thing or two about getting a message out via the press, it's possible to see a number of key elements that informed his decision to go pro. First, there was, by his own admission, some regret over having to leave his friends, teammates, and Coach Knight at IU. No one, least of all Isiah, however, thought that the Hoosier program would collapse upon his departure. Knight was just too good and too experienced a coach to ever let that happen; besides, the veteran IU mentor had always made a point of not building his squads around a single superstar. "I'm pretty sure Indiana basketball will be secure," Isiah predicted. By all indications, nobody on the Hoosiers varsity begrudged Isiah his big shot at stardom. "My teammates are happy for me," he related. "We have a special relationship on the team. I'll miss a lot of my friends, but if they're friends of mine, they'll always be friends."

Second, there was the feeling of indebtedness over having benefited from the facilities and opportunities made available to him as a Hoosier athlete. But as Isiah rightly pointed out in his published statement, his leadership on a team that won two Big Ten titles and one 5 AA trophy more than made up for what he took away from the school. In terms of gate receipts from home games, alumni donations given in the enthusiastic aftermath of a national title, and the recruiting prestige that comes with being able to say that your program won the big one, Isiah more than paid for his education during his two years in Bloomington.

Finally, Isiah addresses the theme of compromising his education by leaving school early. As he said in the published statement, though, he had every intention of completing his degree work over the course of his pro career. It would be easy to foot the tuition bills during the off-season with a pro contract paying the way. "It'll take me a little longer to finish, that's all," he insisted. "I have a chance to do both things now." Indeed, Isiah had to promise mom Mary Thomas that he'd keep returning to college in the off-season until he'd earned his degree. "Just as soon as the last game of the [NBA] season is over," his mom stated, "he's going to pick up those books. That's definite."

Once he'd made the decision to become a professional basketball player, Isiah Thomas had little choice but to sit back and await the reaction of those around him, and of those whose job it is to offer up commentary on such developments in the world of sports. "I feel pretty good about the decision," said a philosophical Isiah after alerting the media as to his intentions. "Financially, I'll be set for life." Keeping in mind the fact that those who find themselves suddenly without financial worries at age 19 often discover that the newly-acquired wealth brings with it an entirely new set of problems, Isiah was determined to keep a level head. "I don't really feel any different," he claimed, mindful nevertheless that whatever pro contract he was soon to sign would make him a millionaire. "I don't want to have to adjust to the money, I want the money to adjust to me. I'm not going to be a jerk just because I have more money now."

Certainly, when Isiah moved, later in his career to management positions with the Raptors, Pacers and Knicks, the whole process of going pro early must have given him some good personal background knowledge of the situations faced by the new breed of young NBA pros, many of whom consider entering the big leagues right out of high school or only after a single year of NCAA ball.

In the same way that his IU teammates took the news that Isiah would be going pro with respect, admiration, and best wishes for their friend and former on-court leader, many Hoosier supporters had only the highest hopes for "their" Isiah on his way to the pros. One student newspaper columnist supported his decision to go pro as a means of supporting the Thomas family, noting that he'd "been a giver at IU, all the way." Another writer maintained that "his true fans are those who now will support that decision all the way," contending that "now, basketball followers must respect his decision to join the National Basketball Association. . . . IU basketball fans now have the task of helping Thomas to go forward without reservations and cheering him on to a successful professional career. With a basketball player as good as Thomas," the writer concluded, "it shouldn't be hard."

While the choice was clear to him, and while he received a lot of support in making it, leaving Indiana early and becoming a professional basketball player after only two years of college was still a brave thing to do. Sure, it was easy for Isiah to claim that this was the smartest move he could make, both for himself as an athlete and on behalf of his family. There was no doubt in his mind — or anyone else's, for that matter — that he would be picked up by an NBA club, likely as one of the first three draft picks. But what then? Surely some big-time exec would be happy to get his signature on a contract, but that would represent just the beginning of a much more complicated series of events, a series that was by no means certain to go in a direction favorable to Isiah Thomas.

First, there was the matter of his age. Despite having overcome what for most people would be a lifetime of adversity and struggle, Isiah was only 19 when he decided to go pro. At such a young age, it would be easy for him to be intimidated by veterans on the court, and attracted by the shady promises of newfound "friends" off it. Life in the NBA would not only mean having to prove himself competitively against some of the finest athletes in the world, but would also require a mature business sense and a great degree of composure away from the game, especially where contract negotiations were concerned.

A second major question regarding the early-entry Isiah centered on his playing ability. Although it sounds almost comical in retrospect, there was by no means any iron-clad guarantee that Thomas would take the pros by storm as a point guard. It was one thing to be able to blow by college guys like they were standing still, but the pros he'd soon be facing were bigger, quicker, and meaner than most of the competition he'd faced while at Indiana. And even if he did have the talent — which, after all, seemed a pretty sure bet — what about the host of outside factors that differentiate the pro game so markedly from the hoops played in college? Injuries, the stress of having to play hard night-in and night-out, the disconcerting effect of constant travel, weird food, strange cities, and unfriendly crowds had been known to take their toll on even the most seasoned of veterans, not to mention sapping the strength of many a promising rookie.

With all of these potential hazards lying in wait, ready to derail the NBA career of the new, post-collegiate Isiah, there were nevertheless a whole host of NBA executives raring to get Thomas to set his Isiah Lord Henry down on a contract bearing the seal of their particular club. Once he'd declared himself eligible for the draft and more than willing to take a crack at pro basketball, Isiah could sit back and watch the guys in suits battle it out for the rights to his roundball services.

The drafting system in place in those days was a straight-forward set-up wherein the team with the worst record in the previous season drafted first, the club with the second-worst record drafted second, and so on. This system had to be altered when it became evident that teams were intentionally losing games in order to be assured of first pick; it was replaced by a random selection of picking order among several of the league's worst teams. But following the old system, the Dallas Mavericks, the not-so-proud owners of a woeful 15–67 record in 1980–81, won the right to pick first in the June, 1981, NBA draft.

The Mavs, an expansion team struggling to move ahead under coach Dick Motta, were seriously considering enlisting the service of the young man from Chicago via the Bloomington detour, and paying him handsomely for his labors. "A true, gifted playmaking guard like Isiah Thomas comes along about as often as a great center," Motta pointed out. "He's a winner and I love winners. When you get a player like Isiah you can be set at point guard for 5 to 10 years." For his part, Isiah allegedly said that he wasn't a big fan of "all that cowboy stuff" he'd heard about in Dallas. This attitude didn't exactly endear him to the Mavericks' front office, and might eventually have been the reason that Isiah never ended up wearing a Mavs uniform.

Other NBA GMs and coaches were as impressed with Isiah's pro prospects as Dick Motta. Jack McKinney, then the coach of the Indiana Pacers, called Thomas "one of the two or three best players in the country. He's certainly the best guard in the country." Predicting that Isiah would be picked among the first few youngsters chosen in the draft — his Chicago playground pal Aguirre and Buck Williams, a superb, Bible-toting rebounder from the University of Maryland were two others mentioned in the same pre-draft breath as he — McKinney shared the prevailing NBA opinion regarding Thomas' future in the big leagues. The Pacers' head coach felt that Isiah had "what it takes to play on a professional level. If he didn't, there would be a lot of teams surprised. When you reach the level that Isiah is on, I think you can step into the professional scene easily."

In the days leading up to the 1981 draft, it appeared certain that the Mavericks wanted to use their first pick to take Mark Aguirre. What wasn't so clear, though, were the reasons why the Dallas club seemed to get cold feet over Isiah and turned instead to his 6–7 friend from DePaul. Isiah denied saying anything negative about the "cowboy" image of the Texas city. "No one ever asked me about Dallas," he claimed. "As far as the Dallas people saying those things, I think there was a misunderstanding. I think words got turned around."

Leaving aside speculations about verbal sniping, perhaps it was simply the case that the Mavericks wanted a bigger player who could shoot well from the outside and pick up points down low. Certainly, Aguirre's flashy game, with its emphasis on scoring, would put fans in the seats for the expansion Mavericks. For Aguirre, who averaged 24.5 points a game at DePaul in his three seasons there, the journey from the Chicago mean streets to an NBA contract was a dream come true, just as it was for Isiah, and not just for selfish reasons. "I left school because I wanted to help my mother," he said, just before signing with Dallas. "I don't want her to do anything she doesn't have to. She's been the light of my life."

The Detroit Pistons had been so sure that Dallas would take Isiah that they'd actively been pursuing Aguirre, and largely ignoring Thomas. But the news that the Mavs had switched allegiances to the ex-DePaul Blue Devil made the Detroit front office very happy indeed. The Pistons had been struggling for years, and lacked both talent and leadership. Upon hearing that Isiah would be available to his club, Detroit General Manager Jack McCloskey was overjoyed. "This is what we've been waiting for," he enthused. "We will absolutely take Isiah — unless somebody makes us such a fantastic trade offer we can't afford to turn it down. I don't foresee trading him once we've drafted him," McCloskey predicted.

McCloskey, brimming with anticipation over the prospect of signing Isiah, knew that the ex-Hoosier was not only a guy who knew his stuff on the court, but someone who, because of his exciting style and captivating presence, would be instrumental in rejuvenating fan support in Detroit. McCloskey called his new target "obviously a player who has charisma, the magic touch and charm. And he is loaded, loaded with talent." In the Pistons' pre-draft strategizing, admitted McCloskey, "it was our top priority to get such a player."

Observers of pro and college hoops alike were quick to note the similarities between Isiah and Aguirre, as well as the nice symmetry that surrounded their 1–2 draft order in 1981. In the draft itself, things went true to form as Dallas took Aguirre first, and the Pistons nabbed Thomas second. Both men had the same agent at the time, Chicago attorney George Andrews, and both signed for a starting pay of around $400,000 per year plus big bonuses for casting their lots with their respective teams.

"This is a great opportunity for me," said Isiah as the flash-bulbs popped and the ink was drying on his new contract. "I can always go back to school, but I can't always make a million dollars." He also repeated his mystification regarding just why

Dallas had seemingly lost interest in him and turned their interest to Aguirre instead. Regarding the draft, Isiah proved that he'd done his homework on the two franchises who had been interested in his services, and that he had a realistic outlook on what the first few years would be like on a team bad enough to warrant a top-2 draft pick. "I'm not unhappy about coming to Detroit. It has the capability of being a winning team," he stated, knowing full well that in the two prior seasons, the Pistons had managed to lose 66 and 61 games, respectively. "I'm not saying that Dallas is a bad organization. But Detroit is closer to winning." Regarding his prospective contributions to the Pistons' offence, Isiah was only half-joking when he predicted that, "In Detroit, I won't have anyone to pass the ball to."

McCloskey had signed his budding superstar. All that remained now was to see how Isiah would adjust to the banging and increased physicality of the NBA game. He'd made the transition from high school to college look easy, but could he do it again? After all, the college competition wore nifty varsity letter jackets, but the guys in the big time played for serious money, a lot of which was going to be thrown Isiah's way as reimbursement for an expected contribution far exceeding that of the average rookie.

Detroit GM McCloskey had big plans for the brand-new point guard, and those who had followed Isiah's career at both of the scholastic levels he'd played in were anxious to see how he'd fare among the giants. He was already being likened to Kansas City's Phil Ford as the game's definitive small guard, but optimists were pointing out that Isiah's outside shot was better than Ford's. On the down side, however, NBA skeptics warned that while Thomas had been able to make up for his lack of size with cunning and quickness in college, the pro league — where the players were both big and fast — was no place for a little guy, and that all of the Isiah-hype would die off once he'd had a taste of some of the rough stuff that comprises the typical NBA outing.

He'd been touted highly, drafted proudly, and signed lucratively, but now that he was on the doorstep of the big time, Thomas would have to prove himself all over again. Luckily, swift and easy transitions were beginning to become something of a trademark for Isiah.

In his very first regular-season game in a Detroit Pistons uniform, Isiah sent a message to the fans, players, and management of the National Basketball Association that he had not foregone his final two years of college just because the pros stayed in better hotels while traveling. Now 20 years old, Isiah had spent a decent exhibition season with the Pistons before they opened the 1981–82 campaign on Friday, October 30, 1981, on the Pistons' then-home floor at the Pontiac Silverdome. Detroit's opponents on that night were the Milwaukee Bucks, a team led by the man who'd be Isiah's match-up on offence and defence, Quinn Buckner. A successful TV analyst after his playing days ended, Buckner is still one of the few players to have won an NCAA title, an Olympic gold medal, and an NBA championship during his career. Buckner had also come out of the Chicago high school system, and had played for Bobby Knight at Indiana. The smart, tough veteran leader of a very good Bucks club that had gone 60–22 the year before, Quinn would prove a formidable one-on-one opponent for Isiah in the rookie's first big league game.

They say there are two sides to every story. The tale of Isiah's pro debut, however, is an exception to this rule. On the good side, Detroit won the opening game of the 1981–82 season by squeezing the Bucks down the stretch for a 118–113 victory. And on the even-better side, Isiah's NBA coming-out party was, by all possible standards of measurement, an absolutely phenomenal success. He scored 31 points against Buckner and the other Milwaukee defenders, and completely took charge of Pistons coach Scotty Robertson's offence. In fact, it was Isiah's leadership that really impressed Robertson — although there was no objection to the 31 clicks he managed to put up on the scoreboard, either. "Frankly, I'm not concerned about the number of points he gets," said Scotty. "That's the last of his assets I want to emphasize. Getting the offence in motion: that's his job."

It was a job very nicely done by the rookie. "If I said he played well, I'd obviously be understating," said Robertson. Quinn Buckner, no slouch himself when it came to analyzing the contributions of a point guard to a pro basketball team, declared, "There's no question he's a player. He makes everyone else play well — that's one of his biggest assets. He's clever. He's good at faking fouls. The officials don't believe a young player has that much savvy, but he does."

Isiah was conscious of Buckner's stature as an NBA player, and simply rose to the occasion in his first regular-season game. What's more, he recognized that the Pistons needed his skills as a floor general and he delivered. It took him only 9 seconds to record his first pro basket, but Milwaukee had opened up a 14-point lead by the end of the first quarter. Detroit battled back and by the half was within 2 points. Actually, they should have been trailing by 5 at intermission, but were even closer thanks to an Isiah shot that even he couldn't claim to be able to make with any regularity: a 50-foot, nothing-but-net three-pointer at the halftime buzzer.

It was that kind of night for the NBA neophyte, one that boded well for a bright pro future. Into the second half, Isiah began putting on the kind of show that he would become famous for in the Motor City over the next 13 years — steals and assists for easy layups by teammates, plus clutch free-throw shooting down the stretch. With 24 seconds left on the clock, he drained 2 from the charity stripe to put the Pistons ahead, 116–113, and with 3 seconds remaining, he knocked down another pair of freebies to ice the win. When asked about his composure when facing those big free throws in the dying seconds, Isiah responded with a mixture of confidence and the realization that each and every NBA contest would be a test of his stamina. "I felt pretty good," he admitted, "but the big thing I wanted to do was get it over so I could go sit down." Isiah had put in 41 tough minutes, and knew that there'd be 81 chances to do it all over again during his rookie campaign. Thirteen years later, established as the General Manager of the Toronto Raptors, Isiah would confront the issue of his star first-year point guard, Damon Stoudamire, and the fatigue and injuries he was facing as he led the struggling expansion club. He knew from first-hand experience what Damon was going through!

How does a rookie point guard come to play his first pro game with the kind of composure illustrated by Isiah — and by his protégé Stoudamire years later — on that night in Detroit? In the end analysis, it comes down to the realization that as a test of wills and brawn, it doesn't much matter where a basketball game is played. It's possible to get psyched by the lights, the uniforms, and the fans, but if you know how to play the game, and in Isiah's case, how to control it, all of the other stuff is just window-dressing. It's the same ball, the nets are the same height, and the rotation on your jumper has got to be identical if it's going to fall. Besides, admitted Isiah, life as an NBA pro in Detroit was, well, maybe one step below the highest possible echelon. Although the noise in the Silverdome took some getting used to, it wasn't impossible, especially considering that "there were only 10,000 people in a place that holds 80,000," as Isiah jokingly pointed out.

In addition, NBA teams do make sure that when their players take the floor for the first regular-season game, even the rookies have some pro experience behind them. There are the two-a-day practice sessions to whip the hoopsters into shape, a chance for the coaching staff to find out who's been diligent about their off-season fitness regime, and who's been catching fish. And there are the exhibition games, which provide teams with the opportunity to work on offensive sets and team defensive patterns, as well as giving fans in some out-of-the-way locations a chance to see real live NBA talent in action. Isiah acknowledged that having played a bit with his new teammates before getting down to the real business at hand had helped take the edge off against the Bucks. "I wasn't too nervous," he revealed. "I was more nervous in the preseason games. Thank goodness for the preseason games."

Thomas concluded his analysis of his first pro game cautiously, despite his great individual performance, showing that he knew better than to expect a cake-walk every night in his rookie season. Life in the bigs was going to mean cranking up the effort, night-in and night-out. "I can't feel too good about tonight," he cautioned. "We've got to play tomorrow night in Chicago."

Even though Isiah was sure to keep this kind of forward-looking attitude in the back of his mind as he launched his first-year assault on the NBA, it was impossible to deny that his first real game as a professional basketball player had been a great one. The Detroit Pistons franchise had every reason to look forward to a lot more of the same from him. Indeed, with Isiah running the show, Detroit won their first three games, against Milwaukee, Chicago, and New Jersey, the first time in 11 years that the team had won the initial trio of games in a season. With that quick start, the Pistons raced out to an 8–5 record, their best showing out of the blocks in 7 years. Basketball fans in Detroit, who had been treated to an incredibly bad 21 sub-.500 seasons in 24 years, cautiously began creeping back to Pistons' games once word got out that Isiah the team leader was for real. One Detroit newspaper carried a full-page ad that shouted, "Hail Isiah, The Savior! See Him Tonight!" and the team's PR department started talking about the "Piston Fever" that was reported to be sweeping the city.

It was a little early to start claiming that basketball madness had taken over the collective consciousness of Detroit sports fans, though. After all, just a bit more than 14,000 combined spectators were in attendance to see the two early wins over New Jersey and Chicago, although Piston crowd support did eventually increase by 83 per cent over the year before. Nevertheless, the Isiah persona was beginning to win over as many supporters as his no-look passes.

Hoop fans had noticed one major characteristic of Thomas' game face right from the start, and the national sports media were starting to eat it up now that Isiah was in the NBA. That characteristic was the now-famous Isiah Thomas grin. Sportswriters noted that no matter what the on-court situation at any given time, Isiah seemed always to be smiling. The grin, as described in *Sports Illustrated*, "starts with a pair of deeply-set dimples and sneaks up each side of his face to his shining, almost sparkling eyes." Another observer, commenting on the ubiquitous nature of the grin, reasoned that, "maybe he can't help it, like when a baby has gas." Even when, completely exhausted from chasing the Bullets' John Lucas (later an NBA coach) all over the court, he shot an airball from the free-throw line against Washington, Isiah grinned from ear to ear. "My mind said yes, but my legs said no," he remembered.

The big smile was really part of a larger, on-court persona that Isiah would carry around with him for the rest of his career, one that was in fact a sort of a two-in-one harlequin mask donned for basketball battles. Sportswriters began referring to the "Angel with the Dirty Face" look, or, less charitably, calling Isiah an "Assassin with an Angel's Smile" in reference to the killer attitude he kept just slightly under the surface of that grinning exterior. Converse didn't mind the image, though, paying Isiah an estimated $100,000 to wear their shoes in his first year. Coach Robertson didn't object to the innocent/vicious routine, either, reasoning that every sports superstar has a smidgen of the carnival showman in him as part of the total package. "All the great ones have a little bull in them," claimed Isiah's new mentor. "The other day he was standing around when the [NFL] Lions walked by, going to practice in the Silverdome. All of a sudden, there's Isiah going through his legs and behind his back."

Luckily, however, this wasn't going to be just a one-man effort. NBA teams that find themselves relying too heavily on the talents of one man often find their fortunes diminishing when the opposition figure out how to shut down the top gun. Actually, Detroit's success was more the product of a two-man, two-rookie effort. While coach Robertson's improving line-up did feature some decent NBA talent in the form of John Long, Phil Hubbard, and former Hoosier Kent Benson, the big stars emerging from the Motor City in 1981–82 were proving to be Isiah and fellow rookie Kelly Tripucka, the Pistons' other first-round pick.

Tripucka had been selected by Detroit at number 12 in the draft, from the University of Notre Dame in South Bend, Indiana, a school known more for its football pulling guards than its basketball shooting guards. But Tripucka was a 6–6 pure-shooting forward who knew how to put the ball in the basket from just about anywhere, provided he had someone to give it to him once he'd gotten open. And that's where Isiah came in. Kelly, who swore he started every day with a bowl of Wheaties, came out gunning in his rookie campaign. He averaged over 20 points a game right from the start, many of them on set-up passes from Isiah. "Isiah and I aren't used to losing," he told reporters. "We'd like to create an atmosphere here like we had in school."

While Tripucka had been groomed as a scorer in college, a big part of Isiah's game had come to focus on passing, and that's just the way Pistons' coach Scotty Robertson was hoping to keep it. Noting that after three months of pro ball, Isiah was leading his club with a 21 points-per-game average, Robertson promised that a team offence in which the point guard led all scorers was a "temporary situation. We've called upon Isiah to shoot early in the season and he's come through. But as a 6–1 guard, his main job is to set up people like John Long, Kelly Tripucka and Phil Hubbard, and he knows it." Long, who had been the Pistons' number-one scorer the year before, obviously had a marksman's appreciation for a guy who was able to supply him with the right kind of live ammunition. "When I get into position," he explained, now that Isiah had joined the team, "I know I'm going to get the ball. I can't be double-teamed now like I was last year, and neither can Thomas, because he'll dish it off to me."

John Mengelt, a one-time Piston and a radio commentator for the franchise, claimed that it was the passing part of Isiah's game that was responsible not only for his ascension to the leader's role with Detroit, but also for the extremely short time it took him to do so. "Those crisp passes are the key to Isiah becoming an instant leader," he asserted, a sentiment echoed by gm Jack McCloskey, who opined, with Isiah in mind, that "if a player does something especially well, the others pick up on it." Perhaps the finest tribute to Isiah's emerging ability to lead a pro team came from a man named Will Robinson, a Pistons scout who had also been the first black to coach a major college at Illinois State and the first black scout in pro football. "I believe God made people to perform certain arts," said Robinson. "Sinatra was made to sing, Jesse Owens was made to run, and Isiah Thomas was made to play basketball."

With all of this glowing praise being heaped on the shoulders of a young man only 6–1 in height and 20 years of age, it was easy for fans to begin believing that Isiah's success had come about solely as the result of heaps of God-given natural talent. Followers of the game were beginning to understand that nothing in Thomas' life had come to him or his family for free, because every game report or feature story about Isiah's on-court exploits was now accompanied by the obligatory description of his rags-to-riches background. This was certainly understandable, since North American sports culture loves a good story, and Isiah's was among the best and most uplifting to come about in a long time. But athletically, people were somehow still convinced that Isiah the all-natural athlete was achieving accolades almost without effort.

Nothing could have been more inaccurate, and those closest to Thomas and the NBA knew it. Quinn Buckner had pointed out as early as Isiah's first pro game that the rookie knew how to work the officials to get the kind of calls he wanted from the zebra-stripes. Coach Robertson was also quick to learn that his prize point guard's arsenal of tricks included a few that if they were not illegal, certainly tested the limits of roundball etiquette, like throwing the occasional elbow or tugging at the odd jersey when the ref wasn't looking. "Isiah is going to do whatever needs to be done to get the job done," explained the coach. "I'm not saying he's going to out-jump Kareem, but Kareem's gonna have to jump!" During the post-season, Isiah did admit that he'd made the adjustment to the physical pro game fairly quickly, due in large part to his knack for discovering what he could get away with. The NBA brand of basketball, he said, is "played much differently. The refs let you get away with pushing and shoving."

The scrappy, do-anything-for-an-edge side of Isiah certainly belied the stereotype of the effortless athlete, and so did a simple fact of NBA life that was beginning to dawn on the young star: butting heads against the best basketball players in the world every night for more than three-quarters of a year exacted a tremendous physical toll on those who chose to make a living in that manner. "People have no idea how difficult it is, playing in the league, how tiring the travel can be," he lamented. "I play for fun, [but] I found out the pressure was this: Now you get paid to play. And now you may play three games in a row in different cities. But the fans expect you to perform. You may be injured or tired, but you still have to perform."

Individually, the hard work paid off. Isiah was named Rookie of the Year by *The Sporting News*, an award that carried extra significance for the winner because it was awarded based on a vote of players, not sportswriters or front-office types. The award was also a noteworthy accomplishment for Isiah because he won it while being the youngest player in the league. "I was never trying to be a rookie of the year or be on the all-rookie team," he maintained. "I wanted to help the team improve, and we did improve — drastically. The award came with the season." And with the season came Isiah's first All-Star nomination. In January, he had been picked to play on the East team, alongside Larry Bird and teammate Kelly Tripucka, and against Magic Johnson in the 1982 version of the mid-season showcase game.

Isiah kept up the pace in his second NBA season as well, maintaining a scoring average of over 21 points a game, along with his per-game assist total of nearly eight. Although sports pundits often refer to the "sophomore jinx" that afflicts outstanding rookies in their second year, Isiah wasn't beset by any such slump. The newly-minted All-Star cemented his leadership role with the Pistons, and indeed, had decided that he couldn't survive in pro ball in any other way than as the floor general of the Detroit franchise. "That's the way I have to play. I'd be terrible if I were allowed to just go through the motions," he asserted. "It's my job to make sure everyone else on the floor is doing the right thing. And if I'm not right, I can't make them be right, either."

Certainly, fellow young revelation Tripucka had been made "right" by Isiah's playmaking, and was firing on all cylinders as well. Kelly led the team in scoring and was also logging big minutes; both accomplishments silenced critics who believed that Tripucka would never make it as an NBA forward.

Another individual success story was taking shape on the Pistons team, this one in the form of 6–11 center Bill Laimbeer. Laimbeer had been traded to Detroit by the Cleveland Cavaliers at a point in his career when it looked like the Motor City would be his last NBA stop. The son of a wealthy corporate president, Laimbeer had played his college ball at Notre Dame alongside Kelly Tripucka, and often joked that he was the only pro basketball player to earn less than his father did. Bill had played in Cleveland with a laid-back, "basketball is just a game" attitude, reporting to the Cavs' training camp overweight as the result of summers spent relaxing. But in Detroit, Bill had responded to the support he'd received after coming there from the Pistons fans, front office, coaches, and fellow players, who believed that with a little discipline, the nearly-seven-foot player could make it in the NBA, even if he was a rich kid. "Everyone showed such confidence in me," he said, "I felt I had to do something to repay them." And repay them he did, with interest, averaging in double-digits in both rebounding and scoring once in a Pistons uniform.

Coach Scotty Robertson had been very clear about the role he envisioned for Isiah on the fast-improving Detroit Pistons team, and with other key players getting better because of Thomas' playmaking and leadership, it appeared that the team was on its way out of the NBA basement it had occupied for so long. People were starting to talk about the Pistons in the same breath as teams like Eastern rivals New Jersey and Washington, clubs in the division's second tier of excellence behind perennial front-runners like Boston and Philadelphia. Thus, it seemed like everything was coming together just perfectly in the Motor City, at least as far as the relationship between Isiah Thomas and the Detroit Pistons were concerned.

This rosy picture, however, had a few rough edges to it. At Indiana, Coach Knight had wanted Isiah to lead the Hoosiers, and he'd taught him to do it the well-rounded way. Knight had realized that given his point guard's many and varied talents, he'd be most effective in combining the several things a basketball player can do to help his team. Sure, a point man should get his fair share of assists on any team, but opposing defences had to tread a lot more carefully around a guy who could forsake the pass on occasion and take it to the rack himself.

With this approach to offensive ball firmly in place from his 2 years at IU, Isiah had begun to feel a little constrained by Robertson's insistence that a point guard had to concentrate on distributing the ball only, and letting the other guys do the scoring. During his rookie year, things came to a bit of a head between the two men. "I'd never done things the way he wanted them done," said Isiah. "I'd always felt I'd played an all-round-game: scoring, passing, playing defence. But it seemed he wanted me to change my priorities: pass the ball, play defence, and then, maybe, score."

In Isiah's second year as a Piston, though, both he and Robertson made some adjustments. The result was greater team success for the club, and an improved outlook for Isiah. "For a time I felt one-dimensional on the offensive end of the court, just penetrating and dishing off," said the point guard after he and Robertson had patched things up. "It was like part of my game was taken away from me. Now I know how he wants things done. I'm a little smarter, a little more mature. But he's relaxed a bit more, too."

Sometimes, a phenomenal professional athlete, caught up in the hype and glamour that surrounds his sport, will come face to face with a crisis that puts everything into perspective and relegates the hyperbole back to the realm of the near-fiction that it truly is. For Isiah, such an event occurred in late 1982, when he learned that his mother, Mary, had suffered a heart attack, aggravating a chronic condition prior to the Pistons game against the Indiana Pacers. Although Robertson had told him he could skip the game if he wanted to, Isiah insisted on playing. "I knew she would have wanted me to play," he said. Paradoxically, taking to the court was the one true way in which Isiah would be able to come to grips with the thought of his mother lying in a Chicago hospital bed, and besides, he was sure she would have insisted on his suiting up against Indiana. "Basketball is the only thing I can do to be free," he told reporters after tossing in 16 points and handing out 10 assists as the Pistons drubbed the Indiana Pacers 115–91. "On the basketball court, it's the only time I have no problems, no worries."

As the 1980s rolled along, so did Isiah Thomas and the
Detroit Pistons. The team just kept on getting better, the
result of some shrewd trades and free-agent signings by
"Trader Jack" McCloskey, and the leadership demonstrated by
his prize catch of the 1981 draft. In addition, Robertson had
been let go; the Pistons management cited his lack of ability to
get the team to play defence as the major reason for his
dismissal. His replacement, Chuck Daly, was put in charge on
May 17, 1983. Daly, who had been a high school coach in
Pennsylvania and an assistant with the Philadelphia 76ers,
responded to the dictates of the Piston's front-office management and concentrated on defence in Detroit. Apparently, it
worked. By 1984–85, the Pistons had rocketed to first place in
the Central Division and actually finished the season just one
game behind Milwaukee for the division crown. "I don't know
when it happened," said Isiah in reference to the point at
which Daly's defensive lectures actually sunk in with the
Pistons players, "but it did. I think defence has saved us a lot.
We go down and throw the ball away, or miss a shot, or make
a mistake, and our defence at the other end saves us and gives
us another opportunity."

After he had been in the NBA for three years, Isiah had the
opportunity to practise some court — actually courting —
skills of a different kind. It was during that summer that Isiah
and the former Lynn Kendall became engaged. Under the
pretence of having to return to IU for a practice session with
Coach Knight, Isiah proposed marriage on the steps of the
library where they met for their first date. Lynn accepted, and
the two were married a year later in Chicago. They settled into
a large home in the Detroit suburb of Bloomfield Hills, near the

Pontiac Silverdome where the Pistons played their home games in those days.

While the Pistons were learning how to play defence under new coach Daly, and Isiah was adjusting to life as a married man, he was also continually being named to the East team for All-Star games. It was, in fact, the events of one such showcase game that generated an incident that has to be categorized as one of the strangest controversies of Isiah's career.

In 1984, the Chicago Bulls had taken Michael Jordan out of the University of North Carolina as the third overall draft choice, behind Hakeem Olajuwon of the University of Houston (who went to the Houston Rockets) and Sam Bowie of the University of Kentucky (Portland Trail Blazers). Jordan's arrival in the NBA was met with much fanfare, and he quickly became a huge attraction wherever he and the Bulls went. Michael's high-flying dunks and tongue-wagging, slashing style added a new dimension of excitement to pro hoops. What's more, the Nike shoe company, realizing MJ's tremendous potential as an advertising icon, quickly brought him on board to promote the brand's shoes and clothing.

At the 1985 All-Star game, though, it was this Nike allegiance that got the young Jordan into some difficulty with NBA vets like Isiah. As the first rookie since Thomas to be named to an All-Star team, Michael could be permitted some degree of hype. After all, what was good for Jordan was good for the sport as a whole. But the fact that the young Bull contested the first two rounds of the All-Star slam-dunk competition in full Nike warmups and gold chains while flashing an all-too-confident grin got a few of the league's more established stars — most notably George Gervin, Isiah, and Magic Johnson — to thinking. Maybe this kid was just a little too cocky for his own good? And maybe he needed to be taught a lesson or two about respect for the game?

As the 1985 All-Star game drew to a close, a powerful rumor began circulating that the three veteran stars had plotted to make MJ look foolish on national TV. Allegedly, the other players had been instructed by the trio, with Isiah the most vocal of the three, to avoid passing Michael the ball, thereby denying him the opportunity to score. Other stories circulated to the effect that Jordan had infuriated Isiah by snubbing him on an elevator, and that he had refused to listen to advice from Charles Tucker, one of Thomas' advisors. Whatever the reason, it certainly looked as though MJ was being ignored on the court during the All-Star contest, despite his being wide open and in good position to score several times.

For his part, Michael was confused and annoyed by the whole thing. "The whole thing has hurt me," he admitted, "really hit me hard." In true Jordan fashion, however, he let his on-court actions do most of the talking on his behalf. Two nights after the All-Star game, he ripped the Pistons for 49 points in a 139–126 Bulls' win. If there really had been a freeze-out orchestrated by Isiah, Jordan had let him — and the rest of the basketball world — know what his reaction was when someone made him mad.

While the Michael Jordan freeze-out incident was certainly stuff made up of many rumors, Isiah was beginning to become accustomed to his every speculation and off-hand comment being treated like a Gospel pronouncement. Because of the predilection of the press to seize upon such tidbits and turn them into "news," it was hard to know what to make of a story that broke in January of 1986, to the effect that Isiah was seriously considering retirement. It was doubly difficult to know what to think of the whole situation when one realized that the details of Isiah's supposedly impending departure as a player were outlined by the respected United Press International wire service, not exactly the Weekly World News of sports journalism.

Adding to the mystery was the fact that right from the start of his rookie year, Thomas had always been up front in his disdain for the high-pressure, high-fatigue aspects of his chosen profession. He'd never hesitated to tell reporters that the travel and the intense competition could really get to him at times. Indeed, only a couple of months into his first season, Isiah had claimed that "I won't be around here [the NBA] until I'm 30." For him, pro basketball was a great way of making a living, but as a labor-relations milieu, the job had some big limitations. "It's amazing how much control the management has over you, how they can uproot you and your family with a trade," he observed. "I'm not gonna be pulling my kids out of school and dragging them all over the country. Not for this."

In early 1986, it looked as though Isiah might be ready to make good on this prediction. A Detroit radio station announced that Thomas, who was sick and had been playing on a bad knee for almost two months, had decided to pack it in. What made things even worse was that the Pistons were going through a 6-game losing streak and had lost 11 of 13 games when the early retirement story broke. "It's been real tough. It's desperate," said Isiah. After a 110–99 loss to Atlanta, which Isiah called "one of the worst things I've ever gone through in my life," he admitted that "I don't know what's wrong. I wish I did.

I'm running out of questions, and I think maybe it's because there are no answers."

As far as answers went, Jack McCloskey wished he'd had a few more regarding his superstar's intentions. McCloskey told the press that Isiah had spoken to him "not at all" about any plans he might have had to retire. But the Pistons' leader was missing games because of fever and the bad knee. Things didn't look good. It was also reported that Thomas had actually quit the Pistons at one point, in frustration with the team's lackluster play and slow-footed approach. Many observers noticed that the Detroit team was avoiding the fast-break style that had served them so well in the past couple of seasons. People were starting to blame newly acquired forward Rick Mahorn, who they said was too slow to keep up with Isiah on the Daly-designed break. Others said it was the loss of hard-working scorer Terry Tyler to Sacramento that was the problem. Daly and McCloskey had even started a feud, which all the local papers picked up and magnified. Whatever the problem was, it was looking like the resurgent Detroit franchise, which had sloughed off its doormat status just a few years before, had hit a snag.

Cooler heads prevailed to deliver the Pistons from this mess, though. Isiah called the team's principal owner, Bill Davidson, to ask his advice on what direction his career should take, and although only those two men know what was discussed, the decision was made for Isiah to stay on. For his part, Thomas produced a true display of class in admitting that he'd have to alter his unique brand of basketball a little in order to adjust to the changes in the Pistons team. "We have different personnel now than the last two years," he observed. "We don't have as quick [a brand] of athletes as we used to. We aren't a fast break team any more." This having been said, though, Isiah was ready to slow down a bit, saying he'd do "whatever is best for our team. This is a challenge to see if I can put my talent into that style and still be productive."

Although the head-spinning universe of the professional athlete could take its toll on anyone — even as cool a customer as Isiah wasn't exempt from the pressure — there were ways to de-stress. Isiah illustrated that he knew one of them, namely seeking out the advice of others as he did in consultation with Davidson regarding an early retirement. But Isiah had developed another method of relaxation which made him a little different than the average All-American jock figure.

Always one to seek answers to life's tough questions from within, Isiah had taken up writing poetry to fill the empty spaces while traveling and in lonely hotel rooms. One such poem was reprinted in *Sports Illustrated*:

I have been to the arena and I
have played the game I've felt
the tension and tasted the sweat
know the pain and I have made
the sacrifice yes I paid the price
to make playing in this arena
my life

Isiah's game on the court had become famous for its free-flowing quality and by his own admission, he tried to adopt the same aesthetic when he wrote verse. "I like poetry because it's free," he said. "There are no rules to it. You are not restricted or confined in any way. No commas, no periods, if you don't want them. That's how I like to play basketball. Free."

Luckily for hoop fans around the NBA and those who supported the Detroit Pistons in particular, all tales of Isiah's demise as a player were greatly exaggerated. As he slowly adjusted to the "new style" Pistons, Isiah started to mold his play to the team that would soon be known as the terror of the NBA, the "Bad Boys" of the league. Given the success of the Detroit club into the late-1980s, it was a good thing that Isiah decided not to retire.

After all, there was still a dynasty left to create.

CHAPTER FIVE

The Bad Boy

Many teams, having emerged from indig-
nity as one of the NBA's laughing-stocks to
the point where they could hold their own
against any club in the league, would have
been content with all that, and simply
stopped improving. After all, there's nothing
wrong with playing slightly above .500 and
making the playoffs every year. Lots of teams have done just
that, without making big waves but without major failures,
either. The Utah Jazz of the late 1980s and throughout the
1990s, for example, were always good-but-not-great squad, and
by all indications seemed content to keep it that way. And, as
any fan of an Eastern Conference NBA team in the late 1990s
and early 2000s will tell you, it's considered a major feat for
many teams to even make it to .500 and make the playoffs.

The "good enough is good enough" approach, though, was
anathema to a pair of key members of the Detroit Pistons

organization. These two men decided that while the improvement that the franchise had undergone in the first part of the '80s was certainly a great thing, there was no sense in stopping now. For General Manager Jack McCloskey and for Isiah Thomas, there was a higher goal, and neither would rest until it was realized. The lure of an NBA Championship trophy drove both men forward, and each in his own way was instrumental in the eventual accomplishment of this highest of pro hoops aims.

In Isiah's mind, winning an NBA title had become something of an obsession. In June of 1982, he had attended the deciding game of the NBA championship finals, and had watched as the Los Angeles Lakers, behind the stellar performances of Kareem Abdul-Jabbar and Magic Johnson, defeated the Philadelphia 76ers to capture the trophy. In the locker room after the game, Isiah was moved to tears as he saw the Lakers celebrating with their families and hugging one another. "Whatever it takes," he vowed, "I'm going to make sure this happens to me."

In 1982, this idealism on Isiah's part might have been cause for a bit of chuckling. After all, at that point in NBA history, the Pistons weren't nearly good enough to be considered serious contenders for a championship. A few years later, though, the Pistons had improved to the point where no-one laughed when Detroit fans started hoping out loud that their team would win the Big One. Much of the credit for this improvement belonged to Pistons GM Jack McCloskey.

As well as having signed Isiah as an Indiana sophomore, "Trader Jack" had brought Bill Laimbeer over from Cleveland, secured the services of Chuck Daly as coach, and traded to get center James Edwards from Phoenix, big Rick Mahorn from Washington, and guard Vinnie Johnson from Seattle. He unloaded a complaining Kelly Tripucka to Utah for high-scoring Adrian Dantley, and drafted a complete unknown out of tiny Southeastern Oklahoma named Dennis Rodman. During the course of assembling his Pistons, McCloskey would also sign John "Spider" Salley, a motor-mouthed 6–11 forward from Georgia Tech, 7–1 William Bedford of Memphis State, and a little-known, soft-spoken guard named Joe Dumars out of McNeese State, an obscure college in Louisiana. These players — although no one knew it at the time, of course — would, by the waning years of the so-called "me" decade, come together to form one of the most feared teams in NBA history.

The awe inspired in the hearts of opposing basketball teams by the McCloskey-built, new-look Detroit Pistons was a terror caused by a combination of skill and physical — even brutal — play. There was no question about the fact that each and every member of the Pistons could play excellent basketball. *New York Times* writer Fred Waitzkin pointed out — correctly — that at least five of the seven Detroit subs could have started for just about any other team in the league. But while a deep bench helped the Pistons win games, critics were quick to add that the team's growing practice of intimidation and hard fouls went a long way towards insuring Detroit's success.

In the NBA, nobody expects an easy time of it when he drives the lane for a layup. For one thing, several giant-sized bodies converging around the basket increases the odds that somebody is going to take an elbow, or at the very least a slap on the wrist. For another, big time pro basketball is played within a decidedly macho context when it comes to physical play near the hoop. There is a lot of woofing and verbal annotation to the play; "in your face," or simply "face!" being one of the milder comments delivered to a player whose shot has been blocked by a defender. The Pistons were well known around the NBA as expert practitioners of this kind of trash-talking.

Competition for rebounds is fierce, with players resorting to all manner of shoves, elbows, jersey grabbing, and the like in an attempt to establish position and box out the opponent. It's even been rumored that Larry Bird, a great rebounder in his day despite his apparent lack of anything even resembling a vertical jump, used to stand on his rivals' feet as they attempted to go up for the ball. Also, during close games and especially in the playoffs, most NBA teams observe a "no free layups" rule, which essentially means that any offensive player who's managed to work his way inside for an up-close shot can be sure he'll get whacked for his troubles, and often ends up having to earn his two points from the free throw line.

Within this milieu of hard fouls and physical play, though, there are limits to the contact that players will make. In the NBA, leaping players' heads often reach rim-level, and the speed and power with which they can come soaring through the key is amazing. But such leaps often leave a player relatively out of control once he's airborne. Thus a shove or a forearm delivered to such a player can be particularly dangerous, both because it hurts on impact and because it can lead to a landing that does not feature the feet as the primary impact-absorbing apparatus. The back, or even the head, is often what hits the court first, and the sickening hardwood thud that follows is a grim sound to even the most blasé of hoops fans.

The Detroit Pistons were beginning to gain a nasty reputation as the NBA's leading practitioners of such nasty tactics. Laimbeer and Mahorn were rightly singled out as the worst offenders, but John Salley and Dennis Rodman were not above the occasional cheap shot, and yes, even Isiah had his fair share of dirty playground tricks in store for unsuspecting opponents. One *Sports Illustrated* full-color photo from 1988 featured Isiah unashamedly executing a perfect, come-from-behind football tackle on the Lakers' Byron Scott as Scott tried to break down-court for a basket in the 1988 NBA finals. Remember the "no layup" rule?

The Pistons, with their increasingly physical play, were necessarily becoming a team of controversy. Opposing ball clubs either complained or retaliated; most usually did both. This in turn led to many games breaking out in brawls more usually seen at hockey games. As the team leader, and increasingly the spokesman of a squad that was coming to be known as the "Bad Boys" — a term coined by team PA announcer Ken Calvert — of the NBA, Isiah was often at the center of the controversy as he attempted to explain why the Pistons constantly resorted to such violence. When asked whether he considered the Pistons a "dirty team," Isiah responded that "playing aggressive is just part of what we do," explaining that tough team defence and a balanced scoring attack were more crucial to the squad's success.

For the league's top brass, the Pistons presented something of a dilemma. On the one hand, after considerable hard work and tremendous expense on the marketing side of things, the NBA had finally managed to create enough hype surrounding the game that fans were starting to follow pro basketball again, after a decade-long period of apathy. Although the Pistons' behavior seems pretty mild by 21st-century NBA standards, a team full of thugs and hooligans was not exactly the image the

NBA wanted to put across in those days. Accordingly, many Pistons, especially Rick Mahorn — the original Bad Boy — and Bill Laimbeer were slapped with big fines and suspensions in an attempt to curb their on-court rough stuff.

On the other hand, though, a lot of fans around the league, and especially those who loved the Pistons, were actually starting to like the Bad Boy image. Even in front of opposing crowds, like the ones that gathered in the Boston Garden to cheer on the Celtics, the Pistons took on a team-we-love-to-hate image. They were showered with popcorn, beer, and profanity by fans upset at their cheap shots and complaints. In order to cash in on this down-and-dirty image, NBA Entertainment, Inc. eventually had the Pistons cut a rap-music video with MTV, in which several Detroit players, including Isiah ("If we're gonna be the Bad Boys, we gotta act like the Bad Boys!") punctuate the music with comments about how tough and mean the Pistons really were. Fans ate it up, purchasing over 20,000 copies at $19.95 each, and NBA officials weren't sure whether to crack down on the Bad Boys' roughhouse antics, or to embrace the persona for its potential promotional value.

With all of the negative press Detroit was garnering, it was nice to see their leader engaged in a truly classy incident during the heat of the 1987 playoffs. The Pistons were embroiled in a fierce playoff battle with the Atlanta Hawks, a series that featured its share of the now-usual roughhousing that prevailed whenever the Detroit Pistons were involved in a game of basketball. In Game 3, Isiah had leapt onto the back of the Hawks' seven-footer Kevin Willis after Willis and Rick Mahorn had started scrapping, and had to be pulled off. The tiff, though, only served to spur Isiah on. "Isiah gets this gleam, this glow about him," said Bill Laimbeer, referring to the occasions when his sparkplug teammate was about to go on a scoring tear. Isiah turned the glow into an amazing, 25-point performance in the third quarter alone setting an NBA record for points scored in a single quarter of a playoff game. Isiah finished Game 3 with 35 points, 8 rebounds, 5 steals, and 8 assists, and much of this impressive total was racked up against Atlanta's Glenn (Doc) Rivers, who had been a Chicago playground pal of Isiah's. Rivers had included Thomas in his wedding as an usher the previous spring, but on that night received no such cordialities in return.

The following matchup, though — Game 4 — set the scene for the touching moment inspired by Isiah. The game itself was classic Thomas. On Mother's Day, with Detroit down 88–87, Isiah nailed a last-second clutch jumper to give the Pistons an 89–88 win. "You have to be mentally tough to take that last shot," said Isiah. The other Pistons confessed that they were looking to him to take control of the game in the final seconds and win it for them. "Zeke was option 1, option 2, and option 3," admitted Laimbeer after the game. Indeed, every kid who has ever dribbled the ball on a driveway and done the dramatic play-by-play announcer routine in his head has dreamed of hitting such a shot. Few players, however, want the pressure of having to actually take it in a real game. "It's one of those moments you dream about in your sleep. Or when you're a kid," Isiah confided. When someone asked him how long he had been willing and able to take — and make — those last-second launches, Isiah responded, "As long as I can remember."

The miracle shot, though, was only the second-best thing to happen to the Thomas household on that particular Mother's

Day, though. Before the game, Mary Thomas had picked up her son's college degree in his stead during a ceremony in Bloomington. Isiah had arranged the whole thing as a surprise for his mom, and the acquisition of the degree had fulfilled a dream for the both of them.

Although Isiah was actually a few credits short of the requirements for his diploma in criminal justice, he expected to finish the work by correspondence through IU and Wayne State University in Detroit. Indiana University allowed such students to graduate in the Spring ceremony. Mother and son spoke via telephone after the Atlanta game. "She was excited, crying, happy, shocked, a lot of things," said Isiah. "She said, 'I'm so happy you got the degree.' She told me that she didn't know I was going back to school." Mary's joy was focused on her son's keeping a promise he'd made to her several years earlier upon leaving Indiana prematurely, and not on Isiah's playoff heroics. "We didn't even talk about that," he revealed. "She didn't ask."

Unfortunately, Isiah's super Mother's Day gift was just about the last pleasant thing he would remember about the 1987 post-season. Yes, Detroit did defeat Atlanta in their round-2 matchup, thus winning the right to go on to face the Boston Celtics in the Eastern finals. Unfortunately for basketball fans in the Motor City, however, the Celtics overcame the Pistons in a tough series that went the full seven games, advancing to play the Los Angeles Lakers in the NBA finals.

The Boston series, though, became an infamous one in the history of Detroit basketball for reasons that were much larger than just the heartbreaking loss. The aftermath of the 1987 Eastern finals would have a tremendous impact on Isiah Thomas' off-court image for the rest of his career.

After the Piston's Game 7 loss to the Celts, Dennis Rodman, whom fans had started to call "the Worm" because of his slippery-but-effective rebounding style and his habit of getting under the skin of opponents, was dejected and angry. When a sportswriter had asked him what he thought of Boston's Larry Bird, whose heroics had almost single-handedly won the series for the Celtics, Rodman answered in his best knee-jerk style, his words given extra venom by the ire he felt at losing. "Larry Bird," announced Rodman, "is overrated in a lot of areas. Why does he get so much publicity? Because he's white." And Worm didn't stop there. In his opinion, Bird was "not God, he ain't the best player in the NBA, not to me." The only reason Bird had won three consecutive NBA Most Valuable Player awards, maintained Dennis, was that "He's white [and] that's why he gets it."

If it had been Rodman — and only Rodman — who had issued such advanced anthropological pronouncements, it is very likely that his words would have created the obligatory uproar, and then promptly disappeared. For Rodman had already cemented his reputation as one of the league's chief eccentrics, and, as fans who witnessed his seemingly unending series of hair-color changes and tattoos later in his career would attest, he was starting to get weirder. In the same way as many observers of the game paid only passing attention to "Sir" Charles Barkley's later claim that as a pro athlete he was under no obligation to replace parents as a role model for kids as just a lot of hot air from a player who liked to stir up controversy, most people would have figured Rodman was just doing his Worm-schtick again.

The problem, though, was that upon hearing his teammate's "Bird is only famous because he's white" theory, the same sportswriters scuttled over to Isiah to get his opinions on the subject. As he was unquestionably the Pistons' leader on the floor and in the department of quotable quotes, the reporters were naturally eager to get some copy from him for their stories. What Isiah told them was reprinted in the following day's newspapers as a complete shocker. Thomas was quoted being in complete agreement with Rodman, saying that if Bird "were black, he'd be just another guy."

It's hardly surprising that this comment, made, as was Rodman's, in the heat of post-game frustration, touched off a major furor. To stanch the bleeding as fast as possible, Isiah flew to Inglewood, California, where Boston had gone to face the L.A. Lakers in the NBA finals. Hastily organizing a press conference that included Bird and about 125 members of the media, Thomas quickly set the record straight. "Comments that were made the other night by me, I was joking about them," he assured the assembled reporters. "I have the tape to prove it that it was definitely laughter and sarcasm at the end of it. Jokingly, I said I have to agree with Rodman, while smiling and laughing, that if he [Bird] were black, he'd be just another good guy. From that, we got this [controversy]."

In other words, it was a sarcastic "yeah, sure" comment and a wink that started the whole mess. The odd part of it, though, was that Isiah Thomas had always appeared to be someone who had used sports as a way of bringing a positive message of achievement and hard work to fans of all ages. "There were a lot of things said, and have been said, about me in regards to racism," said Isiah, who sat next to Bird during the press conference. "I'm a guy who all my life — through basketball — has been trying to bring black, white, purple, green, Mexican, and

Puerto Rican people together. I think I've been successful in doing that through the arena of basketball."

For his part, Bird admitted that he wasn't taking any of it seriously, and bore Isiah no ill will. "I think the main thing is that the statements or whatever was said doesn't bother me so I don't think it should bother any of us," said Larry. Smiling, the pride of the Celtic Green told the assemblage, "Believe me, if Isiah said he was joking, let's take it as a joking matter. I swear to you it doesn't bother me. . . . I just feel sorry for Isiah because just walking into this room and seeing everybody, it must have touched a lot of people and that's why we're here." Bird concluded his comments by promising that when he played against Rodman, "I'm going to bust him so bad!"

The whole racially-tainted incident caused Isiah to draw inward in subsequent years when it came to talking to the press, and to really watch what he said when anyone with a notepad or a hand-held tape recorder came around asking even innocent-sounding questions. But the Bird controversy was also imbued with two powerful ironies that point up several interesting facts about life and sports in North America.

The first irony concerns the initial comments made by Dennis Rodman. The Worm, for all the sensationalism that has surrounded his pro career, and the championships he's won in both Dallas and later Chicago, represents a true, underdog-comes-through story. Having grown up in a tough Dallas neighborhood, Rodman had gotten into trouble with the law and looked to be going nowhere before a late growth spurt gave him enough of a chance to make the basketball team at little Southeastern Oklahoma University. While at Southeastern, Rodman had essentially been adopted by a local family named

Rich, who had a thirteen-year-old son. The kid, Byrne, had been emotionally shattered after accidentally killing his best friend in a shooting incident, but he and Dennis, who was six years older, quickly became best friends. It seems as though Rodman and Byrne Rich, trying to get their lives back together, found support and friendship in one another.

Unfortunately, Byrne's parents started to find that their fellow townspeople were acting strangely toward them after Dennis began spending more and more time at their home. The reason for this rejection was that Worm's new-found parents were white and the inhabitants of that particular part of rural Oklahoma didn't take kindly to such a family taking in a black basketball player. Both family and player overcame this friction, however, and Worm stayed on. Dennis Rodman, the same guy who ripped Larry Bird's abilities as a hoopster because he's white, had actually been accepted by white folks as family during the key, transitional years of his life.

The second ironic element that emerged out of the Bird/racism controversy illustrated just how popular an athlete Isiah Thomas had become, not just in Detroit, but around the U.S. as well. For while Rodman made the initial inflammatory statement, it was Isiah whose opinion on the subject was actively sought and really fanned the flames of a nation-wide controversy. Isiah then had to call the big press conference to straighten everything out, while Dennis got away with just a terse, "it was a mistake on my behalf" apology through the press. Thomas was beginning to learn that when you become a star in the wide world of pro sports, even an off-handed, sarcastic joke on what a volatile teammate has said can explode into a headline-grabbing incident. A controversy he hadn't even started turned into something major to deal with, and resulted in a drastic change in the way he would handle the media for ever after. He'd be much more cautious from now on.

All media controversy aside, the Pistons had truly started to play winning basketball up to and including the 1987 Eastern finals loss to Boston. They kept on playing it into the following campaign as well. After a great regular season and a stellar run through the early stages of the playoffs, the Pistons again got a crack at the Boston Celtics in the Eastern finals. And this time, the Bad Boys were pumped. "To beat the Celtics," said Isiah after Game 4 of the 1988 series, acknowledging just how tough it was to take on a team as tradition-laden as the Celts, "you have to beat more than a basketball team. You have to beat a mind set. The Celtics aren't supposed to lose. And everybody thinks that. . . . Anybody human thinks that."

Human, though, might not be a proper word to describe the proportions of the comeback that the Pistons staged in Game 5 of the series. In front of the rabid fans of the Boston Garden, Detroit staged an astounding resurgence from a 56–40 deficit in the third quarter to tie the game at 92 at the end of regulation time and send it into overtime. With Isiah dumping in 35 points on the night, Detroit pulled away from the men in green, 102–96 in the extra minutes to take a 3–2 lead in the series.

That effort turned out to be a back-breaking one for Boston. Game 6 saw almost 39,000 fans jamming into the Silverdome to watch Detroit hammer the Celtics, 95–90. There was no love lost between the two teams — or in fact between the Bad Boys and anyone they played in those days — and so it was no surprise to see a group of Celtics leaving their bench in the final minute, forsaking the traditional post-game congratulatory handshakes. "That's when I knew we had it, when they were leaving the court," said Isiah, who nevertheless revealed that at least one Celtic, Kevin McHale, had the poise to offer him some advice. "Zeke," McHale told Thomas, "don't be happy just getting to the finals, go out there and win it."

Isiah and the Pistons had every intention of doing so. But first, the man his peers called "Zeke" had to make sure that all of this was really true. The morning after the big win over Boston, Isiah leaped out of bed to check the morning papers. He had to make sure the whole thing hadn't been a dream, and indeed it hadn't. "You can talk about the greatest players," he said once things had sunk in, "but the winners are those who advanced their team to the championship. . . . You can talk about Wilt Chamberlain and Bill Russell, and you say Bill Russell is the best because he won the most championships [even though] Wilt had the best statistics."

Before they could start talking about themselves in the language reserved for NBA legends, however, the Bad Boys would have to get by some other pretty legendary competition in the form of the L.A. Lakers. Los Angeles could boast two of the all-time greats of the game as part of their lineup, guard Earvin "Magic" Johnson and center Kareem Abdul-Jabbar. The Lakers, who were looking to repeat their 1987 title, were much more than just a two-man team. Magic and Kareem were backed by a number of players who had blossomed into NBA superstars in their own right, such as James Worthy, A.C. Green, Byron Scott, and Michael Cooper. Coached by Pat Riley, the Lakers had taken the art of fast-break basketball to a level never before seen, and it didn't look as though anyone — even the rough-and-tumble Bad Boys from the Motor City — would be able to stop them.

The Pistons surely tried, though. Despite the fact that all through the playoffs of 1988 both coach Chuck Daly and leader Isiah Thomas were enmeshed in at-times acrimonious contract disputes (both would settle with Pistons management to their satisfaction), the team managed to stay focused on the task of defeating their West Coast rivals. For Isiah, the Pistons-Lakers finals also represented a chance to do battle with his buddy, Magic Johnson, and the possible fulfillment of the life-long dream of leading his team to an NBA title.

Isiah and Magic had, over the course of their basketball careers, become close friends. Magic had jokingly named a room in his house in Bel Air the "Isiah Thomas suite," and Isiah would often stay at Johnson's place when he visited the West Coast. Magic had his hospitality repaid whenever he was back in Michigan, hanging out at Isiah's home and playing in charity games. They even had a tradition of driving one another back to the visitor's hotel after games. But while the two men were friends whose relationship was cemented by respect for one another's abilities on the court, they nevertheless became fierce rivals after the opening tip-off. "Earvin is my friend," Thomas confided to a sportswriter, "one of the best people in the world. And we have been there for each other a lot. But he's not going to tell me the secret of winning a championship."

For a while, it appeared as though none of the Pistons needed to hear any secrets of success from anyone. They were doing just fine on their own. Playing classic Detroit basketball, the Bad Boys went up 3–2 in the series. In Game 1 at the Inglewood Forum, Isiah knocked down 19 points, ushering the Pistons to a 105–93 win. This game saw Isiah and Johnson exchange the first of their series-long kiss-on-the-cheek rituals at mid-court before the action started. Game 2 saw the tables turn, though, as Magic and his fast-break partner James Worthy took charge in a 108–96 Laker victory.

The series moved to Detroit for Game 3, and this one featured a sluggish Pistons squad being hammered 99–86 by the up-tempo L.A. team. Isiah's 28-point performance was to no avail. The defeat seemed to galvanize both the Detroit players and their fans, however, setting the scene for a classic Pistons effort in Game 4, one that will be remembered for a long time in the Motor City.

The game itself was largely Adrian Dantley's own private scoring showcase. Since he'd been acquired from Utah in that trade for Kelly Tripucka, Dantley had established himself as the Pistons number-one pure scorer. His attitude often seemed to border on the selfish, who-cares-if-we-win-as-long-as-I-score-my-points side of things.

This alienated a few of his teammates somewhat, but they were willing to put up with it as long as A.D.'s individual totals translated into Pistons victories. Dantley notched 27 points in the Pistons' 111–86 triumph in Game 4, but his efforts in a winning cause were overshadowed by the Isiah-Magic sub-plot.

Of course, the two had exchanged their customary pecks before the opening whistle; people were expecting that now. What the 40,000 Silverdome fans weren't expecting, though, was the fight that broke out between the two off-court pals in the fourth quarter. As Isiah took it to the hole past the Lakers defenders, Magic suddenly swooped over and nailed him. Isiah was up in an instant, shoving Johnson in retaliation. A little later, Magic took another shot at his rival point guard. Isiah went back at him again, and this time Laimbeer stepped in as peacemaker. The two chuckled about the contact after the game — Lakers coach Pat Riley laughingly called it "just a lovers' quarrel" — but as NBA legends in the making who had learned their trade on the playgrounds, both knew a thing or two about the need for a little intimidation in the paint when it came down to the crunch.

Unfortunately for Detroit, it was crunches of another kind that were seriously hampering their chances for big-time glory and a series win over their Laker foes, namely the ones that were starting to be felt in a few key places on the anatomy of Isiah Thomas. For Games 4 and 5, he had been forced to take pain killers for his aching back. His physical condition wasn't helped much by the fact that Lynn was eight-and-a-half months pregnant, making sleep a little tough. Before Game 5, though, Isiah's mood brightened with the birth of 6-lb., 5-ounce Joshua Isiah Thomas at the St. Joseph Mercy Hospital in Pontiac, three weeks ahead of schedule but a welcome addition to the family — both Thomas and the Pistons — nevertheless. For the statistically-minded, *Sports Illustrated* reported that "Isiah was present at the delivery, but was not credited with an assist."

In Game 5, an ailing Isiah nevertheless led his mates on to great things. The Lakers had started to gripe about the physical punishment meted out to them by the Bad Boys, and as usual, Rick Mahorn and Bill Laimbeer were getting most of the blame. "He can dish it out, but he can't take it," said Magic of Mahorn before the contest. "He throws out all this cheap stuff, but he doesn't want you to come back at him. Well if it happens in Game 5, I'm going to have to hit him right back." Ironically, however, it was the Pistons' key man Isiah, and not the Lakers, who had taken the most pounding in the series. Bad back and all, Thomas kept the Pistons in it until he was replaced by Vinnie Johnson. Nicknamed "The Microwave" by the Celtics Danny Ainge because of his ability to heat up so quickly, the thickly-muscled Johnson came off the bench to notch 12 points in a 5:50 time frame. Dantley also came up big with 25 points, and Dumars, Rodman, and John Salley performed yeoman service in denying Magic the ball and hauling down key rebounds. Detroit won it, 104–94, and took a 3–2 lead in the series. One more win and the NBA title would be theirs!

They had it in the bag, too. Game 6 was what *Sports Illustrated* would later call "a classic," and for a while, it looked like it — and the coveted NBA crown — would be Pistons for the taking. Isiah put on a spectacular show on his own, burning the Lakers with his deadly outside bombs and drives to the basket. Thomas hit for 25 points in the third quarter alone, pushing the Pistons, who had fallen behind, 53–46 at the half, to an 81–79 lead to start the fourth quarter. Isiah would finish the night with 43, but would also head for the locker room with something much worse — a severely sprained ankle, injured after landing on the foot of his defensive shadow, Michael Cooper. As a mark of the toughness of NBA basketball at the playoff level, Isiah could also count an injured knee, a dislocated finger, and an eye that had been poked by a Laker finger as among his physical woes.

Still, the Pistons were leading 102–99 on a jumper by Thomas and two free throws from Joe Dumars. Then Byron Scott hit a 12-footer to pull L.A. to 102–101. In the dying seconds, the Lakers got the ball back off one of Isiah's rare misses, and went to Kareem down low, who responded by trying to set up his patented sky-hook against Laimbeer.

Incredibly — given that this was the crucial moment of an NBA championship and that he'd surely gotten away with much worse in his career and throughout the series — Laimbeer was whistled for a soft bump of a foul. Wiley veteran Kareem hit both free throws in his best ice-water style and L.A. led by one, 103–102. Detroit had a chance to win it, but a serious miscue between Isiah and Dantley fouled up an out-of-bounds play, and the Pistons were history. They'd need to win it in Game 7 if they were going to win it at all.

They didn't. Almost as an anti-climax, the Lakers beat the Pistons, 108–105 to repeat as NBA champs. Isiah stunned the basketball world by actually playing in this one, despite an ankle so swollen he could barely walk on it, let alone run and jump. The team that had gone the longest of any organization in pro sports without a championship would have to utter what might be the saddest words in the lexicon of the big-time athlete: "Wait until next year."

In reference to the following season, the 1988–89 NBA campaign, Bad Boy Bill Laimbeer had summed up the feelings of every last one of his teammates. No longer are we satisfied with being a much-improved ball club, or a well-respected one, said Laimbeer. Now is the time to get serious about winning the NBA championship. "At some point, we're going to have to do it," he insisted. "We don't need respect now. We need the ring."

CHAPTER SIX

A Detroit Dynasty

Pistons GM Jack McCloskey wasn't about to sit idly by and just hope that his franchise might get lucky enough to win it all some-day. An experienced coach and player in his day, "Trader Jack" knew a lot about what was often termed "team chemistry" and how to create it. There was one element on  the Pistons' periodic table that kept screwing things up every time it seemed like the right basketball mix had been achieved. And while every chemist has committed the short-forms of each of nature's basic elements to heart, so too did the Pistons players and fans come to learn the code letters of that one particular building-block that was constantly inter-fering with the team's chemistry. That element was represented by the letters A.D., and if the Pistons were ever going to win the title, it looked like something had to be done about Adrian Dantley.

None of the Pistons players was a bigger opponent of the Notre Dame grad than Isiah. He and the other Detroit team members had agreed that if any of them were to win the $35,000 that the Walt Disney Corporation was planning to give the Most Valuable Player of the 1988 finals, the money would be split evenly among the whole squad. Dantley, however, had insisted that he would keep the entire sum if he was chosen MVP — even though A.D. was the highest-paid Piston. And this irked Isiah.

It wasn't just Dantley's greed for money that bugged Isiah, though; Dantley was also being greedy on the court. He was constantly complaining that he didn't get the ball enough, and that his individual scoring stats were being hurt by this lack of offensive attention. Isiah and McCloskey knew that an approach like Dantley's was great for creating glory-grabbing superstars, but worthless to a team trying to win a title. Partway through the season, with the Pistons performing decently but nowhere near well enough to win a championship, McCloskey decided to make a move. He shipped A.D. to the Dallas Mavericks, in exchange for none other than Isiah's old playground running mate from the West Side, Mark Aguirre.

The blockbuster trade surprised many, but not those close to the Pistons. Sure, Aguirre had been tabbed a whiner during his days at DePaul and Dallas, and some even wondered whether or not he'd be much of an improvement over Dantley in the attitude department. Even Aguirre's former Dallas teammates were happy to see him go. "Today should be an all-day party because he's gone," said Sam Perkins when he heard about the trade. "Good luck Detroit, because you're going to need it."

But what the skeptics failed to realize was that once Aguirre had committed to playing for the Pistons — his friend Isiah's team — he'd be prepared to give up some of the individual glory for a true shot at the title. Bill Laimbeer told the press he was highly skeptical of the contribution Aguirre would be able to make to the team, but because he was a buddy of Isiah's, he'd give him the benefit of the doubt. The Microwave warned his new teammate that he should prepare himself to get yanked from the game by Coach Daly near the end of a close contest because Chuck favored defence in the crunch. "It's nothing personal," said Vinnie. "It's just how we win." And for his part, Aguirre didn't seem to mind.

"You were a star in Dallas," Isiah told his playground friend. "Here in Detroit, our ninth man on the squad is as popular as you were in Dallas." And if Mark wasn't prepared to give his all and give up the ball when someone else had a better shot, "someone's going to be on your ass," Thomas told him.

No one was saying just how much involvement the Pistons on-court decision-maker had with the team's off-court planners in the Aguirre-for-Dantley trade, but the very fact that it was his friend Aguirre, and not someone else who came to the Motor City, had many people speculating that Thomas was largely behind the move. Dantley's mother, Virginia, was doing a lot more than speculating. "When his Royal Highness wants something, he gets it," she blustered. "For such a little man, Isiah Thomas certainly does have a big ego." More than a few NBA observers and players had to suppress a snicker at the thought of muscular veteran Dantley being defended through the press by his mom, but it really didn't matter. A.D. was history, and if he had been the faulty link in the team's championship chain, it was up to them to prove that they had made a wise choice by substituting Aguirre, the man a sportswriter once called a "whining pudge."

It appeared as though McCloskey had made a great move after all. Aguirre sloughed off his old selfishness and complaining exterior, and, to the amazement of his ex-teammates in Dallas, actually learned to function as part of a team. He still scored his share of points, often leading his new team in that category. But the new-model Aguirre started helping out on defence, and wasn't afraid to pass the ball to a teammate with a higher-percentage shot. And to everyone's amazement, Mark even started get along with his fellow Pistons, allowing himself to take some good-natured ribbing from team clowns Mahorn and Salley.

The big trade illustrated a few significant things about team chemistry in the NBA. Isiah himself shed some light on the intertwined subjects of money-hunger, greed for elevated point-scoring stats, and the whole nasty world of NBA trades and contract negotiations in a conversation he had with Fred Waitzkin of the *New York Times*. "Most of the guys in professional sports come from poor backgrounds," he told Waitzkin, speaking from experience. "Overnight, a guy comes into the league and he's making a million a year. This guy doesn't know how to balance a check book. Overnight, instead of being a college kid, he's a role model. He ain't ready to be a role model. Everyone looks up to him. 'You're great, you earn a million dollars, you can run up and down the court real fast.' It starts to blow his mind."

Once the poor-kid-turned-millionaire starts to believe the hype about himself, he starts letting other people take control of his money and his time off the court. With agents and other hangers-on constantly reminding him how great he is, the player begins to consider just how much he can squeeze out of a given team. This in turn leads to the player looking out for himself, and not playing the kind of basketball that helps teams win. After all, many people had long felt that if Isiah had concentrated solely on scoring and his own stats, he could have been marketed along the same lines as Magic or Jordan. But his game had always been about making the other guys in the same uniforms look better. Isiah succinctly related to Waitzkin just how the me-first dynamic worked in the NBA:

In order to make a lot of money in this league you have to be a good statistical player and in order to have a great basketball team, you can't be selfish. A lot of guys have found the temptation to make money too powerful.

A player sits down with the team's general manager to discuss [his] contract, and he's told, "You want a raise? Let's see what you did last year. You averaged 3 points, 4 rebounds, 2 turnovers, 4 fouls a game. You want a raise?"

Therefore the player says, "OK, in order for me to get a raise I got to get 13 rebounds a night and 14 points. So Isiah comes driving down the lane. I'm not going to try to block his shot. I'm going to hope he misses so I can get that rebound. When my guy gets beat, I'm not going to help him. I'm going to block my man out and be ready. That's two rebounds. That's what this game is about. I got to get my three steals. I'll get one this time. I missed

it. Doesn't matter that my man got a layup. I'm going to try it
every time until I get a steal. . . . And now I got my three steals
tonight, I can sit back. It doesn't matter that I gave up 14 points
to get them.

Now when you got to sit down in the general manager's office,
you say, "I want a raise." And the GM *says, "How can you ask*
me for a raise? The team only won 22 games last season." And
you answer, "Yeah, but I averaged 20 points, 10 rebounds, and,
you know, three steals a night."

Now that Aguirre was contributing to the total team effort, it
was going to be tough to stop the Bad Boys. Detroit stormed
through the regular season after the Aguirre trade, and took out
the Celtics three games to none in the best-of-five first round of
the playoffs. Loyal Boston fans complained that their hero Larry
Bird was injured, but this elicited little sympathy from the
Pistons. Their number one go-to guy, Isiah Thomas had come
out of the opening series of the 1989 playoffs with an excruciating
pain in his shoulder and a broken hand. The hand had been
crushed as Isiah slugged the Bulls' huge seven-footer Bill
Cartwright in a brawl earlier in the year, and his shoulder had
been injured as he reached in to stop the Celtics' 6–9 forward, Ed
Pinckney — who would later be selected by Isiah as one of the
original Toronto Raptors — in the fourth game of the Celtics
series. X-rays ruled out a torn rotator cuff as the cause of the sore
shoulder, but it was incredibly painful nevertheless. As Bad Boys,
the Pistons certainly had a knack of inflicting punishment on
their opponents. But playing this hard as a 6–1 point guard came
with a price, and Isiah had discovered time and time again what
that price was. You could also get hurt if you were a Bad Boy!

The Pistons were going to need to use every last tough-guy trick if they were to get past their next playoff opponents, the Milwaukee Bucks. The Bucks, expertly coached by Del Harris, were a team of hustling overachievers who had knocked off Atlanta in their first-round encounter. What was even more frightening for Detroit was that Milwaukee had beaten them 4 games out of 6 in the regular season, and their one bona fide star, Ricky Pierce, had shot sixty per cent, taking out his anger on a team that had traded him to the hapless San Diego Clippers earlier in his career.

But with Thomas in the line-up despite his myriad physical woes — one cynical Detroit reporter called his ability to play through pain "another Isiah miracle, brought to you by the Detroit Pistons" — the Pistons made it past the Bucks in four straight games, due mostly to an all-team effort and some classic Bad Boys bashing. Next up: Michael Jordan, the Chicago Bulls, and the Pistons' third straight trip to the Eastern finals. In 1987, they had been beaten by the Celtics when they got this far; in '88 Detroit had made it past the Celts only to lose to the Lakers in the league championships. The 1989 version of the battle between the best teams in the East proved to be an all-time classic.

To say that there was no love lost between the Pistons and the Bulls would be like saying the same feelings existed between boxing's Thomas Hearns, another Detroit sports legend, and "Marvelous" Marvin Hagler. This wasn't just a rivalry — the two teams hated each other. Back on April 7, both benches had cleared in the hand-breaking incident between Isiah and Cartwright. Seeing Detroit's scrappy point guard going toe-to-toe, or more accurately, head-to-chest with a man a foot taller and 70 pounds heavier than him seemed to sum up the David-and-Goliath rivalry between the two clubs. The Bulls, behind Jordan and the smooth and deadly Scottie Pippen, were a finesse team that loved to score and run the fast break. They weren't afraid to mix it up, either, but played at a level of phys-icality nowhere near that of their lunch-bucket-brawler foes from the Motor City.

True to form, the very first game featured a lot of shoving, much of it involving Chicago's Dave Corzine and Bad Boy Rick Mahorn. Although the Pistons staged a valiant comeback, the Bulls held on for the win in the all-important first contest of the series. In the second one, Isiah suffered a tremendous shot to a certain extremely sensitive area just below the waist from the knee of Chicago's 6–10 muscleman, Horace Grant. In addition, Bill Laimbeer was ejected due to a cheap shot he laid on Pippen. What happened next, though, will go into the annals of the Detroit Pistons franchise as a truly vintage Isiah Thomas performance, bumps, bruises, and all. He started burning Jordan one-on-one, pulling the Pistons to a 10-point lead, and then to a 13-point one, whereupon Bulls Coach Doug Collins yanked Jordan in resignation. At the end of it, Isiah had amassed 33 points, 4 assists, and 2 steals in the series-tying performance.

More importantly than the personal stats he amassed during the game was the way in which Isiah took control of the team afterwards. He kicked all of the coaches, press, and management out of the locker room and ordered a players-only meeting. It was a brief one, but he'd gotten his point across. The Bulls might be able to win games with one super-star and a lot of strong role players, he told his teammates, but this was not the way the Pistons were going to win it! It wasn't the way he'd learned to play basketball at Indiana, it wasn't the way Daly coached, and it wasn't the way McCloskey put together his team.

When the meeting ended, the sportswriters rushed in to ask Isiah what the Pistons had talked about. "I said it's not good for a basketball team when one guy has to score as many points as I did tonight," he told them. "What makes our team good is that we've got six or eight guys that can get in double figures . . . and that's when we can look at the stat sheet and say, okay, this basketball team's playing pretty good."

But that hadn't happened in the first two games against the Bulls. The Pistons, Isiah felt, were just standing around, and when it came to crunch time, were looking to him to pull them through. They were going limp, both on offence and defence, and ignoring the fundamentals of good, tough, Bad Boy hoops that brought them this far. "The problem with these last two games," said Isiah, " is we're just passing by guys in the night. You can't set a screen if you just pass a guy by — you've got to stop and set it. . . . It's just a matter of getting out on the basketball court and setting the damn screen."

In a fantasy world, the Pistons would have responded to Isiah's let's-get-it-together-guys exhortations and stormed back to crush the Bulls in Game 3. In the real-life world of the NBA, however, the Pistons botched a 12-point lead and lost. Michael Jordan hit for 46 points, including a miracle bank shot with 3 seconds to put the Bulls up by 2. Doug Collins' instructions to his players as they huddled to prepare for the final shot illustrated the team's approach to offensive basketball in a nutshell. "Get the ball to Michael," Collins ordered, "and everybody else get the fuck out of the way!" Bill Laimbeer, who was beginning to feel he had been placed "under a microscope" by the refs, was called on an unbelievably soft foul — again, he'd gotten away with a lot worse contact — as he barely touched with Jordan with 9 seconds to go, setting up the Bulls' star's winning basket after the time-out. Dumars had a chance to win it at the buzzer, but just missed a three-pointer as time expired.

For the rest of the series, though, it would be all Detroit, and lots of Isiah Thomas. In Game 4 he was everywhere, burying three-pointers, dishing off, picking the pockets of the Bulls dribblers, doing it all in a Pistons win. Detroit also took Game 5, 94–85, courtesy of a wicked defensive effort by John Salley and Dennis Rodman that even forced Michael Jordan into the unthinkable — an airball! In Game 6, the most physical one of the series, Chicago built up a 12-point margin behind Jordan's scoring tear, but the Pistons surged back. In the final quarter, however, a funny thing happened.

Cameron Stauth, a writer who was lucky enough to be able to follow the Pistons around the league for the entire 1988–89 season, describes the drama that put Game 6 on ice in *The Franchise*, his book about the Pistons:

Isiah Thomas came out of the time-out with his face rigid, looking a little amused, if anything. Then he took over the game. He hit a jumper, then drove on Jordan, drew a foul, and made both shots. Then he hit another jumper and grabbed a rebound. As he came down with the ball, Daly put his palms out flat: slow it down. Isiah worked [Bulls guard] John Paxson into a frenzy, collected another foul, and swished both. Suddenly, the lead was 10. Jordan missed a free throw, Isiah pumped in another jumper and now the bench was standing, grinning. . . .

When it ended, Isiah Thomas threw his arms around Mark Aguirre. "I got us in it," said Thomas. "Now you've got to win it for us."

Only one more best-of-seven series lay between the Pistons, Isiah, and the ultimate NBA goal. By now, playoff basketball was becoming a familiar thing to the Bad Boys, and the guys they'd have to face in the 1989 finals were familiar too — the L.A. Lakers. After all, as the old saw goes, "the devil you know is better than the one you don't." In the case of the Pistons, there would be no big secrets in facing the demon Lakers. Another Magic-Isiah duel, another Laimbeer-Kareem battle of the big men, another style-and-finesse vs. rough-and-tumble bout of basketball philosophies. "This is as it should be," said Pistons GM McCloskey, "the two best teams fighting it out."

If anybody knew about the effort it took to win an NBA championship, it was Isiah Thomas. Before the series started, he offered his opinions about how to conquer the mighty Lakers. The secret — as always — was to play team basketball. "It's hard not to be selfish," he said. "The art of winning is complicated by statistics, which for us becomes money," he continued, indirectly invoking memories of the departed Adrian Dantley. "Well, you gotta fight that, find a way around it. And I think we have. If we win this, we'll be the first team in history to win it without having a single player averaging twenty points. First team. Ever. We got twelve guys who are just totally committed to winning. Every night [during the regular season and the opening round of the playoffs] we found a different person to win it for us."

They kept it up against the Lakers in the 1989 finals. Isiah, Vinnie Johnson, Aguirre, Salley, Laimbeer, Rodman, even Rick

Mahorn, all chipped in with major contributions in a series that can best be described in one word — "sweep." Joe Dumars won the MVP for the series, but the whole thing was a total team effort, a 4–0 broom-job against a demoralized Lakers squad. Isiah Thomas' contribution, for all his team-play rhetoric, put him first among equals on the Pistons team. With an 18.2 points per game average and 8.3 assists per contest, Isiah was at the top of the club's playoff stat charts in those categories. After all, even total-team-concept franchises need their leaders, in terms of both sheer numbers and emotional boosting. On the newly-crowned, 1989 NBA champion Detroit Pistons basketball club — the notorious but successful Bad Boys — Isiah Thomas was unquestionably that leader.

The following season, the Pistons moved out of the great team category and into the dynasty classification. Mowing down their regular season and playoff opponents — including the hated Bulls in another brutal Eastern finals — with a regularity alarming to their NBA rivals, they came face to face with the surprising Portland Trail Blazers in the league championships. The Western division's perennial powerhouse L.A. Lakers had surprisingly been taken out in the second round by Phoenix, who in turn were bounced by Portland in six games.

That was as good as it was going to get for the Blazers and their coach Rick Adelman, who later went on to coaching success with the Sacramento Kings. Detroit and Portland had met twice during the season, and each had won one game. The Trail Blazers' attack featured some tough players, like Clyde "The Glide" Drexler, guard Terry Porter, huge Kevin Duckworth, and a sharp-shooting Yugoslavian named Drazen Petrovic. But in the 1990 finals, Detroit took out the Trail

Blazers in five games; only the second one, which Portland won in overtime, was really close.

It was Isiah's series to control, and he did it in classic style. Veteran NBA scribe Jack McCallum of *Sports Illustrated* called it a "studied, mature orchestration of the Detroit Pistons' NBA championship." According to McCallum, "Thomas kept the tempo at a controlled, even pace . . . and when he wasn't doing that, he was creating something from nothing, with long-distance jump shots, body-twisting drives and steals in the open floor."

There was no better example of Isiah putting his stamp of ownership on the 1990 finals than in the first game of the series. In a 5-minute burst in the fourth quarter, Isiah took the Pistons from a 10-point deficit to a 5-point lead, a surge that totally broke the Trail Blazers' spirit. And in the space of one minute during that spurt, Thomas made a steal, hit two free throws, nabbed a rebound, and hit a three-pointer. Shortly after that, he nailed a jumper, and then another trifecta.

"It's will, not skill," he told reporters who wanted to know how a human being in shorts and a tank top could do so much in such a short time. "Everything comes into focus. . . . Everything on the court seems to get slower . . . Gets clearer . . . Everything slows down," he told them, trying to describe the feeling of being in the "zone," that mysterious and uncontrollable feeling that players talk about when they've felt that every shot they take is going to fall. "Everything you do goes right," explained Isiah, "be it rebounds or shots or passes. . . ." He would later say that this was the best "zone" game he'd ever played.

The series win over Portland, in which Isiah was named the Finals MVP, was so one-sided that its major function as far as Pistons fans were concerned was simply to cement the team's position as an historic NBA dynasty. Unfortunately, two sad off-court events followed the Bad Boys' second consecutive league championship, a pair of happenings that overshadowed the actual basketball games to a large extent.

Detroit had always been known as a rough town. Its violent streets had earned it the nickname "Murder City, U.S.A." in the 1970s. The decade before that, 43 people had been killed there in a civil rights riot in 1967. Still, no one was really prepared for the widespread violence that erupted in the Motor City following the Pistons' 1990 championships. Seven citizens — including 3 kids under the age of 16 — died senselessly in a night of rioting. Hundreds of people were shot. Although many members of the Pistons had attempted to spread a message of non-violence to the city's youth, including Isiah, who a few years earlier had organized a "No Crime" day with Detroit Mayor Coleman Young, the idea seemed not to have sunk in. In all, it was a terrible end in the streets to a great season on the court.

The second deleterious controversy that emerged out of the 1990 finals involved Isiah Thomas in a very direct way. Less than a day after the Game-5 win over Portland, Isiah came home to find Lynn crying. She had just seen a news report on Detroit TV station WJBK that troubled her immensely. The report claimed that her husband was somehow connected to a federal investigation into a nation-wide gambling ring, because of his involvement with a friend named Emmet Denha. Denha, a big supporter of the Pistons and the owner of a Detroit supermarket, was also Joshua Thomas' godfather. The WJBK report said that while Thomas himself wasn't officially under investigation, authorities wanted to know more about some checks that Denha had cashed for Isiah, since

Denha was under investigation by the feds. What's more, the TV people claimed that Mark Aguirre had "apparently" approached a former FBI man with the news that Isiah had a gambling problem, and had played "high-stakes" dice games. Aguirre, though, denied even knowing the ex-federal agent, let alone having spoken to him.

Through his attorney, Isiah told the press that the whole thing was nonsense. The alleged amounts of the checks he cashed had been highly inflated, and what's more, the rumors about the dice games were exaggerations as well. Sure, said Isiah, he had played a few casual dice games in Detroit, but these were for stakes of $10 and $30, hardly big-time occasions.

In addition, Isiah maintained that the only reason he'd cashed the checks through Denha's store was that he wanted to avoid the usual commotion that occurred whenever he appeared in public in the Detroit area. Several of Isiah's current and past teammates also told *Sports Illustrated* that their friend did not have a problem with gambling. "I'm really mad," said Isiah, "because none of this has anything to do with fact. I'm sure it will all blow over — at least my part in it — and will not affect the team." He also claimed that he'd be "totally shocked" if his friend Denha was found to have any involvement in the alleged gambling ring. (A few years later, though, when Isiah was in Toronto and in the midst of trying to build the Raptors into an NBA contender, the allegations about Isiah and gambling would be raised all over again in a book called *Money Players.*)

Amidst all of this post-season controversy, there had also begun to emerge some speculation around the league as to just how good the Pistons really were in comparison to some of the classic teams of the past. Whenever a team wins two consecutive league championship titles in any sport, it's never enough to satisfy many fans and media pundits. Soon, they'll begin talking about three in a row, or the "three-peat," a hideous appellation apparently coined by ex-Lakers coach Pat Riley after his team took NBA crowns in 1987 and 1988. Sure enough, basketball observers started pondering the possibility of the Bad Boys going for a trio of NBA titles just as soon as the champagne had stopped bubbling after the last game of the Portland series.

The Pistons couldn't pull it off in 1990–91. They tried, though, blasting off to the best November start in the team's history. At Christmas, both Isiah and Bill Laimbeer defied team orders — and were fined by Jack McCloskey for doing so — by refusing to leave their families on Christmas Eve to fly to Chicago for a game against the Bulls on Christmas Day. The two eventually chartered their own plane in time to make it to the Windy City for the game. Both were unapologetic to team officials at having not traveled with the team. "Seeing my little boy open presents, you just can't buy that," said Isiah. "We played, didn't we? It isn't like we missed the game or anything."

Thomas had begun to notice a change in his ballclub around the time of the Christmas matchup with the Bulls. After losing to the Jordan-led squad, he put it into words. "From the coaching staff on down to the players," he predicted, "we're not going to get it done with this attitude. We may have to look in a new direction. New people, new enthusiasm. . . . We slowed to a crawl. We don't have the same emotional energy and enthusiasm in the second half. That seems to be our pattern this year. . . . This is a totally different attitude than we had last December."

After an 11-game winning streak into January, it was beginning to look like some of that old intensity had returned.

Strained ligaments in his right wrist, however, made things tough for Isiah. In typical fashion, he insisted on playing despite pain in his shooting hand. The injury got worse, and the only option was surgery. Doctors predicted he'd miss 12 weeks of action, in other words, the rest of the regular season and likely some of the playoffs. The layoff was only about 6 weeks in total, but in the meantime trade rumors had surfaced. People around the NBA were starting to speculate that McCloskey might be considering shunting Isiah off to another club. The rumors were totally bogus, though, and as *Sports Illustrated* opined, anyone who thought that a mid-season slump would be enough to get the Pistons' brass talking about trading Isiah were missing out on a fundamental reality that governed Detroit basketball: "June, not January, is Thomas' time to shine."

Upon his return to the lineup, Isiah quickly re-took control of the team. "Isiah looked like he never missed a beat," said Coach Daly. But Thomas had grabbed the reins of a club that was ailing. James Edwards, John Salley, and Mark Aguirre all had bad backs, and the Pistons dropped three games in a row shortly after Isiah's return. It was time for him to deliver another blast to his mates, injuries or no injuries. "Nobody gives a damn around here any more, and that includes the coaches," he informed the sportswriters, for their part always eager for news of internal dissension to fill their columns. "We've become comfortable with losing. It doesn't bother anyone any more. Nobody cares." Losing should bother anyone associated with a back-to-back championship ball club, said Isiah, and the fact that it didn't seem to was ticking him off. "It doesn't even hurt any more when you lose," he griped.

The 1990–91 Pistons ended up at 50-and-32 on the season, a record many pundits figured wasn't bad given the raft of injuries the team had endured. In the playoffs, there was some reason for optimism. It seemed as though everyone's ailments had healed, at least to the point where playing hard on them was possible. But the physical element of the game is only a part — some would even say a small part — of the game of pro basketball. And on the psychological side, the Pistons just weren't into it. Feuding and team miscommunication were starting to creep into the picture. They squeaked by the Atlanta Hawks in the first round of the playoffs in a series that went the full 5 games. It was in the fifth game of the Hawks match-up that the Pistons showed flashes of their customary brilliance, Isiah hitting for 26 points on an aching hamstring, Dumars scoring 22, and Worm Rodman hauling down an incredible 20 rebounds.

In the next round, Isiah's play against the Celtics was limited, due to an ailing foot picked up in the Atlanta series. How many more body parts could the guy injure? And how much more pain could he take? People could say what they wanted about the virtues of the plucky little man bashing heads with the giants of the NBA, but this play-through-pain thing couldn't last forever, could it? Still, playing when he could, Isiah chipped in mightily against Boston. In game 6, a contest that went into overtime, Isiah tallied 17 points on the throbbing foot. The Pistons had qualified for the Eastern finals for the fifth consecutive year!

The bubble burst — some would say mercifully for the ailing Isiah and his teammates, who had begun to fear the worst about their chances for a three-peat — against the Bulls in the Eastern finals. It was a fast-bursting bubble, too, as Jordan &

Co. put the once-Bad Boys out of their misery in four straight. In the final game, mindful of all of the cheap shots both teams had thrown at each other over the years, remembering the gloating comments of the Bulls about a sweep when Detroit was down 3–0, and above all aware of how sweet it was for Chicago to finally crush their arch-rivals, Isiah and Laimbeer engineered a concluding snub. The Pistons starters, relegated to the bench during the final few seconds of "garbage time" simply walked away from the court, without shaking the Bulls' hands and without congratulations. "Was it choreographed?" Isiah asked rhetorically after the game. "Of course it was. They didn't show us any respect. Why should we show them any?"

Dynasties, by all historical standards, are short-lived in the National Basketball League, and the one established by the Detroit Pistons was no exception. They had earned their place in the annals of the game, and now, having gotten an emphatic dose of the old broom-treatment by the Bulls, it actually felt good to have it over with. "I'm going to relax my body, relax my mind. Sit in the sunshine," proclaimed Isiah in obvious relief. "And you don't know the pressure . . . because you're not under it. I don't think anybody realizes what we've been through all these years. It's a cruel form of torture. There's nothing to compare what we've gone through, what we had to endure physically and mentally."

Physically, at least, there was a litany of injuries — hand, wrist, ankle, hamstring, shoulder, knee to name but a few — plus too many bruises, scratches, and cuts to keep track of. The toughness of the NBA was really starting to take its toll on Isiah, and fans wondered how much longer he was going to put up with it.

With the Pistons going into obvious decline in subsequent years, it looked as though Isiah Thomas would have one last bath in glory before his career would came to an end. This final dose of hoops acclaim, everyone thought, would come in the form of Isiah's membership on the 1992 U.S. Olympic basketball team. The international basketball community, realizing that the growing worldwide popularity of the game would only be helped by such a move, allowed the U.S. to include pro players on its Olympic squad for the first time. The resulting "Dream Team," announced at the start of the 1991–92 NBA season, featured such stars as Michael Jordan, Karl "The Mailman" Malone, and Charles Barkley. It did not, however, have Isiah Thomas on its roster.

Pistons fans were incredulous at the omission, especially considering that the Dream Team's coach was none other than Chuck Daly. But in the pros, rivals don't often forget their grudges, and that was what kept Isiah from being a Dream Team member in the end. Inside sources claimed that Michael Jordan had insisted that Thomas be kept off the team, and that Scottie Pippen had even gone as far as to say that if Thomas got to play, he wouldn't. You just didn't walk off the court on the Chicago Bulls in their moment of glory, it seemed, and expect them to forgive you just like that. For his part, Isiah insisted in taking what he called "the high road" and wouldn't say much, but for one of the game's all-time great point guards to be excluded from the historic 1992 Olympic squad was a painful slap. "I've never felt such a mix of emotions as I feel right now," he said. "All of these guys are taking shots at Isiah, and I'm just sitting here not saying a thing. It's not the most disappointing moment of my life, but it's close. It's a bitter pill to swallow, and I just want to get the taste of out my mouth as soon as I can."

More than a decade later, as many top NBA players were trying to decide if risking a trip to Athens for the 2004 Olympics was worth it in the face of a possible terrorist threat to the Games, Thomas had a chance to comment on his exclusion from the 1992 edition of Team USA, and in particular the role that Jordan might have played in his being left at home. "All I can do is take [Jordan] at his word," Isiah said. "He said he didn't block me. For my peace of mind, I have to believe him, because I really wanted to be part of that Olympic experience and never got the chance."

To make matters worse, Olympian Karl Malone decided he'd send another anti-fan-club message to Isiah during the early part of the 1991–92 season, just in case he hadn't gotten the picture from his Dream Team exclusion. The Mailman, who fancied himself as something of a bodybuilder and played with a crashing, straight-ahead style, aimed an elbow at Isiah's head during a Utah Jazz-Pistons game. No problem, all part of the physical world of the NBA. Unfortunately, this elbow opened up a huge cut over Thomas' left eye, which took 42 stitches to close and made it difficult to focus his vision for a week. Unbelievably, Isiah took it all in the stride of man who'd come to understand all of good and bad aspects of his chosen profession.

"I think Karl Malone intended to hit me," he said, "and I think he intended to give me a hard shot. I don't think he intended to give me 40 stitches. Now, do I dislike him for it? No." For Isiah, dealing with an errant forearm, no matter how viciously it might've been thrown, was standard operating procedure in the pros. A few years later, Brendan Malone, then a Pistons assistant coach and later the Isiah-picked inaugural coach of the Toronto Raptors, would report that Thomas had actually returned to play out the game against Utah after his head had been sewn up. "Sometimes you have to swallow bad medicine," Isiah confessed. "My philosophy is hurry up, get some water, swish it around and get out the bad taste . . . because you've got to take it. It happened."

At the beginning of the 1993–94 season, another unpleasant burst of publicity surrounded Isiah, and this time the headlines concerned not only him, but his teammate and friend Bill Laimbeer as well. People had always wondered how, and why, these two men had become such close friends. After all, Isiah had had to scrap and scrape for everything he'd ever gotten in life, while "Lamb" had always had it easy, reminding people that he didn't have to play hoops for a living. Isiah came from the inner city, Bill from the 'burbs. Isiah's relationship with his father was tenuous at best, due to Isiah II's absence and personal instability; Laimbeer's dad was a wealthy executive who provided for his family. Bill was white, Thomas black; Isiah a little guy, Laimbeer a giant. Yet with all of those glaring differences, the two had become close friends. It was the passion, the drive that both shared for winning — winning at all costs — that had brought them together, and had solidified the bonds of comradeship between them.

That's why Pistons fans and management went into a state of near shock when they learned that Isiah and Bill had been fighting in practice. Laimbeer, having been relegated to second-string center, had nailed Isiah with an elbow in a scrimmage game, breaking two ribs. Then, in another practice session about a month later, Isiah retaliated with a sucker-punch to

Laimbeer's head, fracturing his own hand on contact. The injury put Thomas on the disabled list for six weeks, and confirmed the suspicion that team morale had really gone downhill in Detroit.

Rumors had it that Laimbeer wanted to wait until Isiah came back to action until he retired from the game, believing it would look bad to do so with his teammate absent. In the end, both players made up, but fans couldn't help remembering a time in the not-too-distant past when it was the Pistons opponents who were on the receiving end of the elbows and punches emerging from the "Zeke and Lamb show." For Isiah, the fight with Laimbeer signaled something significant, something with an element of finality to it.

Maybe the glory days of the Bad Boys were a thing of the past. Perhaps it was time for Isiah to leave this game and move on to something else?

CHAPTER SEVEN

From the Back Court to the Front Office

Although Isiah had enjoyed a Hall-of-Fame career with the Detroit Pistons, it was beginning to look like it was time for number 11 to hang up his sneakers and start looking for a new challenge. He had easily taken over as the Motor City franchise's all-time leader in scoring, steals, total games  played, and assists. In addition, Thomas had been voted the NBA's Most Valuable Player no less than three times.

Perhaps more importantly, Isiah had gained a reputation as the greatest "little man" ever to play the game. Although the Boston Celtics' Bob Cousy is usually also mentioned as a contender for this particular title, it has to be said in all fairness to the great "Couz" that while he did popularize some of the nicest playmaking innovations in the game — like the behind-the-back dish and the long bounce pass — his 1950s opponents were not exactly of the same caliber as ones named

Jordan, Bird, Kareem, or Magic. Take a look at some highlight film from the glory days Bob Cousy, and then look at, say, footage from one of the fiercer Pistons-Lakers games at the peak of Isiah's career. It doesn't even look like it's the same game being played in both; there's no comparison. For sheer talent, determination, and creativity, Isiah Thomas was — and still is — the greatest small guard in history.

Isiah realized early on in his pro career that as a smaller player, he would have to develop his game in such a way as would not only enable him to compete, but to succeed in the NBA. In fact, after he had retired, Thomas would reflect on his career with pride, much of it based on the fact that he was able to hold his own against much taller, heavier opponents. "I look back on what I got from my body, that I was able to compete with those guys, and I almost can't believe it," he remembers. "You shrink all those guys down to 6–1 and 175 lb., and see what happens."

But playing as a little man in a game dominated by giants eventually has to take its toll. Something was gradually starting to go missing in Thomas' game after about 1992 — a half-step slower on defence here, the formerly automatic jumper slightly off there. Thomas' complete and total ability to take over a game when he wanted simply wasn't there any more.

A couple of years later, retired from play and comfortably ensconced within the Raptor organization, Isiah reflected on the warning signs of athletic decline which were beginning to make him realize that his time in a Pistons uniform was coming to an end. "I had played and got as much out of basketball as I possibly could," he recalls. "If I'd played another year without having the type of passion that had more or less died in me, then I would have been cheating somebody out of some money. I'd have been getting money for something that I really didn't deserve."

When a superstar professional basketball player begins to lose the abilities that have catapulted him into the limelight, he can go in a number of different directions. He can keep right on playing, reasoning that if he was one of the best when he was at the top of his game, he should still be good enough to be better than most — even if he isn't quite the player he used to be. This appeared to be the case with, for example, the legendary "Ice Man," George Gervin. A prolific scorer with the San Antonio Spurs, Gervin ended his NBA years with the Chicago Bulls. While Ice's game had certainly dropped off in the latter stages of his career, he still seemed to be able to score enough points to be useful to his team.

In the same vein, a canny veteran might understand that there are some parts of his overall game that haven't suffered too much with age, even though other elements have fallen apart. Even though it would take an extreme cynic to contend that the post-baseball and Washington Wizards version of Michael Jordan had "declined" in his abilities, it's still pretty obvious that he had changed his game later in his career. He would still take it to the hoop like he used to, but the second and third editions of Jordan seemed to favor lots of pull-up jumpers and three-point attempts. He was always a scorer, but by emphasizing his outside game more on offence, Jordan was definitely working on extending his shelf-life.

But when a player starts firing on anything less than all cylinders, there will always be fans clamoring for him to get out while the getting is still good. It certainly helps to have retired pretty close to the top of one's game when it comes time to be chosen for the Hall of Fame balloting. And nothing is sadder for the true NBA fan to see someone who formerly had the game under his complete control gradually start to get beaten under the boards or off the dribble by lesser mortals. That's why, in Isiah's case, it made sense to start thinking about retirement at the end of the 1993–94 season.

In fact, Thomas remembers that it was one specific day that crystallized his thoughts about retirement, and caused him to announce that he'd be leaving pro basketball. "I woke up one morning and went to practise and I remember sitting in the gym and we practised for an hour and I didn't take one shot," he reminisces. "I walked away from the gym and went back up to my hotel room. And I sat at the edge of the bed and I said to myself, 'Something's wrong,' because that was the first time I'd ever walked in the gym with no desire to play basketball. When that happened, I just knew it was time to move on to something else."

At the time, only Isiah knew what that "something else" might be. But on April 19, 1994, whatever forces control the fates of basketball heroes determined that, whatever Thomas' intentions were for a life after basketball, his career as a point guard would conclude in a very abrupt manner.

On that fateful evening, hordes of Piston faithful had flocked to the Palace in Auburn Hills to see Isiah's final home game of the season against the Orlando Magic. The team that had formerly terrorized opponents as the Bad Boys of the NBA were floundering through to a 20–62 season. That season, they would not be going through to the playoffs. Since their schedule had them playing out their final three games on the road, Isiah would be saying good-bye that night to the loyal fans who supported him during his 13 years as a Piston. At half-time, Isiah jogged to midcourt, took a big bow, and enjoyed the 4-minute standing ovation showered upon him by the Palace crowd, which included his mother, Mary.

The ovation, however, was as good as it got on this night during which the Pistons would get blown out, 132–104, by Orlando. With 13 minutes to go in the game, Isiah threw one of his patented dribble-drive moves on the Magic's Anfernee "Penny" Hardaway. The result, unfortunately, was the real-life actualization of an old playground joke: Isiah went one way and his right Achilles tendon went the other. Typically, Thomas fought off all attempts by trainers and teammates to help him off the court — he was going off under his own steam this one last time.

A few weeks later, on May 2, 1994, Isiah limped into a press conference on crutches and announced his retirement as a professional basketball player. Surgery had been performed to repair the ruptured Achilles, but Isiah was much more interested in talking about closing out this particular chapter of his life. After scoring more than 18,000 points and leading Detroit to two consecutive NBA titles, three straight trips to the finals, and five Eastern Conference finals in a row, Thomas wanted to reflect publicly on what it all meant. Wiping away some tears, he tried to put his career into perspective. "The hardest thing for an athlete to do is to know when to quit," he explained. "When do you let go of the thing that has shaped your entire life?"

After 13 seasons in the pros, Isiah Thomas was still only 33 years old — aged, perhaps, for an NBA player but relatively young in the "real" world of stockbrokers, teachers, and insurance agents. "I've never had to give a retirement speech before, so at my young age, you're going to have to bear with me," Isiah told the media. He was quick to point out that basketball had, above all, afforded him some astounding opportunities — possibilities most athletes can only dream of. "I had a tremendous time, made a lot of friends, got a chance to travel — see places I never would have gotten to see growing up on the West Side of Chicago," admitted Thomas. "Basketball has brought me a long way."

Luckily for North American hoops fans, though, none of this meant that Isiah Thomas was finished with NBA basketball. Not by a long shot. Anyone who had seen him in action during his 13-year playing career knew that a man of such tremendous energy would never be able to opt for a quiet retirement and a lot of time on the golf course. What was next for Isiah? What could he do for an encore after his magnificent years in the Motor City?

Throughout his career, Isiah Thomas had stuck with only one team — the Detroit Pistons. He had always stressed his loyalty to the organization, and as his years as a player were coming to an end, it appeared as though the Pistons would repay him for remaining faithful to them. Originally, the Detroit brass had signed him out of Indiana University to a four-year, $1.6 million contract. After that, Isiah had almost single-handedly turned the team from a 21–61 squad to one that won 49 games in his third year, going over .500 for the first time in seven years. The Pistons' management tore up the original contact with a year left on it. Isiah then signed a 10-year, $12 million deal that both he and the Detroit front office hoped would make him a Piston for the rest of his career.

In fact, Isiah often described himself as a "Piston for life." Several major U.S. newspapers reported in January 1994 that

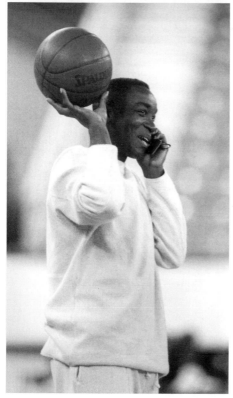

Thomas would sign a gigantic $55 million deal, sweetened with a part ownership of the team. However, all of these articles were punctuated by information from "unknown sources" and barely-substantiated rumors. In fact, none of the Pistons' key figures — owner William Davidson, president Tom Wilson, player personnel director Billy McKinney, or coach Don Chaney — would comment on the purported mega-contract.

Isiah had earlier been rumored to have been on the trading block, with the New York Knicks being named as the most likely recipient of his talents. Indeed, New York sports columns were rife with the speculation that Thomas had "used" the Knicks to get what he wanted from Detroit. Isiah refused to discuss any of this, and would only comment that "I don't want to discuss my personal agreements with anyone." As far as he and the Pistons' ownership were concerned, "we've discussed our mutual intention of continuing my relationship with the Pistons after my playing and we've agreed not to announce or discuss any specific roles until I retire."

Both the Pistons and Isiah have remained absolutely tight-lipped about the entire matter of the deal he was supposedly offered to remain in Detroit. Neither side would say then, or has ever said, much at all about what had transpired between them. But recent history bears out some pretty clear evidence that Thomas and the Pistons' management were unable to reach an agreement whereby he would continue in some front-office capacity in the Motor City after retiring.

Suffice it to say that in 1994, Isiah became the GM of the Toronto Raptors, and has moved on to play key roles with two other NBA clubs, the Pacers and the Knicks — and thus will never be considered a "Piston for life." In fact, with all three of these post-Pistons teams in the NBA's Eastern Conference, Isiah has had to face his old franchise as an opponent on a regular basis. For his part, Thomas has never stooped to bad-mouthing anyone involved with pro hoops in the Motor City, and will only comment that "the business of doing business got in the way" and that "it just didn't work out . . . all the jobs were full" during his final months in Detroit.

Despite this setback, Isiah had been wisely preparing himself for a second career during his later years in Detroit, one that would begin just as soon as he got done playing. Although an Associated Press report of his retirement press conference tersely stated that Thomas "was not sure what he would do next," it was nevertheless true that he had been laying some pretty sound foundations for the future. Using the same kind of foresight and dynamic calculation he had brought to the Pistons' backcourt, Isiah had done much more than the typical NBA star to ensure that once he left the game, he would be able to continue to accomplish significant things in the world of business and commerce.

In 1989, Thomas had become the star of a special "ambush marketing" campaign for the Puma USA shoe company. The campaign centered on a 60-second video production starring Isiah, entitled "The Puma Challenge." Advertising execs in charge of promotion for Puma decided to run the spot in eight major U.S. cities — Baltimore, Chicago, Dallas, Detroit, Indianapolis, Milwaukee, St. Louis, and Washington — in movie theatres during the busiest back-to-school-shopping weeks of September. The video featured Isiah as a military commander landing a Stealth-like bomber, whereupon he and crew members divest themselves of flight gear and begin playing basketball. The campaign was also bolstered by a series of bill-boards and magazine ads. The entire result was to establish Isiah Thomas as the firmly-identified spokesman of Puma shoes. What's more, he learned a valuable lesson about self-promotion and making money based on image.

Another venture into the area of marketing, merchandising, and promotions was instigated by Thomas in 1992. He approached a Michigan company named Morley Candymakers about the possibility of manufacturing the "Isiah Bar." Morley agreed, realizing that Isiah's fame as a basketball star would translate into big sales, at least on a regional level. Indeed, in the first few months of the candy bar's shelf life, the "peanuts and caramel slam-dunked in milk chocolate" treat was purchased by over 750,000 consumers in Michigan and Northern Ohio. And while the success of the Puma shoe campaign and the launching of a personalized chocolate bar might not have reached a level comparable to, say, Nike's "Air Jordan" bonanza, these exercises nevertheless taught Isiah something about marketing his name. They also prepared him for the marketing challenges that would face him in Toronto. Sneakers and candy bars aside, by the time he was finished on the court, Isiah had spent some serious time learning about the ins and outs of how corporations work.

By now, sports fans are getting tired of the old saying that "sports is big business," and one begins to wonder: if this dictum is so true, why don't more ex-athletes trade in on their fame and find success in the corporate world upon retirement? An article in *Forbes* magazine on December 19, 1994, attempted to answer this question, using Isiah Thomas as a model for success. The cover of this particular issue featured a smiling

Thomas sitting courtside in ASICS sneakers and baggy sweats — holding a lap-top computer. The front cover copy next to Isiah's head reads: "My celebrity created a natural deal flow." Emphasizing that Thomas had calculated that it was far more prudent to go into business while he was still in the public eye, the article recounts how he had acquired a company called American Speedy Printers with partners in 1993. In fact, Isiah and a partner named Rick Inatome — with whom Isiah formed I.I. Ventures — bought the copying franchise for about $4 million. In addition to the printing company, Isiah also acquired a chairmanship of an event marketing company called Event Horizons, and was an executive with Omni Banc Corporation, an African-American banking concern. "I believe that the leverage you have, the accessibility you have to people while you're playing, is a hundred times greater than when you quit," Thomas told Forbes.

The leverage Isiah Thomas could wield as a player, however, didn't exactly disappear when he retired from the Pistons. It looked pretty definite that he would not be included in the Detroit franchise's front office plans any time in the near future, but another opportunity had presented itself just across the border. And this one looked too good to pass up.

A Toronto group, headed by a young Canadian business-man named John Bitove, Jr., had won the right to begin assembling an NBA franchise. Bitove's team, which included former Ontario Premier David Peterson, had earned the stamp of approval from the NBA Board of Governors late in 1993. Bitove's group beat out competing bidders that included a team comprised of Earvin "Magic" Johnson and entertainment giant Michael Cohl, and another headed by Toronto entrepreneur

Larry Tanenbaum backed up by the Canadian Imperial Bank of Commerce and Labatt Breweries. In the end, the NBA was so impressed by the Bitove group's high-energy campaign they awarded them permission to start planning to bring the league to Toronto.

In choosing a name for the new Toronto team, the ownership went to the public. The odd name "Raptors" had in fact been chosen through a fairly lengthy process conducted in early 1994, which included a cross-Canada survey of names gathered from responses by over 100,000 Canadians. Once the names had been narrowed to a manageable list, a fan vote was held. The name "Raptors" garnered 24 per cent of the 152,000 votes cast, beating out the Dragons and Bobcats, the next two most popular names.

Soon, hoops fans and fans-to-be throughout Southern Ontario were decked out in all manner of garb that featured the ferocious-looking prehistoric mascot. Market analysts noted that the team name and logo would take advantage of the existing craze for dinosaurs brought on in part by the popular film Jurassic Park. Those with a slightly more paleontological turn of mind observed that in the dinosaur world, a raptor was a creature that spanned between about 6 and 7 feet in height and could run and leap well. Given the characteristics of the typical NBA player, it did sound appropriate.

While the selection of the team name was essentially left up to the chance of a fan vote, it was not by random coincidence that John Bitove wanted Isiah Thomas to become Vice President of Basketball Operations for the Raptors. The Toronto businessman was a devoted fan of the game, and had attended Indiana University as an undergraduate during Isiah's time there. Watching IU win the NCAA's under Thomas' leadership only seemed to fuel Bitove's interest in hoops. Sportswriters have been quick to point out that Bitove was also attending the University of Windsor Law School — just a short tunnel-ride away from Detroit — while Isiah was tearing it up with the Pistons in the Motor City. It was only logical, then, that the Toronto-born Bitove, who the local press often portrayed as "star-struck" because of his connections with Isiah and hockey great Wayne Gretzky, should go after the roundball star as soon as he became available.

For Bitove, the choice was based as much on his sense of Isiah as a businessman as on his admiration for him as a basketball player. In talking to Thomas, Bitove relates that Isiah "brought a lot of new, good ideas on how the game would and should change on the basketball side." And Bitove also noted that Isiah, along with his day-to-day duties of running the club, was also committed to being a part-owner of the team. Some sources put Thomas' share of the Raptors' ownership at 4.5 per cent, others at nine percent, still others at ten percent. General agreement in the media seems to put Isiah's ownership slice at nine per cent, and sets his initial investment in the team at around $4 million. Concludes Bitove, "I and the rest of the partners have the fullest confidence in him."

This confidence might have been based on Isiah's attractiveness as a superstar — one cynical Toronto sportswriter even wondered in print if the Raptors were actually Bitove's attempt at a private "fantasy camp." More likely, Bitove's belief in Thomas' abilities was born out of Isiah's willingness to throw some financial support behind the team as an investor. What is certain, though, is Bitove's belief that Isiah Thomas was the right man for the expansion franchise. He gave three reasons why he thought this way. "No. 1," said the new President, "we've got a proven winner." The second reason, explained Bitove, was that in Isiah, "we've got someone who has been involved in judging talent in his leadership role with a successful basketball organization," alluding to the fact that Pistons' GM Jack McCloskey and owner William Davidson had often allowed their superstar considerable say in personnel matters. And reason number three was simple: "He has a desire to work." All of these elements added up to a impressive package for John Bitove, Jr. who concluded of Isiah that, "Of all the factors we considered, he was the most capable in the league" to take over as GM of the infant Toronto Raptors.

For his part, Isiah seemed pretty confident that he would be up to the task of running a big-time basketball team. After all, he'd done it numerous times on the court on the West Side, at St. Joe's, and at IU. For countless years with the Pistons, his leadership was rarely questioned. But knowing how to beat a full-court press only goes so far when the shorts and tank-top are traded in for a suit and tie. "I think if I had not had the kind of background I do on the administrative side I would not have been as comfortable with the role I've got," Thomas explained in a reference to his various existing business ventures and his degree work in college. "Every night you had to make a choice: Am I going to stay in and hack at this computer or am I going to go out and hang out? I thought that staying in was pretty important."

Everyone knew that as a player, Isiah Thomas moved quickly off the dribble and toward the hoop. But that was nothing compared to the speed with which he moved out of the Piston's backcourt and into the Raptors' front office. In an unbelievably quick turnaround, Isiah was announced as the Raptors' GM on May 24, 1994 — just three weeks after his last game as a Piston and only two weeks after announcing his retirement as a player.

Originally, Bitove and his staff had planned to wait until the summer to make the official announcement, but moved the date forward in response to rampant speculation that Isiah would indeed be named GM of the new Toronto franchise. Raptor director of communications Tom Mayenknecht indicated that while the initial plan had been to delay the announcement until early June before the NBA draft, Bitove & Co. "wanted to make this next move sooner rather than later," to respond to several published reports that Thomas would be taking over. By the time a press conference had actually been called, the *Detroit Free Press*, the *Toronto Star*, the *Globe and Mail*, the *New York Times*, and the *Financial Post*, among others, had already printed announcements of the hiring.

In a special ceremony at Wayne Gretzky's restaurant in the shadow of Toronto's SkyDome, Isiah Thomas, who had been "smuggled" into the proceedings dressed as a cook, burst out of a giant paper box with the Raptors logo on it. Holding a basketball and dressed in a brand new Raptors jacket, Isiah sat down to face the media in his first press conference as a basketball executive.

Inevitably, the questions quickly came around to what plans Isiah had for his new team. From the outset, Thomas asserted that he was planning to tackle his new job the same way he approached basketball as a player. "I've [always] been under the gun to perform," he said, "and I've had to live with cynicism, criticism and accolades." Thomas set the tone for his management style by telling the assembled members of the media that "my job is to get the job done and your job is to evaluate that. I'm very confident that when all is said and done, you'll be pleased with the way the Raptor organization runs itself and how the players perform." But pleasing fans and reporters wasn't going to be easy for the Raptors, if recent expansion-team history was any indication.

NBA expansion teams are always faced with tough decisions in the early years of their existence in the league. There are always those — rival GM's, players, sportswriters, or play-by-play announcers — who are willing to go on record criticizing each and every perceived mistake made by a new club as lacking foresight, being too concerned with immediate gain, ignoring potential fans, whatever. The obstacles facing the Raptors' new management team were no different than those faced by the Charlotte Hornets, Miami Heat, Orlando Magic, and Minnesota Timberwolves a few years before, and their cross-country expansion partners the Vancouver Grizzlies in 1994. Most of the franchise's basketball decisions fell squarely on the shoulders of new GM Thomas. And that meant that the pressure of making choices to determine the fate of the fledgling franchise was about to be cranked up under the close scrutiny of the media and Isiah's front-office peers around the league.

Would Thomas decide that it was better to draft players who could make an impact right away, or invest in some future "projects"? Go with youth in the hopes that they'd one day mature into champions, or build the team on solid, proven veterans? Pick a team suited to a run-and-gun offence, or one more likely to win games through tenacious defence? And what about coaches? Select a staff committed to winning as many games as possible in the first year in order to establish respect around the league right away, or go with patient mentors who'd put winning second and concentrate instead on quietly bringing players along with the intention of one day finding the right mix. For the rookie GM, there were more tough choices to make than face a ballhandler trying to get through a full-court press.

Adding to this pressure was the fact that several members of the Toronto media — who, in all fairness were rookies themselves in the business of covering the NBA — kept insisting on drawing unfair comparisons between Isiah and Pat Gillick, the GM of Toronto's baseball Blue Jays. Gillick had become something of a minor deity in Toronto for his role as a patient franchise-builder. Gillick's patience and long-term foresight was eventually rewarded with back-to-back World Series championships.

Baseball GM's, however, can rely on a well-developed farm system, and have the luxury of being able to bring players along over time courtesy of the feeder teams and the longer shelf-life of baseball players. At least Gillick was one Torontonian who was prepared to admit that his knowledge of hoops was limited, confessing that while he did see the hiring of a rookie GM as "a bit of a risk" he nevertheless saw Isiah as "pretty intelligent, well organized in his thought processes, very professional," concluding that "Based on the little I know about him and based on his playing career, I don't see why he can't do a commendable job."

Right from the word go, Isiah realized that people were expecting big things from him, and he in turn was ready to respond. "There's the feeling in me that I've got to perform," he told the media. And when reporters asked the standard expansion-team question about winning lots of games quickly or coming along slowly, Thomas was ready with an answer: "Our goal is to win a championship, hopefully in our sixth or seventh year," he explained. "We'll be cautious and conservative, not do crazy things. We don't plan to be winning 40 games one year and 20 games the next."

With Isiah in charge of their new NBA team, people all over Toronto rushed to learn more about the man who would be taking control of every basketball-oriented aspect of the franchise. Folks who had been following the NBA prior to the expansion needed no introduction, of course, but for the new breed of fan — and make no mistake, the Raptors were wisely going after the youth market, especially teenagers — there was a lot to be learned. There were some vague notions that this Thomas fellow had once been a pretty good player in his day, but that was about it. What with Michael and Shaq and Sean Kemp around in 1995, who needed to remember the old guys? One playground pickup game in downtown Toronto cracked up when some of the older players — guys in their early thirties and thus old enough to remember the Bad Boys Era — couldn't contain their laughter at the assertions of a pint-sized hoopster who identified Thomas as "that little dude who was always kissing that Lakers guy."

Slowly but surely, the media machine began to churn out the necessary parts of the Thomas legend — the hardships as a kid, the NCAA title at IU, and the dynasty in Detroit. In addition, Raptor-mania and interest in Isiah heated up even more in the summer of 1994, as Toronto and Hamilton, Ontario, hosted the World Championships of Basketball. This event broke every attendance record in the tournament's 44-year history, thanks largely to the U.S.A.'s Dream Team II, which featured Thomas as an injured, non-playing member. The U.S. easily beat Russia in the final in a game watched by over 32,000 fans at SkyDome.

In the excitement and hype that surrounded the announcement of Isiah's hiring as GM, it was easy to overlook that a few milestones had been reached. For starters, Thomas had become only the fifth African-American to attain such a management position in pro sports. As a part owner of the Raptors and a member of a racial minority in North America, he was even more of a rarity. Isiah had been president of the NBA Players' Association for five years, and his former colleague in the NBAPA, Charles Grantham, observed that "it appears as though the newcomers in the league are far more color-blind than here in the U.S.," and commended the Raptors on what he called the wise choice of "a tough, hard-nosed winner."

In addition, several NBA analysts were also pointing out that the involvement of an ex-professional athlete — no matter what his race — as a shareholder of a big-league team was unusual, especially one so recently retired. No one could imagine the same thing happening in the NHL or the NFL, but sports fans had come to view the NBA as the one North American pro league that usually led the way when it came to progressive moves like this one. Of course there have been former players who have moved on to front office and coaching positions in all the major sports, but retired stars becoming actual investors is another story. And so is the type of almost total involvement with the day-to-day operations of a team that Isiah was being promised in Toronto. Drafting, trading, finding a coaching staff, cramming the team's salary under the dreaded league-imposed cap, and determining the Raptors' on- and off-court image were all duties that would be left up to Isiah Thomas, following his burst through that paper cut-out at Wayne Gretzky's and into the world of front-office leadership.

And he couldn't wait to get started.

CHAPTER EIGHT

Assembling the Personnel

Isiah Thomas' first major task as GM of the Toronto Raptors was to select a coaching staff. As much as he might have liked, Isiah couldn't do everything to raise his baby Raptors by himself. Taking to the court and actually playing was out, and, although coaching had always been a goal so was  standing behind the bench to call plays on game nights, at least now. He needed to assemble a group of experts to guide the team on the court, scout the opposition for future games, motivate players, run practices, and plan strategy. One of the reasons that John Bitove, Jr. had hand-picked Isiah to be VP of Basketball Operations for the new expansion club was that as a former Detroit Piston, Thomas possessed considerable familiarity with the day-to-day details of a winning franchise. Almost a year had gone by since he had been named GM, a year of hype and fanfare to try to get Torontonians excited about the NBA. Now, it was up to the rookie to deliver the goods and to prove his worth as a team-builder. He needed to start with the coaching staff.

It must be hell to be the head coach of an NBA basketball team. Like perhaps no other sport, the fans at a typical pro hoop game are right on top of the teams' benches. What's worse, there have been several notorious "super fans" through-out the league's history who have been more interested in hurling verbal abuse — much of it aimed at the opposing team's coach — than in cheering for their favorite squad. If the fans at away games aren't bad enough, there are always your own team's supporters ready to second-guess the guy in the suit. And from a labor-relations perspective, coaching in the NBA means being employed by a corporation to supervise and guide the work of employees who are usually much better paid than you. To make matters worse, the NBA has become known as a "player's league" and a whining superstar can get a coach fired if he's paid highly enough and complains loudly enough, as was the case at Golden State with Don Nelson and his high-priced star, Chris Webber, and, reportedly, Michael Jordan and Doug Collins in Chicago.

When a team wins, it's usually the players who get the credit. But when they lose, that's the time when the media and fans decide they're all basketball Einsteins and jump on the blame-the-coach bandwagon: He should have let someone else take the last-second three-pointer. He told them to foul the wrong guy. They should have gone long on the inbounds pass. The list of second-guesses can be endless, but the whole nail-biting situation leaves one wondering why an otherwise intelligent, business-minded person with a passion for basketball and a nice collection of suits would want to spend night after night trying to make high-pressure decisions in front of thousands of nasty critics, instead of just watching from the stands or at home with a cold beer and some popcorn.

The answer is the same one that explains why players like Isiah Thomas go all out to win, despite injuries, tough defence, and seven-foot shotblockers. Something in their mental makeup continually compels them to keep trying to attain that elusive rush that can only come through scoring more points than the other guys. Some coaches — like Nelson or Chicago's Phil Jackson — were pretty decent players in their day, and made it to the higher ranks of college or even professional ball. Others might have found themselves too short or too slow or too heavy to keep up on the court, turning instead to the world of chalkboard X's and O's and early-morning shoot-arounds. Whatever the route taken, basketball coaches — especially professional ones — are driven by winning. So while love of the game certainly plays a part, the most important things concerning coaches have to be the won-loss numbers.

During his playing career, Thomas played for three of the basketball world's best coaches at each of the sport's three major levels. Gene Pingatore at St. Joseph's, Bobby Knight at Indiana, and finally Chuck Daly in Detroit all imparted to him a tremendous amount of knowledge about the specialized skills needed to get five men working together like a well-oiled machine. This exposure to successful coaches and mentors made up a big part of his hoops background, and so Isiah knew what he was looking for when it came time to lead the Raptors. "There are two schools of thought for an expansion team," he said while searching for the right coach for the Raptors. "You can hire a guy who's been around the league for a while, have him come in and get your program started — for about three years. Then you can bring in another coach who can more or less take it from years three to five or seven. I don't think we have the luxury of doing that."

Thomas noted that since NBA teams get most of their players via college and trades with other teams, they don't have the possibility of "grooming" players — bringing them along slowly and honing their skills over time — through any kind of farm system. This need to get the most out of players right out of college was for Isiah option number two: "So you want to find a person who philosophically agrees with what you're trying to do from a basketball standpoint," he continues. "You also want that person to have had some type of success, or winning ways in his past. You want him to be a good communicator because a lot of the players we're going to get in the expansion draft won't necessarily be the cream of the crop. They'll have a lot of learning to do — probably a young team."

Finding the right coach for the Raptors was going to be a tough sell for Thomas. In addition to the fact that whoever was chosen would have to spend time working with young, mostly unproven talent, NBA expansion teams simply don't seem to be able to win many games in the first few years of their history. Unlike new franchises in the NHL like the Florida Panthers, or in baseball like the Colorado Rockies, it's usually a long road from expansion team to playoff team in the NBA. (The Orlando Magic are a notable exception, having entered the league in 1989–90, and having reached the playoffs in 1993–94.) Isiah realized this pro basketball fact of life, and admitted that when it came to looking for a coach, "you . . . want the guy to have some patience and some discipline in himself to understand that you're going to lose a lot of games."

The important thing for whoever took the position, according to the rookie GM, was not to "become a loser within yourself. And that's tough, very tough when a guy's getting beat every night, for him to maintain the attitude and philosophy that he's a winner and to teach winning ways."

All of these requirements made up a pretty demanding wish list for the man who would become the coach of the Toronto Raptors in their inaugural campaign, and Isiah knew it. "Looking for all that in one person is difficult," he admitted. "You're going to have a team full of role players competing with a team full of superstars — on a nightly basis." In the end, though, the major task confronting Thomas was to uncover a coach who would somehow take the players chosen by the Raptors and create the right combinations, the right mix — what sports fans call "chemistry" — on the court and in the locker room. In the high-stakes world of pro basketball, it's often sheer chemistry that has propelled teams like the Chicago Bulls, the L.A. Lakers, or the Boston Celtics to championships ahead of equally talented rivals.

And so into the pressure-cooker that is the lot of the NBA head coach, Isiah Thomas cast a man named Brendan Malone, who had recently been let go from his job as an assistant coach with the Detroit Pistons. Malone had once coached at Power Memorial Academy in New York City — the alma mater of Kareem Abdul-Jabbar, then known as Lew Alcindor — and in addition had been head coach of the University of Rhode Island, as well as an assistant at Yale, Fordham, and Syracuse, and with the New York Knicks under Hubie Brown. Drawing on his Detroit connections, Thomas had initially asked Malone to run a three-day training camp for free agents at a suburban Toronto school, Seneca College. After watching Malone in action overseeing the Seneca camp, Thomas was so impressed he decided to offer Malone his first NBA head coaching job.

The move surprised many people in Toronto who were just beginning to become attuned to the strange rhythms of this new league called the NBA. For weeks, the two main names being tossed around in the papers as probable contenders for the job of Raptors' head coach number one were Chicago Bulls assistant Jim Cleamons, and former Portland Trail Blazers star and Phoenix Suns assistant coach Lionel Hollins. But when on June 2, 1995, Isiah announced that it would be Brendan Malone who would be taking the reins, it wasn't only the NBA newcomers who were shocked. According to Malone, a father of six, "I never thought of the [Seneca] camp as a job application. Isiah asked me to run the drills and that's all I was thinking about."

For Isiah, the free agent camp had been a real learning experience. It taught him, as he says, "not to pigeon-hole people" regarding their capabilities on and around a basketball court. He had always known Malone as a hard worker from his time in Detroit, what other NBA coaches called a "good X's and O's guy." But when he saw Malone motivating players at Seneca, he had to change his opinion. "From working with Brendan in Detroit, I had always seen him in the assistant's role; I never really got to see him perform head coach's duties," said Thomas. Isiah, who was trying to get people around the league to look at him now as GM and not merely an ex-player, was willing to bet that Malone could also change roles effectively as an NBA rookie himself. "I told Brendan that he was like a beautiful woman at the office who wears glasses and wears her hair pinned up," joked Thomas. "You really don't pay much attention until she takes off her glasses and shakes her head. Then you go 'Whoa!'"

In his comments about why he wanted Malone as his team's head man, Isiah was already starting to leave his mark on the Raptors' on-court personality. What attracted him most to the former Pistons assistant was his "tireless work ethic, his work ethic was very similar to mine as a basketball player, wanting to get better, wanting to improve." It looked, before the team had even signed a single player to its roster, that the new Toronto entry into the NBA would have bring many of the same characteristics to the league as Isiah Thomas did as a player — hustle, determination, and a constant striving for improvement.

For his part, Malone was overjoyed to be given a chance at a head coaching job, whether it was with an expansion team or not. The 50-year-old admitted that "it would be Pollyanna of me to suggest that we're going to win the NBA championship next year," but stressed nevertheless that as far as his role in coaching the new team went, "I want to be able to compete in the NBA and have guys there who will work hard and [have] character."

It wasn't merely that Thomas had been impressed at the way Brendan Malone had yelled at a few free agents at a training camp, then admitted that he'd been wrong in considering him a life-time assistant, and eventually changed his mind about Malone based on some romantic ideas about hard work and character. That kind of approach might have made for good PR, but it simply isn't the way Isiah Thomas operates. Instead, he carefully sought out advice from experts on the nuts and bolts of franchise building and high-pressure coaching.

Two such allies were Tex Schramm, who owned the Dallas Cowboys during their rise to glory as one of the NFL's most respected franchises, and Don Shula, the legendary coach of the Miami Dolphins. Isiah had always stressed his interest in building the Raptors on a success model based on winning franchises in all sports, like the Cowboys, the Dolphins, and the San Francisco Forty-Niners. The one thing he said he discovered in his analysis into what made teams into dynasties was the concept of continuity of personnel. "I think when you have a lot of change, a lot of upheaval and a lot of turnover, it doesn't breed the type of consistency that it takes to win," reasoned Isiah. "So I don't expect to change coaches in a year or two or three years. I expect this to be a long-term situation." To Isiah, Malone looked like a solid, long-term bet as head coach.

And in the same way that Brendan Malone stated explicitly that it was going to be difficult to begin life in the NBA at anywhere near .500, Isiah knew enough about life as an infant NBA franchise to express some reservations about the team's early prospects, despite his confidence in the new coach. "If we can get through the pain and the misery and suffering that we're going to have in the next couple of years and live with each others' sins and ups and downs," Thomas said, "I think in the long term this will be a happy marriage for all of us." By the end of the season, though, Raptors fans would realize that this patient, long-term outlook had undergone some revision in the minds of Thomas and others in the front office.

The position of head coach having been filled by Brendan Malone, it was time for Isiah to pick some assistants to help him. Here as well, observers were quick to point out that the Pistons connection had been working in the background. In fact, Isiah had offered a position within the Raptors organization to his Pistons pal Bill Laimbeer even before hiring Malone. Laimbeer, who declined his ex-teammate's offer, citing his desire to continue in business. Having patched up their earlier differences, Thomas and Laimbeer were back on friendly terms. Although the aggressive former center was not willing to go to work for the Raptors, Isiah maintained that if Laimbeer "should ever change his mind and want to be involved in our basketball organization, though, he'd be a welcomed addition to our staff."

There were also rumors that former Piston Bob Lanier — whose scoring records Isiah had broken in Detroit — and Thomas' former Indiana University teammate Randy Wittman would be joining the Raptors, but neither panned out. All of these overtures to ex-teammates prompted one Detroit source to comment regarding Isiah's attempts to build his team that it was "obvious he's trying to surround himself in Toronto with as many friends as possible." For his part, Thomas would not commit to speculations about his desires to rebuild a mirror-image franchise of the Pistons north of the border, saying that "the way we conduct our business in this organization will not be public knowledge."

One ex-Piston who did make it into the Raptors' off-court line up was former guard Darrell Walker, who had played with Isiah for a season and a half in the Motor City. The two ex-guards' relationship went even farther back than their time with the Pistons, as the two had shared backcourt duties in a high school All-Star game between Illinois and Kansas. Walker who had also spent time in the pros with the New York Knicks, was a respected defensive stopper as a player, and had been working for the NBA Players Association. He was chosen by Thomas as an assistant to Malone along with long-time NBA scout Bob Zuffelato and former pro player and Southern Methodist University coach John Shumate.

Given Walker's concentration on defence as a player and his relationship with Isiah in Detroit, he was a natural to help Malone behind the bench, even though he admitted that he had been working more on his golf game than on analyzing the finer points of the pick-and-roll before getting the call from Isiah. Eventually, the Raptors would find themselves in considerable Isiah Thomas-caused coaching turmoil at the end of the 1995–96 season, and it would be Darrell Walker who would emerge as one of the key figures in the whole mess.

With the coaches in place for 1995–96, Isiah turned his attention to actually putting together a team of professional basketball players. Much has been made of the Raptors' selection of Damon Stoudamire as their first pick in the 1995. What started as a draft-day booing at SkyDome when Damon's name was announced ended up as a NBA Rookie of the Year season.

Although it's pretty safe to say that Isiah does not actually own a crystal ball, it is still amazing to see how Stoudamire worked out in Toronto and how Ed O'Bannon — the player for whom the assembled armchair experts chanted "We Want Ed!" on draft day — didn't fare nearly as well as a New Jersey Net. Of course it would have been ridiculous to expect O'Bannon to have stepped in and single-handedly turned the woeful Nets around, but even by his own admission, the ex-UCLA star did not perform up to expectations in New Jersey. He illustrated his class, though, by going on record toward the end of the 1995–96 season as saying that he was partially to blame for the Nets' poor finish, a fact that didn't prevent some fans at the 1996 draft held in the New Jersey Meadowlands, from booing him when a clip of the previous years' draft was shown. Comparisons between Damon Stoudamire and Ed O'Bannon aside, it is safe to say that as the Raptors' rookie point guard's stock was beginning to rise throughout 1995–96, many were beginning to praise Isiah's faith in him as nothing short of psychic. Selecting an unproven first-year player to run an expansion team — thus completing an unprecedented quartet of leaders: rookie team, rookie GM, rookie coach, and rookie floor general — seemed nothing short of insane, given the conventional NBA wisdom about such things. But anyone who had been keeping close tabs on the plans Thomas was making for his team would not have been so surprised on his picking Stoudamire, and in the way the whole thing worked out so well.

People around the league were beginning to realize that Isiah Thomas made front office decisions for the Raptors in exactly the same way he had made on-court decisions for the Detroit Pistons. On the surface his moves might have looked risky and flashy, but behind them there was logic, calculation, and reason. In his published comments in the Toronto *Globe and Mail*, Isiah had gone a long way toward tipping his hand about what kind of players he was looking for in compiling the first edition of the Raptors. Thomas said that he "was not necessarily looking for a point guard or a power forward or a center, just the best players available." And the secret to predicting which college stars would go on to make it big in the pros was more than just looking at the stats and paying attention to which players got the most press. "Not only do you have to evaluate the player," he explained, "you have to evaluate the program he plays in, and the coach he plays for because some systems do not allow talent to grow at the college level, do not allow the player to display his skills."

Once a player is evaluated within the context of his college program, though, the GM of a brand-new NBA franchise still has to decide whether or not the youngster will fit into the overall game plan that has been designed for the team. "It starts basically in terms of what you see happening in your head and trying to make it transpire on the court," said Isiah. "We definitely want a team that's versatile, in terms of having players that can play different positions. We want an athletic team. We want a good defensive team. You want people who can score, can shoot, you know, you want it all." Of course, Thomas was speaking in terms of Platonic ideals regarding the players he wanted; the ones he actually got from the dispersal draft, who after all had been left unprotected by their former teams, might not be quite such all-round stars. And with seventh pick overall in the college draft, Isiah was realistic enough to admit that the Raptors would be unlikely to draft "a franchise player, unless we get lucky and some people make mistakes" in their choices ahead of Toronto. Whether it was luck or not, Isiah's judgment regarding Stoudamire couldn't have been better. Pundits who were contending that the ex-Piston was trying to re-create his old team in Toronto bluntly suggested that in picking Damon, Thomas was merely drafting himself to start building a team.

In sports-talk, "chemistry" is a hard-to-define element that every great team possesses. It's the secret ingredient that enables players to get along well on the court. It results in cordial relations between the front office and the athletes. It's a satisfying mix of personalities and styles that produces co-operation at every level.

Now that he had a group of coaches to lead the team in practice and from behind the bench and a promising floor general to lead them on the court, Isiah had to start putting together the rest of his side. He had been up front about his desire for a head coach who would be able to achieve the right chemistry with the Raptors, and he was equally adamant that chemistry would be the buzzword in the front office and when it came to choosing players as well.

"The most important thing we believe in this organization is chemistry," Isiah insisted. "The type of chemistry that you have at the top will ultimately be the type of chemistry that you see on the floor. . . . We may pass up some of the best people [players and coaches] simply because we want to make sure that the chemistry is right in the organization and on the floor." And while sportscasters, newspaper columnists, and casual fans of the game can debate the relative merits of on-the-court harmony among basketball teams until they drop, getting in synch was absolutely crucial to the new Raptors GM. As a point guard, he had learned that maintaining a balance of emotions among his teammates was a responsibility that fell to him as team leader. Knowing when to shoot, when to pass off to a team-mate to get him involved in the offense, even when to throw an elbow to rile up the other guys — these were just some of the ways in which an experienced floor leader like Isiah would try to generate the right chemistry among his Pistons teammates. In fact he had been doing it his entire career, and was uniquely qualified to comment on the importance of psychological factors and their relationship to winning. "From all my experiences in sports — grade school, high school, college, professional level — talent is always secondary to chemistry," he said. "Always."

Isiah had certainly been around enough successful coaches in his life to make him feel that Brendan Malone was the right choice as the Raptors' first head coach. And in the same way that he had picked up tips on successful coaching by spending time around some of the best in the business, Thomas had built a relationship with one of the most accomplished — and shrewdest — GM's in the history of the NBA when he played for Detroit. Jack McCloskey had been known affectionately, and not so affectionately, around the league as "Trader Jack" because of his willingness to deal players in an unending quest to win championships. The strategy had worked, and the son of a Pennsylvania coal miner became a hero in Detroit, where sportswriters never tired of mentioning the fact that there was only one person in the entire Pistons organization who wanted to win as badly as McCloskey: Isiah Thomas.

McCloskey had selected Thomas with the second pick of the 1981 draft, and the careers of both men had taken off in the Motor City from that point on, culminating in the Pistons' back-to-back championships. McCloskey taught his protégé a lot about chemistry, and had made some moves that while unpopular with fans turned out to be successful on the court. Recall how earlier, one such deal involved trading high-scoring Adrian Dantley away from the Pistons to Dallas in exchange for Mark Aguirre, who had been a friend of Isiah's since boyhood. Dantley's selfish attitude had alienated him from many of the Detroit players, especially Thomas, and following the reunion of Isiah and Aguirre, the Pistons won their first of the back-to-back championships in 1989.

It was all about finding the right mix of players, even if it meant getting rid of a superstar, and the lesson was not lost on Isiah. In fact, toward the end of his career as a Piston, Thomas was consulted regularly on most major personnel decisions facing the team, a process that constituted a kind of a "GM in training" exercise. Later, as Isiah took his place in the front office in Toronto McCloskey was listed in the Raptors program as "Consultant, Basketball Operations," and continued to help the team with various projects for many years.

Isiah was tight-lipped early on regarding exactly which players he wanted in the dispersal and college drafts. He would say only that "Our players will clearly connect with the logo, creating the image. You'll look at our players and say, 'He's a Raptor.'" While this statement seemed cryptic and prompted *Sports Illustrated* to wonder "Will he draft prehistoric guys with two toes?", things came into focus after Stoudamire had been picked to run the team.

The Raptors already had two point guards before Damon. B.J. Armstrong had enjoyed a successful career with the NBA Champion Chicago Bulls. A former University of Iowa standout, Armstrong had enjoyed the luxury of being brought along slowly on the powerhouse Bulls squad, and had improved his pro game to the point of being a highly-regarded passer and outside shooter. His namesake, B.J. Tyler, who had played with Philadelphia, had also been picked up in the expansion draft. But Armstrong, the Raptors' first pick in the expansion draft, was adamant that he didn't want to play in Toronto. Armstrong was clearly being seen as trade bait by Isiah, who eventually shipped him to Golden State on September 18, 1995, for five players including Victor Alexander and Carlos Rogers. In a bit of poetic justice, Armstrong was booed by the SkyDome crowd when the Warriors visited Toronto a couple of months after the trade, and proceeded to brick a late three-pointer to seal the loss for Golden State. And Tyler, a lightning-quick player who had been primarily a backup in Philly, wrecked his 1995–96 season after falling asleep with an ice pack on his leg that caused severe nerve damage. So Stoudamire was definitely the man who was going to lead the Raptor charge, and Isiah needed to find the guys to run with him.

In obtaining Carlos Rogers in the big trade with Golden State, Isiah found a player who had developed a reputation as something of a trash-talker and an eccentric. But at 6–11 and 220 lb., Rogers was also a fantastic leaper with a knack for blocking shots, going hard to the hoop, and crashing the boards as well. Veterans Willie Anderson and Alvin Robertson could both be counted on to add experience and defensive skill to Stoudamire's playmaking abilities in the Raptors' back court, where they would be joined by another rookie, Michigan's Jimmy King, and Italian star Vincenzo Esposito. Veteran "Easy" Ed Pinckney, journeyman Tony Massenburg, and youngsters Martin Lewis and Dwayne Whitfield would combine up front to give the Raptors some size and rebounding ability. As well, Croatian Zan Tabak, formerly of the NBA Champion Houston Rockets, and ex-Celtic Acie Earl were two promising centers who would help out inside.

As usual, there was a Detroit Pistons connection at work. John "Spider" Salley, a teammate of Isiah's during the championship years with the Bad Boys, was picked by the Raptors in the expansion draft. While Salley was clearly a talented forward, he always seemed to fit into the category of the "now you see him, now you don't" type of player. When he was fired up, he was a fantastic, hustling rebounder who could also score. But other times, the Spider's mind seemed somewhere else, and on these occasions he almost invariably received a verbal lashing from none other than Isiah Thomas. Eventually, the Pistons decided that Salley, who was notorious for his clowning and penchant for making TV commercials, was too erratic and traded him to Miami. But fans were interested in seeing whether Salley and Isiah could recreate some of the magical chemistry that had worked so well in Detroit.

The other ex-Piston to come to Toronto was a center named Oliver Miller, who, while never having played on the same team as Isiah, must nevertheless be classed as on of the rookie GM's "project" players. Miller had been a standout at the University of Arkansas and had played decent ball with the Phoenix Suns and then Detroit, but had frustrated coaches and teammates by his propensity for putting on weight. He was exposed by the Pistons to the expansion draft because even though he had a well-developed game that was strong in all areas, he simply couldn't — or wouldn't — meet the demands of his coaches by keeping the pounds off. But Isiah was willing to gamble that he and Brendan Malone could motivate "the Big O."

With these players comprising the nucleus of the first Raptors' team, the fledgling franchise was ready to take to the court in the fall of 1995. Everything was in place — the front office, the coaches, the players. But one thing had to be taken care of yet. What if nobody showed up to watch?

Of course the idea of a 1990s NBA franchise with no fans in the seats is ludicrous, but it might have been a little less so with an expansion team in a city like Toronto. After all, this was the beginning of the NBA's regular-season life any place outside the U.S., and it was taking place in a city where hockey could only be described as a religion. Whether the Toronto Maple Leafs are playing well or not, a ticket to see the NHL in the city is always tough to get. The Raptors would be competing head-on with the Leafs for fans during the cold Canadian winter, and the entrenched hockey mentality would make selling the NBA even tougher.

During the 1946–47 season, there had been a short-lived Toronto franchise in the Basketball Association of America (which would soon evolve into the NBA) called the Toronto Huskies, but that was the extent of the city's actual involvement with top-level pro hoops. Toronto had also supported a team in the Continental Basketball Association for a short while, and almost ended up adopting the Cleveland Cavaliers in the 1980s, but when the NBA decided to move to Hogtown, 1995–96 marked the start of the big time.

Educating and converting fans had to be the first step — even the most casual of sports fans knew automatically what a power-play was in NHL lingo, but who could tell the difference between a point guard and a power forward? Isiah knew that one of his principal tasks was to teach Canadians something about basketball, how the game worked on the court and its cultural trappings off it, before getting them hyped on the game. Even his office staff, who were sometimes unfamiliar with some of the well-known basketball names who called Thomas, needed some coaching. "I'm here to create a framework where a basketball team can perform," he claimed. "But first it starts with educating your staff. I feel like a professor sometimes. NBA 101."

The Toronto market, however, was extremely receptive to the Raptors, who in turn made no bones about the fact that the team had a special interest in targeting young people in their marketing efforts. David Strickland, the Raptors' consumer products director when the franchise began, noted that when it came to purchasing basketball-related products, "the 12- to 17-year-olds drive sales. . . . They are the future. As they grow up they provide the key 18-to-35 market." The NBA was considered cool by young people in Toronto and all over Canada. Attending Raptors' home games first at SkyDome, and later at the Air Canada Centre one definitely gets the sense that it's a young crowd, night in and night out. Junior high and high school field trips to games seem to be a particular specialty. But what accounts for the Raptors' — and indeed the entire NBA's — popularity among Canadian kids, who after all are supposed to be hooked on hockey?

One theory that might explain this phenomenon is that many of the youngsters attracted to pro basketball come from first- or second-generation immigrant families, and as such have not internalized the hockey-as-national-religion ethos in the same way as kids from long-time Canadian families might. Indeed, it's amazing to look around the Raptors' home crowd on game night, or indeed on any playground court, and see young people from all ethnic backgrounds completely homogenized by the NBA-approved garb they're wearing. The official Raptors photo of the unveiling of the team's home and away uniforms features Isiah flanked by two school-aged kids named Everol Bennett and Daphne Tran and serves as sort of a basketball-tinted snapshot of the Canadian cultural mosaic.

Another explanation for basketball's growth in Hockey-Land is that it's hard for anyone, Canadian or not, to resist the hyped up media campaign of pro hoops. Indeed, going to a Raptors game can at times seem like a sensory overload. It's as if some basketball-crazed soul decided that it would be disastrous to have even one second of silence in the house when the Raptors play, and so the giant scoreboard, the Raptors' Dance-Pack, the team mascot, and ear-splitting music combine to create an unending sensory bombardment. Who cares if most of the fans don't know what an illegal defence is? It's all about the hype — and they love it. Before the first game had been played, sales of Raptors' merchandise had zoomed up to eighth in the league.

More significantly, however, the Raptors took on a role of responsibility in the community, a role that involved several initiatives to assist kids who might well not have been able to afford even the cheapest of Raptor souvenirs. One such program was the Raptors Foundation Community Sports Facility Fund, a joint venture with Nike that put $1.5 million over 5 years into the construction of parks and recreational facilities around the city, including resurfacing basketball courts. Isiah, who was instrumental in the project, realized the importance of the playground as more than just a place to shoot hoops. "The basketball court represents many great things to a youngster," he says, remembering his own youth in Chicago. "It's a place to learn leadership and teamwork. In this time of [government] cutbacks, the needs of our young people are greater than ever but the opportunities are dwindling."

The theme of the athlete as a role model is a common one in North American life. It's often argued that the very reason that cultural groups excel at certain sports — Francophone Canadians at hockey, U.S. blacks in basketball, Brazilians at soccer — is that within these cultures, athletic success is something that is prized highly and emulated by young people. Consequently, it was not surprising that many of Toronto's black leaders looked to Thomas as he began putting the Raptors in motion. Speaking to the city's Black Business and Professional Association, Isiah contended that "the expectations and the demands of myself and of my time have, and always will be different from others. I don't know why that is. But my life has been that way since, basically, college." It wasn't just that people expected him to be good at hitting three-pointers or throwing bounce passes, there was always something more: "I've always been asked or expected to do more than just play basketball or run a basketball organization."

Being a role model — no matter what Charles Barkley says — is part of the territory for the pro athlete. But as *Toronto Star* writer Rosie DiManno pointed out in a front-page feature after talking to Isiah, black athletes seem to carry a double burden when it comes to being public figures: they are often expected to come up with answers for an entire group of people, to somehow explain away certain behaviors with a kind of all-seeing insight. When DiManno asked Isiah what was expected of him and of his new team regarding their part in race relations, he answered wisely, "I'm a newcomer. I can jump up and give you nice rosy answers that will sound good philosophically. But do they have any meat on 'em? Probably not. You tell me. What should we do?"

With all the hype that surrounded Isiah's selection of a coach, a team, his ascension to a high-profile figure in the Toronto media, and the general mania about the NBA among young people, it's worth remembering that the 1995–96 basketball season came pretty close to not happening at all. Due to a labor dispute between the league's owners and its players, a lockout occurred that resulted in some serious concerns in Vancouver and Toronto about whether or not those two cities' new franchises would ever actually play a game. At the very least, some momentum was lost due to the fact that it's hard to get potential fans in a new market excited about a sport they might not get a chance to see. Professional baseball witnessed first hand what a lockout of players by owners can do to fan enthusiasm and therefore ticket sales, especially in Toronto where attendance dropped dramatically for the Blue Jays after play resumed when the baseball strike had ended.

Isiah had a unique perspective on the whole situation. Having been a long-time president of the Players Association, he could sympathize with their demands. But as "one of them" — an owner and front-office guy — now, he had some considerable interest in protecting the interests of the league's ownership. And given the relationship between pro sports in labor disputes and subsequent fan support, Thomas was understandably a bit nervous about the upcoming year. "It's going to be interesting to see how everybody reacts to the labor unrest," he said. "I wonder if fans will understand that players and management more or less bit the bullet on the new collective agreement in order to keep the momentum of the league progressing. Even though we avoided any lost games, given what happened to baseball and hockey, there will certainly be some questions to be answered."

With no strike or lockout imminent, it was getting to be time for the Raptors to finally take to the court. Pre-season press conferences and new uniforms are great, but such things really can be no more than lead-ups to what really matters — playing basketball. Now it was time to see what kind of team Isiah Thomas had built for himself and for the city of Toronto. On one hand, nobody who knew much about the NBA would be expecting much in terms of wins in this first season. But the fans and media in Toronto, who after all were relatively new to the sport, would not be pacified by expansion-team excuses for ever, and would demand a team that if it wasn't winning all the time was at least coming close and putting on a good show doing it. Of course, you could expect packed houses and home fans cheering for the visitors when guys like Jordan or Shaq came to play, but that wasn't the point.

What was the point was that after all the hoopla, it was finally time for Isiah Thomas to move on to the next stage and the next challenge. Now the Raptors actually had to get out there and play night in and night out, on the road and at home, through injuries and successes. How good had Isiah been at picking his team, his coach, his staff? Would he be forced to make some adjustments as the season progressed? Would Toronto like their new NBA team as much as the pre-season hype seemed to suggest? And would the Raptors' rookie GM be as good at making decisions off the court as he had been at making them on it?

The questions were all there, just waiting to be answered, as the 1995–96 season got underway.

CHAPTER NINE

Raptors Hit the Court

As the newly-minted, number-one Raptor, Isiah had a few decisions to make regarding his life now that his place of work had shifted to the metropolis north of the border. For a while, he and Lynn considered moving from their home in Bloomington Hills, Michigan, with son Joshua and  daughter Lauren to the Forest Hills area of Toronto. But for the duration of the 1995–96 season, Isiah was content to do lots of cross-border commuting in his role as GM, staying in a prominent downtown hotel while in Hogtown.

The symbolism of his ascendance to the front office of an NBA club wasn't lost on Isiah, or on his mother. "She never thought that black people would have these opportunities," he reveals. "And it's funny it had to happen in Canada."

Funny, perhaps, but not so surprising, considering that the Great White North was the place for an earlier barrier-breaking event in sports. Some decades before, baseball's Branch Rickey sent Jackie Robinson to Montreal to play in the minor leagues, reasoning that race relations in Canada differed from those in the U.S. to the point where Jackie could develop as a player without having to worry about things like personal safety or harassment. Things certainly have changed considerably since then, but it still might be argued that Isiah's position as GM of Canada's expansion Raptors wasn't a complete coincidence.

Before actually opening the 1995–96 NBA campaign, the Raptors had completed a decent pre-season. Although it's usually difficult to predict how a team in any sport is going to perform in the regular season based on exhibition games, it was evident that the team would at least be able to handle themselves as a pro squad. Isiah was pleased with what he'd seen in the pre-season, and liked the way in which the young team was adapting to the coaching style of Brendan Malone. "I've been pleased with the work ethic of the players and coaches," he said. "Brendan has thrown a lot at the players in a short time and they're responding well. The lockout really hurt us, but we've made up for lost time."

Just as the regular season was about to begin, Thomas made what was to prove to be his most successful free-agent signing of the year. In the Raptors' exhibition games, Isiah had noticed — along with just about every basketball fan who was paying attention — that Damon Stoudamire was already proving himself to be a legitimate pro player. Indeed, he finished the pre-season averaging 18.1 points per game, and caused opposing defenders fits as they tried to keep pace with him. Unfortunately, it didn't take long for the Raptors' rivals to adjust their defensive schemes in an effort to stop the rookie point guard.

Isiah knew his team needed another scorer on the floor to keep opposing defenders honest, and that's why on October 31, 1995, just three days before the Raptors were to take on New Jersey to begin their NBA lives for real, Thomas inked Tracy Murray, formerly of the Houston Rockets, to a one-year contract. "We've seen through all the exhibition games that Damon would get double-teamed when he crossed half-court," explained Isiah. "A player like Tracy would allow us to open things up a little more." Murray, a 6–7 forward and a standout at UCLA in college, actually led the NBA the year before in 3-point shooting percentage. But the Rockets, the defending back-to-back NBA champs, just couldn't find enough floor time in their rotation for him, and had to leave him unprotected as a free-agent. Murray, however, was overjoyed to be coming to Toronto where he'd be allowed to do what he liked to do best — shoot the ball — even if it was for only $250,000 a year, a paltry sum by NBA standards. "This is a new start for Tracy Murray," the modest 24-year-old native of Los Angeles enthused. He'd be rusty after missing the pre-season, but the Raptors were in no position to be choosy. They needed someone who could score, and Isiah had found him.

With Murray in a Toronto uniform for the first time, the Raptors took to the court at SkyDome on Friday, November 3, 1995, thus beginning their first NBA season. Their opponents were the New Jersey Nets, the team that a few months earlier had drafted Ed O'Bannon, the player that Isiah was "supposed" to have picked in the college draft. The game couldn't have been scripted better, as the Raptors went on to defeat the Nets, 94–79, with Alvin Robertson scoring 30 points in front of 33,306 fans. Stoudamire had only 10 points, but Acie Earl came up big with

16 in place of the suspended Oliver Miller. Tracy Murray and John Sally both had 9 for the winners. "Hats off to Isiah Thomas," enthused the *Globe and Mail*'s Stephen Brunt, commenting on the new GM's selection of Damon Stoudamire as team leader and the assemblage of talent on the inaugural Raptors squad in general. "This one, it seems, he got very right."

Once the opening fanfare surrounding the first game of the 1995–96 season died down, the Toronto Raptors got busy with the night-in, night-out process of playing NBA basketball. And early on, the infant franchise gave their hometown fans something to go wild about. On November 21, the Raptors took the SkyDome floor to face the Seattle SuperSonics, perennially one of the strongest teams in the NBA's Western Conference. The Sonics, under head coach George Karl, fielded a balanced lineup. They were led by point guard Gary Payton, who would go on to win the NBA Defensive Player of the Year in 1995–96. Seattle, which had gone an impressive 120–44 over the last two regular seasons, also had high-flying slam-dunk king Shawn Kemp and clutch-shooting German forward Detlef Schrempf, as well as the canny Nate McMillan in the backcourt with Payton. Indeed, the Sonics would go on to win the Western Conference Finals and take on the Chicago Bulls for the NBA title that season.

The Raptors, however, weren't intimidated, even though the matchup with the SuperSonics was only their seventh home game and their eleventh NBA confrontation overall. In a game that seemed to be played with playoff-like intensity by both clubs, the Raptors prevailed 102–97 behind veteran Willie Anderson's 22 points and clutch jumpers down the stretch. Oliver Miller was the Raptors' high scorer with 23, and

Stoudamire had 20 in front of a North American TV audience. The Raptors' bench and hometown fans went wild after the final buzzer had sounded, as if the team had just won game seven of the NBA finals and not an early-season contest. Indeed, coach Malone cited the rabid support of the "sixth man" as one of the reasons for the win.

Isiah couldn't have been much happier about the win against Seattle. As the GM of an expansion club, he knew the importance of knocking off a powerhouse team like the SuperSonics. No matter what the Raptors' record was at the end of the season, the yeah-but-we-still-beat-some-great-opponents argument would go a long way. Looking at the big picture, Isiah maintained that "you can't stop progress. Winning has its own timetable," sounding for all the world like a guy who'd occupied his front office position for years. "You can't control winning and you can't control development. You can only manage it."

Thomas knew, too, that the victory over Seattle was important for another reason. It marked the third consecutive win for the Raptors, a definite improvement over the seven-game losing streak the squad had suffered through shortly before that point. "It has surprised all of us the way they've come together quickly, the way they play, and the way they've learned from their mistakes," he asserted. "We were all concerned about how the [seven] tough losses might affect them. There aren't a lot of old players. There are a lot of kids on the team and we know there are going to be some rough stretches."

As an NBA veteran himself, Isiah knew all about slumps and how to come back from them. Remember that this was a guy who, as a rookie, joined an awful team that had a lot of improving to do before it was able to make it as a legitimate title contender. "If 30-game fatigue sets in, or mental concentration slips and boredom sets in," he said after the win over Kemp, Payton, et al., "that's when the pros have to be pros. When that process takes place, you know what kind of men you have."

Toronto basketball fans didn't have to wait very long before they were able to cheer about something else of significance. Expansion teams, after all, have to take victories when they can get them, and wins are even sweeter for freshman clubs if they're notched over NBA powerhouses. That's exactly what happened at SkyDome on December 17, 1995, as the Raptors took on the Orlando Magic in front of 25,820 fans, many of whom showed up to witness first-hand the looming presence of Shaquille O'Neal. Unfortunately for the Magic — who would eventually make it to the Eastern Conference finals against the Bulls — budding actor and rap star Shaq, superstar guard Anfernee Hardaway, long-range artist Dennis Scott, and the rest of the team were simply having an off night. Toronto took advantage of O'Neal's foul trouble and the Magic's overall malaise to win, 110–93 behind Alvin Robertson's 20 points. Tracy Murray had 16 points off the bench, a total matched by Miller and Anderson, with veteran forward "Easy" Ed Pinckney chipping in 14.

Raptors fans, players, and coaches took particular delight in watching Damon Stoudamire going up against Shaq. "Mighty Mouse" showed little fear in taking it to the rack despite O'Neal's huge presence and equally big reputation for blocking shots. The Toronto morning papers feature photos of the two players in action side by side, and the contrast in their respective body sizes couldn't have been more pronounced. Even the normally dour Brendan Malone couldn't resist a quip when he saw the little guy going at Shaq. "Damon versus Goliath," he quipped.

At about the midway point of the Raptors' inaugural season, Isiah Thomas took the opportunity to mix business with the more pleasurable side of being an ex-NBA-superstar-turned-front-office-executive. On February 17, 1996, the Raptors traveled to Detroit for a game with the Pistons, and on that night Thomas was honored by the only pro team he ever played for in a special ceremony at the Palace in Auburn Hills.

Although Toronto ended up losing the game 108–95 despite Oliver Miller scoring 25 points against his former teammates, Raptors historians will remember the retirement of the No. 11 Pistons jersey that night in Michigan far longer than they will the defeat. Accompanied at half-court by his mother, Mary, his wife, Lynn, his son and daughter, and four of his brothers, Isiah responded to the tribute graciously, reminding the 21,500 cheering fans that he couldn't have done it without those closest to him. "This is my family; this is what Isiah Thomas is all about," he said. "This is my biggest accomplishment."

In addition to retiring his jersey, the Pistons renamed a road leading up to the Palace Isiah Thomas Drive, unveiled a painting of him in action, awarded a scholarship to St. Joseph's in his name, and presented the family with a trip to Hawaii. Any animosity that might have been lingering around the issue of Isiah's never having been made a "Piston for life" in the team's front office was ignored on this night, and Isiah was quick to give credit to the Pistons for what was a very classy tribute to the franchise's all-time greatest player. "I owe a debt of gratitude to everyone who put this on," he declared. "People did things from their hearts, said things from their hearts and that's very special to me."

Others who had helped — and been helped by — Isiah during his playing career were quick to thank and praise him. Bobby Knight told the faithful Piston crowd that what set his former pupil apart was his intelligent approach to using sports as a vehicle for success in other areas. "Isiah stands out in my mind as someone who used basketball to the fullest," said Coach Knight. "There is no better example in the world today of what an athlete should do with his basketball ability." Pistons' owner Bill Davidson thanked Isiah "for making my dream [of winning an NBA championship] come true," while league Commissioner David Stern told him that "I represent hundreds of millions of fans around the world to say 'Thank you.'" And the other four Pistons who have had their numbers retired — former Bad Boys Bill Laimbeer and Vinnie Johnson plus Bob Lanier and Dave Bing — were also on hand to honor Thomas.

Typically, though, Isiah deflected much of the praise heaped upon his abilities as a player and a leader by crediting others who had helped him through some difficult times. Fans, even those well-meaning ones who show up on tribute nights like this one, often forget that having to perform game in and night out under the harsh scrutiny of the public gaze exacts a toll that is more than just a physical one. Isiah told the Palace crowd that over his 13 years as a Piston, "You watched me grow from a young man into adulthood before your eyes. You got to see the good in me and you got to see my sins. You got to discuss and criticize it. That was very difficult for me. When I'd go home alone and none of you were there, I would go to bed and sit there and cry and it was [Lynn's] hand that guided me through the night."

As the 1995–96 season moved toward its mid-way point and the annual All-Star game, sportswriters, broadcasters, and fans were beginning to notice a rather alarming pattern within each of the Raptors' games, a pattern that in fact continued right up to the end of the team's first campaign. The trend was a simple one, but it was nevertheless disturbing for everyone connected with the franchise. Simply put, Damon Stoudamire was single-handedly carrying his team in almost every game. The Raptors would usually begin their battles strongly and then, through a mixture of inexperience, and fatigue, start to see games slipping out of their control only to have Damon keep them close by doing it all — scoring, dishing, playing defence, occasionally even rebounding.

Sports Illustrated thought so much of Stoudamire's contributions that the authoritative weekly ran a feature article on "The Mouse That Roars," a play on Damon's "Mighty Mouse" nickname (which is in turn inspired by a tattoo he wears of the cartoon character). Isiah told *SI* that for him, Stoudamire was "a show all by himself. Watching Damon makes you want to jump up and holler." Isiah was also credited for teaching his young charge a lot about how to play point guard in the pros, and for emphasizing the mental aspects of basketball more than the physical ones.

The importance of the brain-driven side of the game was made plain to Damon in the Raptors' 103–100 loss to the Utah Jazz on November 13, a game in which he was completely dominated by John Stockton, for years one of the NBA's best all-round point guards and a perennial All-Star. Skeptics treated the Stockton-Stoudamire battle as sort of an "I-told-you-so," a way of proving that the youngster still had a long way to go before he could be considered a legitimate NBA star. But according to Stoudamire, his GM used the experience as something positive to build on. Recognizing that Stoudamire had allowed the wily Stockton to dictate the pace of their one-on-one matchups, Thomas was quick with some pointed advice first honed on the playgrounds of the West Side. "Isiah took me aside and told me never to be passive, no matter who I'm playing," Damon told *SI*'s Phil Taylor. "He told me his motto: Go attack them before they attack you. Ever since then that's what I've tried to do."

Of the clause that Thomas included in Stoudamire's contract that made it mandatory for him to attend the NBA finals, Isiah commented: "I want him to see what he's chasing." If Damon was to be the future of the team, he'd have to get to know first-hand the kind of high-pressure atmosphere that surrounds a league championship game. "This franchise isn't in it [only] to go to the playoffs some day," said Thomas. "We're here to work toward winning a championship, and anything short of that is failure. That's one of the reasons we wanted Damon. He comes across as the kind of player who won't be satisfied to have a good career and no ring."

The *Sports Illustrated* article said a lot of positive things about the early play of Damon Stoudamire and the wisdom that Thomas had shown in selecting him. But it also noted that at 41.4 minutes a game after the season's first two-and-a-half months, Stoudamire was already second in the league in minutes played, unheard of for a rookie. Folks who could remember back far enough recalled that when Isiah hit the NBA, he carried the Pistons as a rookie point guard and made them a much-improved team.

SI also mentioned that NBA rookies often seem to hit some kind of psychological and physical "wall" after about 40 games. Damon's comment was that "if you don't think there's a wall, there's no wall," but the amazing amount of time the rookie was spending on the floor was beginning to worry a lot of people in Toronto, even after Damon proved fresh enough to win MVP honors in the all-rookie All-Star game. Eventually, the issue of his excessive playing time would lead to a lot more than just worry within the Raptors' organization. Sure, young hero Damon Stoudamire was carrying the Raptors, but at what cost?

What made the fatigue-induced woes that Damon was suffering even harder to explain was the fact that earlier in the year, the Raptors had passed up a golden opportunity to sign a solid back-up for him. Chris Whitney, who eventually went to Washington, was willing and able to play the point for Toronto at a price reported to be very close to the NBA minimum. But Isiah failed to sign Whitney, and Stoudamire was faced with the prospect of racking up big minutes on his own.

Given the unfortunate patterns that the Raptors had slipped into, it has to be remembered that in reality, the team wasn't going through anything radically different from the usual woes experienced by most NBA expansion teams. The very fact that they were actually holding their own against some pretty decent big-league competition in their first campaign while under the leadership of a rookie coach, a rookie GM, and a rookie point guard, had more than a few observers — like NBC's Bob Costas at the All-Star Game — referring to the "surprising Toronto Raptors."

Nothing surprised people more, however, that the stunning events that took place at SkyDome on March 24, 1996. On that night, in front of over 36,000 people — easily the largest crowd ever to watch a basketball game in Canada — the Raptors shocked the Chicago Bulls in a nail-biter, 109–108.

Now, it might be argued that a good portion of the fans who assembled that evening had come to the Dome solely to witness the wizardry of one Michael Jordan, likely the greatest player ever to pick up a basketball. It would be hard to dispute that assertion, but it also bears keeping in mind that as great as Jordan is, the 1995–96 edition of the Chicago Bulls for whom he played might well have been the most dominant team ever assembled. Certainly, the 72 wins they amassed that season is an NBA record eclipsing the 69-win mark established by the legendary 1971–72 L.A. Lakers. Indeed, "Da Bulls" lineup for 1995–96 has to compare favorably with the great Lakers, Sixers, Celtics, Knicks, and Pistons squads of the past — the ones usually invoked when the greatest-team-of-all-time arguments get started in sports bars around North America. Besides Jordan, the 1995–96 Bulls featured perennial Olympian and All-Star Scottie Pippen, who undoubtedly would be "the man" for just about any other strong NBA team if it weren't for the bald guy playing next to him. There was also Dennis Rodman, Isiah's old running mate on the Pistons, now gone completely wacko with his alternating blond-red-green hair dye jobs and an amazing array of tattoos, but still hauling down more rebounds than anyone in the league. Rodman, however, would have to sit this one out, missing the game against the Raptors as he served a 6-game suspension for head-butting a referee.

Alongside these three hoop giants, the Bulls were comprised of a frighteningly good lineup of role players, many of whom would have starred for just about any other NBA franchise but were willing to put their personal ambitions on hold for the greater glory of sharing the Championship trophy: Croatian Olympic star Toni Kukoc, guards Ron Harper and Steve Kerr, Australian center Luc Longley, Canadian big man Bill Wennington, and former Raptor John Salley to name a few. And against this juggernaut — the same one that eventually romped through the post-season playoffs to a virtually uncontested 1996 NBA Championship — the baby Toronto Raptors came up big. Huge, in fact.

Earlier in the season, Toronto had given the Bulls a pretty good run for their money, losing 117–108 on November 7 in Chicago. Bulls' coach Phil Jackson commented after the game that the Raptors "gave us a handful — it took us a while to figure them out." In the re-match, however, it looked as though it was the Raptors who'd been doing most of the figuring. Tracy Murray was hard to stop on this afternoon, firing in 23 points and collecting 12 rebounds. "This game," he said later, "meant more to me than winning the championship [with Houston] last year." One of the keys to the big win was the defensive play of recently-acquired guard Doug Christie, who had been acquired by Isiah from the New York Knicks. While Christie did not exactly shut down Jordan — nobody does that — he did cover the superstar well for most of the game, even blocking one of Jordan's shots with 24 seconds left. Jordan himself gave a lot of credit to Stoudamire, saying that he "played like a veteran." The loss put the Bulls at 60–8 on the season and moved Toronto to 18–49, illustrating that while the Raptors had notched a nice win, there were still light years separating a good expansion team from an NBA powerhouse. As a final note, John

Salley, who'd been let go from Toronto, failed to exact any form of revenge on his old team, scoring a measly 2 points.

As 1995–96 wore down, fans began to reflect that individually, there were several bright spots besides the play of Damon Stoudamire for the Raptors during their first year. Most notably, Tracy Murray had justified Isiah's faith in him by emerging as one of the league's top three-point scoring threats and was in contention for the NBA's "Most Improved" award. Guards Doug Christie and Alvin Robertson showed they could both excel on defence and keep up their ends of the scoring responsibilities. Oliver Miller played well most nights in the middle, and Zan Tabak showed flashes of brilliance down low as well. And lightly-regarded Acie Earl went on a manic scoring tear toward the end of the season — perhaps, the cynics said, in order to improve his attractiveness as "trade bait" — in which he averaged over 20 points per game and hit for 40 against his former team, the Boston Celtics.

As 1995–96 drew to a close, it was time for Isiah to begin taking stock of how his first year as an NBA GM had gone, and how the team was going to move on to the future. Given the fact that the franchise's attendance figures had been phenomenal, many observers believed that the Raptors would use the huge gate proceeds they had earned to purchase themselves a big-time, high-powered superstar free agent. Nothing, however, could have been further from Thomas's intentions, although he was prepared to admit that in the hype that followed the big win against the Bulls, it would have been easy to get carried away, forget about pre-season plans and exuberantly blow a bundle on a marquee player. "We have a policy regarding free agents and it won't change," said Isiah, invoking one of the

Raptors later-season acquisitions. "We traded for Sharone Wright [from Philadelphia], instead. The price was reasonable. . . . A comparable player, as a free agent, would be at least twice as costly. We decided this was a better way to go."

The game plan, then, was straightforward and simple, yet smart and very much concerned with the details of not losing one's head. "While the attendance figures are gratifying, we're not exactly rolling in dough," said Isiah. For a first-year franchise, there were many start-up costs to cover before anyone could start thinking about big profits. And even though defeating the Bulls was something to be proud of, Thomas maintained it wasn't worth endangering the franchise's future over. "I have to make sure nobody — least of all me — is seduced by the smell of sweet success," he cautioned. "It's tempting to say 'Hey, let's go for this up here,' when it's so important we continue these baby steps down here — the ones we agreed on from day one."

Fans in Toronto had long enjoyed comparing the growth of the Raptors with that of the baseball Blue Jays, and for once Thomas was prepared to draw similar parallels, noting that "the Jays stuck with their program. The fans remained patient. Look how it worked out eventually." Given the fact that the Jays' patience paid off with back-to-back World Series titles, and given also that Isiah had stated several times that he was interested one day in winning an NBA title in Toronto, the patient approach advocated by the Raptors' baseball brethren seemed to be the wisest plan of action. "Like if you're selling popcorn and you're accustomed to moving a certain amount," he explained by way of an analogy. "Suddenly, you sell an enormous quantity. Do you immediately change your entire policy, or do you carry on with the systems that have been working? Of course!" Although the Raptors didn't have the Blue Jays' benefit of a farm system and players with long careers, the overall philosophy was still the same: good things come to those who wait!

Such abstract reflection on Isiah's part, however, was short-lived. There were much more concrete problems beginning to emerge in Toronto, and they needed his immediate attention.

Everyone in the Toronto Raptors organization, most pro basketball fans in Canada, and a good portion of the folks in and around the NBA knew that Damon Stoudamire was being given too much floor time by head coach Brendan Malone. With his average still up over 40 minutes a game and approaching 48 in many contests, the idea that Damon was being overplayed was little more than a no-brainer. The far more intellectually challenging issue, however, revolved around the potential disasters that might be brought about by this absence of pine-time for the rookie sensation. As long as the Mighty One kept logging the big minutes, the Raptors were staying close and occasionally even pulling out a win or two. But how long could he keep it up, and what — if anything — would force him to stop? And why didn't Malone give him more rests? Why hadn't Isiah held on to Chris Whitney? It was almost as though hoop fans in Toronto were watching some kind of injury-waiting-to-happen, high-wire act being carried on as a sub plot to the actual games themselves. And this high-wire routine in turn marked only the beginning of a much larger disaster in the front office of the young Toronto Raptors.

On Tuesday, March 26, with the team still basking in the afterglow of their huge triumph over the Bulls, the Raptors lost to the Atlanta Hawks at home. Damon Stoudamire played all 48 minutes of the game. The next night the Raptors lost to the Philadelphia 76ers in the City of Brotherly Love. What's worse, Damon had to miss the entire game because of severe tendonitis in his left knee, a classic overuse injury among athletes in all sports that usually worsens over time when opportunities for rest and healing are denied. As opposed to broken bones or muscle tears, tendonitis is not an injury that goes "snap" but rather gets more serious with continued stress. And by all indications, this one had been going chronic for a while, because Damon was also forced to sit out much of the action two nights later as the Raptors were completely crushed by Orlando, 126–86 at SkyDome.

It quickly became apparent that the Raptors were just not the same team without Damon Stoudamire, and it wasn't long before people started pointing the finger at the man they felt was responsible for his injury woes: head coach Brendan Malone. Observers noted that all along, the game plan for the new franchise had been clearly set out as one of patience, and that meant bringing younger players along gradually. "When we first hired our coach," said Isiah, referring to the time not so long ago when he introduced Malone to the Toronto media, "I said that in an expansion situation you can't judge a coach on how many games he won or how many he lost." That having been said, it followed that one guy receiving an excessive amount of floor time in order to ensure victory didn't make a lot of sense. But where the logic gets twisted is when one considers that as an NBA head coach — and a first-year one at that — Brendan Malone wanted to win as many games as he could. And to do that, Damon Stoudamire had to be on the court.

Following the Philadelphia loss, Thomas was clearly concerned, but not yet overly agitated, with the injury to his prize protégé. "It sparked some front-office concern," he related. "Any time you have a player who's injured and who's still playing a lot of minutes, it's concerning to all of us. [Damon's] a young guy who never wants to sit on the side, he competes and he's got the heart of a warrior. He would never complain and the way he goes is the way we go." Stoudamire's bravery notwithstanding, however, Isiah realized at this point that without caution, his plan for bringing things along slowly was in danger of falling apart. He warned that "we have to be smart enough to understand the big picture."

The sound of the alarm bells of controversy being rung by Brendan Malone were almost audible. "Coaches coach to win and players play to win," he said in his own defence. "The Toronto Raptors were the talk of the NBA this year because of how hard they have played." What's more, claimed Brendan, the fact that the star point guard was getting so much time on the court was both helping his development as a player, and was essential to his team's success. "If Damon were only playing 32 or 35 minutes, do you think he'd be considered a serious candidate for rookie of the year?" Malone asked rhetorically. "He wouldn't be happy either. Damon is a gamer, he's a winner. He knows when he's off the floor we don't have a shot to win." And while Toronto's morning radio sports pundits were already whispering that the coach/GM differences over the issue of playing time would soon cost Malone his job, Isiah himself was not speaking in such dire tones. "Hopefully, this is a situation we can manage as opposed to there having to be total breakup," he said.

As if to enforce the Damon-doesn't-play-and-we-can't-win theory, the 40 point loss to Orlando came on a night when Stoudamire played "only" 29 minutes on his bad knee in front of 35,700 fans. And on this same night, it appeared as though Isiah's desire to see some of his lesser-used Raptors in action was satisfied. Dwayne Whitfield saw his first significant minutes in the blowout, and Jimmy King also played far more than usual.

As if to point up how difficult an NBA head coach's job really is, sportswriters and radio commentators jumped all over Malone for apparently giving up the ghost against the Magic. The expansion coach couldn't get a break — he was ripped for overplaying his stars, and then accused of lying down when he tried to get the younger guys some action! But despite the media howling, it seemed as though the Thomas-Malone tensions had abated a bit. Isiah assured reporters that the head coaching job was not in danger, and Malone even admitted that "my competitive spirit sometimes gets in the way of the big picture."

But two nights later, it appeared as though things were going back to their usual messy state. In front of over 36,000 fans at SkyDome, Toronto lost a 111–106 squeaker to the Los Angeles Lakers and the recently-returned Magic Johnson. Incredibly, Malone used only six Raptors in the entire game, with Carlos Rogers and Oliver Miller playing the full 48 minutes, the still-ailing Stoudamire going for 45 and Tracy Murray logging 43 in a 32-point, 10 rebound performance. As unbelievable as it sounds, Malone said that in using only six players against the Lakers, he was "just trying to win," and, repeating a now oft-used Malone-ism, asserted that "coaches coach to win and players play to win" in the NBA. Although Isiah was in New Jersey to scout out the NCAA Final Four and missed this game, his presence was not required in order for observers to start seriously wondering about the relevance of Malone's "coaches coach" chestnut to the situation of a first-year expansion team.

The Raptors next took the floor on April 2 at home against the L.A. Clippers, and pulled out a 104–103 win in overtime. According to Brendan Malone, his team was very focused for the matchup and had "completely divorced itself from the publicity in the papers." In this one, Damon put on his usual superstar routine, tallying 44 of 53 minutes on the court, and scoring 29 points, dealing out 12 assists, and hitting a big 3-pointer with 43 seconds left in OT to win it.

For his part, Isiah, while impressed with Stoudamire's guts, was anything but pleased with the decision to use the rookie so extensively. "Just because a player is willing to die for this organization," he fumed, "doesn't mean you have to kill him." In response to questions about Malone's head-coaching life with the Raptors, Isiah would only comment that "our staff will be evaluated on all 82 games, not just a few." This stated practice of long-term assessment being the case, though, one has to wonder just how important it really was for a team that had already been eliminated mathematically from playoff contention to play its injured best man so much, just for another win.

Rumors about Malone's fate abounded. There were stories about front-office communiqués being slipped under his door at night, informing him of his termination. Some people claimed that Raptor PR personnel were being "planted" at press conferences in order to ask questions that would embarrass the coach. There was even speculation that Brendan had, for all intents and purposes, been fired well in advance of the Clippers game, and was just riding it out until season's end.

While Malone obviously wanted — needed? — the victory over the Clippers, the game itself was, from all appearances, the straw that broke the coaching camel's back as far as his career in Toronto was concerned. It was after that particular contest that Isiah Thomas began in earnest to set in motion the events that would lead to Brendan Malone's departure as the Raptors' number-one man behind the bench. And while it may seem ironic that the very game in question was in fact a victory for the Toronto hoopsters, this irony simply points up the crux of the Thomas-Malone feud: the GM wanted simply to develop a young team, while the rookie coach wanted to win games.

The actual mechanism first used by Isiah to speed Malone on his way out was an old-fashioned one: the radio. Following the fateful Clippers game, Isiah appeared on two Toronto stations, the all-sports "The Fan" and CFRB, the station that broadcasts all of the Raptors' games. Stressing that Malone's employment status with the Raptors would not change until the very end of the season, he nevertheless expressed concern with the heavy dose of injuries the Raptors had swallowed in the late season. "Our team doctors are very concerned about some of the injuries that are cropping up with some of the players at this time of the year," he explained. "Some of those players are carrying heavy, heavy minutes and we're seeing backaches and pains and strains now."

In the end, though, it wasn't what Isiah was saying about Malone and these injuries — these comments were obvious and repeated often in the media. Rather, it was how he was saying them that was significant. Here was the GM of a major pro sports team taking to the airwaves to publicly chastise his coach. While the CFRB program was booked well in advance, Thomas actually volunteered to go on The Fan to speak his mind. Certainly, this bold and very public move signified trouble for Brendan Malone.

Following the win over the Clippers, Damon Stoudamire's injured knee soon forced him into day-to-day status, and eventually into total inactivity. With the rookie sensation on the bench, it was all the Raptors could do to painfully finish out the season. Painfully, because no one likes losing and even more so because, as Isiah had indicated, major-league pains and bruises were spreading through the Raptors players like mad cow disease through a herd of bovines. Carlos Rogers had a neck strain, Zan Tabak a groin strain, "Big O" Miller was suffering from a bruised right calf, and Sharone Wright from back spasms. Dwayne Whitfield had a sore knee, and B.J. Tyler's freak nerve-damage injury to his leg had still not healed. Rumors swirled around SkyDome in April that maybe some of these injuries were less serious than reported and were in fact being accentuated in order to speed Malone's exit. It certainly is not hard to imagine members of a team fighting for a playoff spot being somewhat more willing than the Raptors were to play through the pain. Remember Bad Boy Isiah Thomas and all of the painful injuries he played through during the Pistons' play-off drives in the dynasty years? Whatever the story, the 1995–96 season was winding down, and the injury-ridden Raptors were going out with some loud whimpers.

The end of the coaching controversy finally came on April 21, 1996 as Toronto faced Philadelphia. Just about everyone who knew what a Raptor was, expected that this would be the last game behind the bench for Brendan Malone after Thomas had begun criticizing him about 3 weeks earlier. "I'm not going into the game thinking it's my last game," said Malone, ever the plucky fighter. "I'd like to win the game, by the way. Get number 22. But if it happens, it happens. . . . I think I did the best job possible for the franchise in laying the foundation for the Raptors, and we've far exceeded [the expectations] . . . of everybody . . . in that we've made ourselves competitive." The game, which was won by Philly, 109–105, put the cap on a 21–61 season for Brendan Malone and the Toronto Raptors in their inaugural NBA campaign. But no sooner were the details of the contest transferred into agate type for the morning papers than the crucifixion of Brendan Malone began.

The first to go after the soon-to-be-ex coach were, as might well have been expected, Raptor big men Oliver Miller and Carlos Rogers. Both men had played well during 1995–96, but their reputations for "talking trash" on and off the court were at least as big as their games. Miller claimed that Malone "didn't respect us enough as people . . . and he didn't give everybody a chance to show what they've got." For Rogers, playing for Malone was simply frustrating. "I played less this year than I did [with Golden State] in my rookie year and he never told me why," Rogers said. "He didn't talk to me; he just ran over me. It got to the point where I didn't want to dress for games. I was a victim of his system."

In his defence, Malone contended that many of the Raptors actually liked playing for him, mentioning that "after the [final] '76ers game Esposito and Tabak thanked me and Alvin [Robertson] embraced me." As far as Malone was concerned regarding the issue of respect and his Raptors, "they showed me respect by playing hard night in and night out."

But given all the talk about respect that was flying around Toronto hoop circles at the end of the season, the thing that really must have hurt Brendan Malone was the criticism leveled at him by Damon Stoudamire. Carlos Rogers and Oliver Miller were one thing — even the fans in SkyDome's cheap seats knew that those two were loudmouths. But Damon, the guy Malone once compared to Jimmy Cagney? What made it worse was that the rookie sensation seemed prepared to go on at length about his coach's shortcomings. "We respected Brendan to a certain extent, and I guess he did as good a job as he could," said Stoudamire, "but I felt at times he didn't respect us. I thanked him for the minutes he gave me, but I went out and did the work. The reason I reaped the rewards was through my hard work and through my playing; it wasn't because of the coach. When you have a style like Brendan's, you want to win so bad you'll do it at all costs. But the young players didn't play enough, so they weren't prepared for pressure situations."

Ultimately, though, players don't fire coaches — General Managers do, although as the case of Brendan Malone illustrates strongly, players can certainly cause coaches to get fired. Going into the last game of the 1995–96 season, Isiah had remained true to his word that he would not make any coaching decisions until the last layup had been shot. "I intend to sit down with Brendan to see if we can have a meeting of the minds," he said, indicating his plans for after the final buzzer had sounded.

This meeting of the minds settled on just one state of consciousness, however, and that was that Brendan Malone no longer had a job as coach of the Raptors. While Malone maintained that he was never made aware of the "big picture" regarding the proper balance to strike between winning games and developing players, it is extremely hard to imagine that given the size and scope of the Raptor organization and the importance of its first year in a new NBA country, that some communication did not take place regarding a coaching mandate. "I never went into the season being told that I should win, lose, or play people," claimed Malone. "Nobody put the brakes on and said 'do this.' I was under the impression that we were developing a winning attitude." Diplomatically, Isiah would only state that as far as he and Malone's outlooks were concerned, "Our philosophies are different in our visions of the future."

Typically, Malone remained without much bitterness, choosing instead to remember the team's first exhibition game in Halifax and its special importance for basketball in Canada: "10,000 Canadians standing up and cheering in unison, happy that the NBA is in Canada and cheering for 12 Americans in a sport that they're not familiar with." The ex-coach could, at least from a financial standpoint, afford not to harbor any major feelings of animosity, as he had initially signed a guaranteed 3-year deal at around $300,000 per year. One nasty rumor was that while Thomas wanted to continue paying Malone, the coach could in fact have been fired for breach of contract, that is, for not having followed the directives sent to him by the front office. Ultimately, Malone and the Raptors settled for a reported $325,000. In his parting comments Malone denied any animosity toward his former GM or anyone else in Toronto. "I thank Isiah for the chance to coach this team," he said, and then repeated his favorite media-mantra: "Coaches coach to win and general managers live for tomorrow. . . . I feel good about myself, I hold no grudges."

Oddly, Malone recounted a story of a telephone call he received from Thomas after he had been let go. "Isiah called me a week after he fired me and he told me I'd done a great job, that I'd kept the team in games we had no business being in," recalls Brendan. "He said I would be a very good coach for this team in three years if I wanted to be, or I'd be a very good coach right now for a team in the playoffs. I thanked him for the offer and then cut the conversation." In fact, Isiah's prediction of Malone's suitability for a team in playoff contention was not far off. It wasn't long before the ex-Raptor received another telephone call, this time from the Seattle SuperSonics, who wanted him to scout teams for their playoff drive. In a nice bit of irony, Malone stayed with Seattle throughout their championship run and thus made it to the NBA finals in 1995–96 after all! His credentials were also seriously considered by the Milwaukee Bucks, the New Jersey Nets, and the Charlotte Hornets. Ultimately, Brendan Malone ended up being hired that July as an assistant coach with the New York Knicks. (And even stranger, Malone would end up being an assistant coach under Isiah, when Thomas was behind the Pacer's bench from 2000–03.)

For his part, Isiah Thomas maintained that cutting Brendan Malone adrift would be the best move for the team as a whole, and would be the only way it could move forward within the vision for an expansion team that he had set forth from the beginning. "I feel bad we just couldn't have had a resolution. I wish we could've seen eye to eye," said Isiah. "His competitive nature made him short-sighted in terms of seeing the big picture. Winning 21 games the first season was a good start, but we want to move forward, to win the championship." And moving forward was something that Malone was seen to be incapable of, being blinded by his ultimate goal of winning lots of games in his, and the team's, first year. Ultimately, according to Thomas, Malone was let go in favor of the "long-term health and future of this organization. Brendan was a guy who loved the game. He was a tireless worker. Everything he did was about winning."

The strange paradox here was that, in the end, Coach Malone was fired for wanting to win too many games! Lack of desire for success isn't usually grounds for dismissal in the NBA, but in Brendan's case, the timing was simply off.

How is one to put the whole Brendan Malone firing situation into perspective, especially if one wants to look at it from the angle of reviewing Isiah Thomas' first year on the job as the Raptors' GM? Perhaps Chris Young, who covers the NBA expertly for the *Toronto Star*, put it best when he said that when the whole thing is taken into consideration, "just one thing makes you flinch. Thomas gave Malone a six-inch leash and asked him to look a mile down the road, hardly ideal conditions whether you're ambulating on four legs or two."

The image of a short leash is doubly paradoxical here when you remember that the big themes in Isiah's early comments about coaching and the new franchise were continuity, stability, and relative longevity. Even so, Thomas waxed philosophical about going back on these earlier promises. "I wouldn't categorize it as a failure," he maintained. "I would say, however, that it's unfortunate that the organization and the coach couldn't see things the same way." Simply put, given a difference of opinion as major as the development-vs.-winning one seemed to be in Toronto, radical changes and even firings have to take place, no matter what promises were made to the media.

Chris Young calls the whole thing a classic "failure to communicate. Not good managing on Thomas' part. Not good wind judgment on Malone's part. Two guys learning on the job." Given the relative inexperience of the two, this is certainly an appealing way of looking at it. After all, Malone ended up in New York, on his feet and definitely in line down the road for another head coaching job somewhere in the NBA. And Isiah's still the GM — a wiser and more experienced one now. "Have I learned anything?" he said after the firing. "Ask me that question in two or three weeks, after I get a chance for some self-analysis."

Isiah did not look very far for a replacement for Malone. In fact, he searched no farther than the Raptors' bench, where he found assistant coach Darrell Walker willing and more than able to take his first job as an NBA head coach. Into Walker's position moved Jim Thomas, Isiah's old back-court mate at IU and formerly a Raptors' scout.

Of course the main initial reaction among Raptor-watchers was that Isiah had simply hired an inexperienced yes-man with past connections to the GM. The new coach, however, would have none of this talk. "I wouldn't say I'm a puppet," countered the happy Walker. "I'm going to be running the basketball team. And no matter what you say, it's kind of hard for Isiah to coach a team from . . . up at the office or when we're on the road and he's at home in Birmingham, Michigan."

Isiah and others in the organization liked Walker's NBA playing experience, an asset he shared with such coaching greats as Lenny Wilkins, Pat Riley, and Phil Jackson. Damon Stoudamire contended that "he's played in the NBA and he understands what we go through as players. I don't think Brendan could relate; he didn't play the game at this level."

For Isiah, Walker's knowledge of what it means to lose, and how teams go about winning, was a great combination. "He's played on a team [the Knicks] that won only 22 games, then he played on the Chicago Bulls team that won a championship," reminds Thomas, "so he knows the things it takes to become a winner, and he's got the intensity to carry it through." Having gone back as far as boyhoods in Chicago, Walker and Thomas had a lot in common, and both spent time at an early press conference remembering those shared roots. "It makes you feel good from that situation we all came out of, we survived," Isiah told new coach Walker. "You were able to come out intact, able to have a wife, kids and everything else — the American dream, so to speak."

With the 1995–96 season in the books, it was time to look forward to the post-season, and beyond. On May 15, 1996, to the surprise of very few NBA observers, Damon Stoudamire won the Schick NBA Rookie of the Year Award. With 76 votes for R.O.Y. honors, Damon was way ahead of Portland Trail Blazers big man Arvydas Sabonis who received only 17. The shortest player ever to win the award, Stoudamire told the press conference at the SkyDome Hotel that he was surprised to have won by such a wide margin. Isiah, however, wasn't. After all, he was the one who believed enough in the little guy to have drafted him the year before. "He said he was going to do great things and he really put us on the map in terms of credibility and respectability," said Thomas. "As a former player, there are not many young guys these days that us old guys respect, but Damon's got special qualities. He's rare."

Stoudamire having been such a success emanating from the previous year's draft, it was only logical that the 1996 draft would garner as much attention as it did. The early buzz had U Mass's Marcus Camby a lock to come to Toronto, but sportswriters, fueled by speculation from Isiah and others, also considered that Cal's Shareef Abdur-Rahim and U Conn's Ray Allen might end up wearing a Raptors' jersey in 1996–97. But when commissioner David Stern announced Camby's name as the second pick overall, and the Toronto Raptors' first-round choice, no one was really surprised. Given last year's shock pick, was Isiah becoming predictable? Maybe so, especially since he had written that piece in the *New York Times* giving his support to underclassmen deciding to pro early, and since Camby, a junior, fit the bill. "We got the guy we wanted. We liked him all along," said Isiah, from Wayne Gretzky's restaurant on draft night. "We feel we got the number one player in the draft. . . . Marcus has proven he's a champion at every level."

In fact, both Philadelphia and Toronto got the "best" player in the draft for their specific needs. The '76ers needed a point guard. And given the Raptors' need for some size and shot-blocking in the paint, Camby seemed like a good addition. And given, too, the precedent set by Damon Stoudamire whereby a youngster responds to the faith shown in him by one of the greatest players of all time and a new-but-learning GM, hoop fans in Toronto can hope that Camby will be another great judgment call by Isiah Thomas.

It seemed as though Camby was a person cut in much the same mold as his new GM. On September 10, 1996, Marcus was welcomed to Toronto by Isiah at the Raptors' Foundation charity fund-raising golf tournament. It had been announced earlier that Camby had signed a three-year deal with Toronto for almost $7 million.

There was a lot of talk about whether or not Camby had the strength and stamina to make it as an NBA big man, but his most notable — and most Isiah-like — comments were being made about just what he planned to do with his new-found millions. Marcus revealed that he had purchased a new house for his mother and two teenage sisters, as well as a new Lexus car for his mom.

"I think I'm more happy for my mom than anybody because she raised me and my two sisters by herself and there's nothing that I can do or buy to repay her but just say thanks," said Camby. "Me, coming from the housing projects in Hartford, I never thought this [day] would happen," he continued. "What are the odds of a guy making it to the NBA? They're real slim. But I worked hard, I overcame a lot of obstacles in the course of my life. I'm just thrilled."

Sound familiar? Just as Isiah had attained the NBA paycheck in realization of a family dream fifteen years earlier, Camby was finally paying back the family that had helped him get to the big leagues.

While Raptors fans rejoiced in the team's selection of Camby, a sadder note emanating from the post-season — other than the few hours the players were locked out of practice because of an NBA labor dispute that was quickly resolved — was the club's failure to re-sign Tracy Murray. As one of the league's most-improved players and one of the Raptors marquee stars, Murray could certainly command a lot more than the lowly $225,000 per year he was making in Toronto.

While the Raptors released little-used but highly-paid Italian guard Vincenzo Esposito to make room for Murray under the salary cap, it wasn't enough. Tracy signed a much more lucrative deal with the soon-to-be-renamed Washington Bullets — the team name had been deemed too violent — in mid-July.

What made the team's loss of Murray even stranger was a weird disagreement that erupted between the Toronto expansion club and their counterparts on the west coast. According to John Kernaghan, who followed the Raptors with a practised eye for the nearby *Hamilton Spectator*, the team asked the NBA to waive a league rule regarding the salary cap that would enable them to ink Murray and Oliver Miller to new contracts. While this was OK by the league brass, the Grizzlies said that allowing Murray to sign a contract for more than a 20 percent increase in pay (as usually prohibited by the cap) would prevent them from signing four free agents they were after. Thus, the Grizzlies said "no way" to the league's offer to waive the salary restrictions concerning Murray, and he was forced to look elsewhere for his proper monetary due.

The Vancouver veto, according to Kernaghan, caused "much mirth in Raptorland," since at least two of the free agents being sought by the Grizzlies couldn't reasonably expect a similar pay raise to the one the Raptors wanted to give Murray. "In any case," says Kernaghan, "count on this feud to be continued."

Looking ahead to 1996–97, Raptors fans could anticipate a much-improved season because of Isiah's acquisition of some pretty exciting players to complement Stoudamire, Rogers, Wright, Tabak, and Christie. While Isiah was still cautious about getting too over-anxious for early glory by losing sight of the big picture of an NBA title for six or seven years down the road — "The last time I checked they weren't giving out rings for 30- or 40-win seasons" he said — it was tough not to get just a little bit happy about some of the big-time talent he'd brought to Toronto to go along with the stars of the first season.

Guard Hubert Davis and forwards Popeye Jones and Walt "The Wizard" Williams all promised to help the team tremendously in the key areas of rebounding, scoring, and defence. Add Marcus Camby and Coach Darrell Walker to the mix, and it wasn't hard to understand the buzz surrounding the 1996–97 Raptors on the streets of Toronto.

Whatever the team's prospects for the sophomore season, 1995–96 had been a heck of a rookie year for the Toronto Raptors, and for Isiah Thomas in particular. Defeating what might be the best basketball team ever. Wins also against the Western Conference champs and the Eastern Conference finalists, but losing to enough mediocre ones to finish at 21–61. A Rookie of the Year find in Damon Stoudamire. Injuries galore. Getting rid of a rookie head coach, only to replace him with one that has even less coaching experience. Trying to find the right on-court chemistry through trades and free-agent signings. A big-time draft pick. Bringing the NBA to a new country. Selling the game, and the culture that surrounds the game, to a brand new audience.

If the GM of the Toronto Raptors could do all that in his very first year, fans around the league could only sit back and wait to see what Isiah Thomas had up his sleeve for the future.

CHAPTER TEN

The Bid for Control

By the end of the 1995–96 season, things were looking good for the Raptors as they planned ahead for '96–'97. Marcus Camby, the team's first-round draft pick for the upcoming season, looked as though he had the potential to make it big in the NBA, and, perhaps more importantly, looked like the  kind of rookie who would be able to help the Raptors make a significant improvement on its record of 21 wins in the previous campaign. By adding Popeye Jones, Walt Williams, and Hubert Davis to the Raptors, Thomas was also showing his commitment to building a well-rounded team that could score, rebound and play some defence as well.

These player acquisitions were only the beginning of a series of even more dynamic, history-making decisions in the front office, though — moves that would keep his name in the forefront of the pro basketball media over the next year. And ultimately, they would see Isiah's career path move in a way that was a lot different than what Raptors' fans imagined when their new GM burst through that big team poster just a few years ago, announced he'd arrived to take the new franchise to the NBA promised land.

● ● ●

By signing Camby, Jones, Williams, and Davis to the Raptors' lineup, Isiah Thomas had established himself as a shrewd judge of NBA talent and the career trajectories of those who play the game. Indeed, his acumen in finding players — guys like Jones, Williams, Davis, Oliver Miller, Carlos Rogers, or Doug Christie — who'd reached crucial, transitional stages in their careers and giving them enough rope to either hang themselves or pull themselves into the NBA's upper echelons, had become something that other GMs were starting to admire.

Kevin McHale, who had battled Isiah on the court while a member of the powerful Boston Celtics and was now building a promising team as the GM of the Minnesota Timberwolves, told Jackie MacMullan of *Sports Illustrated* that "there have been a few times already where I've seen a deal Isiah made and just kind of shook my head and said, 'Yep, that's Isiah for you.'"

Donnie Walsh, GM of the Indiana Pacers, had similar praise for Isiah's ability to judge talent and to assess which players would make good building blocks towards the ultimate goal of every GM — an NBA Championship. "He's aggressive, he's smart, he has a lot of knowledge on who can play and who can't play. He's out there for real; he's not fooling around," asserted Walsh to Chris Young of the *Toronto Star.* "When you call him on trades or anything like that, he's protecting his franchise. He jumped right in and became a GM — not an ex-player."

Part of the Thomas secret lay not only in knowing which hoopsters available in any given trading or free-agent scenario could score or play defence, but also in determining which ones would flourish in the Raptors environment. When players came to Toronto, they'd have to be aware that they would be contributing their skills to a young but improving team, one that was probably a few years shy of playoff contention. For his part, Isiah made it clear that he wasn't interested in pursuing athletes who were looking at Toronto as a place to comfortably play out their NBA lifespan, exerting minimal effort on the court while collecting a safe paycheck.

"We don't want expansion to be a place where people come to rest or live out their careers," he revealed to Young. "We want them to rehabilitate or restore their careers." And to that end, Thomas set about building a team of contributors, guys who in one way or another would chip in to help the team in the short run as it prepped for its second big-league campaign, and in the long-term as well, when Isiah's often-stated plans of making the playoffs and even winning an NBA crown would become practical and attainable goals.

As the summer of 1996 and the basketball off-season came to a close, the Raptors had to confront the reality of the squad's sophomore season and the immediate prospect of improving on their 1995–96 efforts, in which they managed to win 21 games. Such a record was good, perhaps, for a first-year expansion club, but far from satisfactory for competitors like new coach Darrell Walker, team leader Damon Stoudamire, or Isiah himself.

While Isiah Thomas was certainly beginning to establish himself among his fellow league GM's as a truly cagey assessor of talent and a builder of expansion basketball teams, it's important to remember that an NBA season did actually take place between October 1996 and June 1997, a series of games that enabled the men he'd assembled to hit the hardwood and strut their stuff. It is only within the sweaty arena of real, live, 48-minute games that the true worth of an NBA general manager can be tested, because it's there that games are won and lost. All of the noise about potential, resurrected careers and the promise of an expansion team adds up to just a lot of hot air if some progress is not made in the win–loss column.

But before much action happened on the hardwood, front office dealings grabbed the headlines. Very early on in the 1996–97 season, sports history in the city of Toronto was altered dramatically in a turn of events that centered on the fledgling NBA team. In mid-October, co-majority owner Allan Slaight, the broadcasting magnate who up until then had kept a fairly low profile in the day-to-day operations of the club, pulled what came to be known as a "shotgun clause" on the other majority owner John Bitove. In short, this meant that Bitove had one month to buy out Slaight's 39.5 per cent share of the team. If he could not raise the money, Slaight would then be legally able to buy out Bitove's 39.5 per cent, thereby becoming the Raptors' sole majority owner.

Although there hadn't been a public blow-up between the two, Slaight and Bitove had disagreed almost from the start on the construction of a playing facility for the Raptors. Bitove wanted to build a special stadium to be used exclusively for basketball, and had even gone so far as to sell naming rights on the site to Air Canada for tens of millions of dollars. Slaight, though, believed a basketball-only facility to be the next best thing to financial suicide, what with an NHL team in the same city competing for fan dollars. Given the fact that the Maple Leafs seemed to have outlived their tenure in the Gardens, it seemed logical to try to combine hockey and basketball in the same building, as was done in several cities in the U.S.

This apparently sensible approach — combining the two professional winter sports under the same roof — had a few flaws when applied to Toronto. For one thing, Leafs' owner Steve Stavro was a cousin of Bitove's. For another, Stavro had gone on record as saying that any type of combined hockey/basketball facility would be fine with him, as long as his group could "control all aspects of construction and operation of the building." The NBA, Stavro was saying, was going to have to be a tenant rather than an equal partner if it wanted to share space with the NHL.

This reaction — an understandable one, perhaps, in a country where hockey has never taken, and probably will never take, a back seat to another sport — provoked a violent response from NBA Commissioner David Stern, a man not used to being told what to do. Stern, whose assistant at one time had been NHL head honcho Gary Bettman, told James Christie of the *Globe and Mail* that Stavro's we-call-the-shots remarks were "a kind of bullying from a team that's had the city to itself and doesn't like the prospects of competition." What's more, it was clear that, of the two owners, Stern favored Bitove because of his love for basketball and, more importantly, his vision of a basketball-only building in Toronto.

Slaight's move had important implications for Isiah, who still held the 9 per cent share of the team given to him as part of his initial contract as GM and Vice-President of Basketball Operations. After all, it had been Bitove who had selected Isiah to run the team. Now that Thomas' fellow Indiana University alumnus was in danger of losing his share of the Raptors, was the GM in a position to lose his job as well?

When the 30-day shotgun period was over, John Bitove was unable to raise the estimated $88 million he needed to buy out Slaight, and so lost his share in a counter-buy-out. In a tearful goodbye speech, Bitove, accompanied by the Raptor mascot, said farewell to the team he'd helped launch. It was obvious that this was a man who had truly — perhaps desperately — wanted to be a part of a pro sports franchise but who had simply fallen short in getting the financial support needed to make his dream last any longer.

For his part, Slaight assured everyone that Isiah's job was safe. "He has no reason to feel insecure. . . . He's a class act in sports and in business," the new majority owner told the *Globe and Mail.*

Isiah had conflicting emotions about Bitove's departure. "You're OK with the franchise moving forward, and you're [glad to be] done with the in-house fighting," he concluded, "but you feel bad for John being the loser after he put his heart and soul into it."

Early in the aftermath of the takeover by Allan Slaight, Isiah began to send out feelers about increasing his ownership share in the club if the opportunity arose. On the day of Slaight's takeover — November 15, 1996 — the *Globe and Mail* reported that Thomas had been working feverishly to put together his own package of investors to purchase the team. Before long, the basketball world would discover that this was not idle speculation on the part of the former All-Star.

The shotgun blast heard around the NBA took place in October and November of 1996, the very beginning of the 1996–97 season. With the takeover complete, there was still lots of basketball to be played. For fans of the team, the Raptors' antics on the court evoked a nostalgia of a different, more recent vintage that was nevertheless filled with emotional ups and downs. In the team's first season, Toronto hoops followers were treated to an unusual and at times frustrating pattern in the Raptors' performance. The team had shown that it could play brilliantly, notching victories over some of the NBA's finest clubs. But they'd also found themselves slammed by squads more accustomed to serving as the league's doormats. In 1996–97, the confusing pattern continued.

At one point, the Raptors were the only team to have beaten all four NBA divisional leaders, having knocked off the L.A. Lakers, Utah Jazz, Chicago Bulls and Miami Heat at least once each during the season (although L.A. ended up being overtaken by Seattle in the Pacific division), as well as beating the powerful Houston Rockets. But Toronto also managed to lose to such relative weaklings as Boston (three times) and Vancouver, the league's two worst clubs, as well as to hapless squads like Golden State and San Antonio.

In reality, it was just the inexperience of a young team that led to this up-and-down performance over the long haul of a full season. With all of the talent the Raptors had on their roster, it wasn't surprising that they could get geared up to face giants like Michael Jordan, Shaquille O'Neal and Alonzo

Mourning and even overcome them. But it was equally plausible that, given their youth, they'd be unable to psych themselves up to beat the weaker teams in workman-like fashion when the glory of giant-killing wasn't at stake.

While Isiah was hard at work building a team he hoped would develop into a championship contender in the near future, his exploits on the hardwood hadn't been forgotten since his retirement just a few years earlier. In keeping with its 50th birthday festivities, the NBA selected an official "Top 50 Players of All Time" team, a squad on which Isiah joined such luminaries as Larry Bird, Wilt Chamberlain, Bob Cousy, Julius Erving, and George Mikan. The group was honored in a special ceremony at the All-Star game in February 1997.

Over the course of the team's second season, Raptors' fans took special interest in two of the team's highest-profile players, second-year guard Damon Stoudamire and rookie Marcus Camby. Stoudamire had another great season, averaging 20 points, 8 assists, and 4 rebounds a game, despite the fact that opposing defenders had had a full year to try to figure him out. Damon simply came up with new ways to baffle opponents, and in the process reinforced his position as the team's spiritual leader.

Marcus Camby was one of the players who at times got a bit of a tongue-lashing from Damon, at least at the start of the year. Nobody doubted Marcus' ability, least of all Isiah, who'd made him the team's first-round draft pick out of college. But Camby began the year with a series of injuries that had more than a few fans wondering about the big guy's mental toughness and tenacity. After all, this was the NBA, where a few bumps and bruises are as much a part of the game as plane travel and hotel room service. If Camby couldn't take a few shots here and there, maybe he should have stayed at U. Mass for another year.

Happily, Marcus really started to turn his game around late in the season. By mid-March, fans started to wonder if his spectacular performance on the court might net him Rookie of the Year honors. Unfortunately, it was a case of coming to the party a bit too late, as Philadelphia's Allen Iverson took the award based on his spectacular season. Camby's chances for Rookie of the Year were no doubt hurt by the 15 games he missed due to various injuries at the start of the season, but he still finished with an average of almost 15 points a game to go along with 6 rebounds per contest and a total of 130 blocked shots in just 63 games played. And seeing the determination with which he blocked shots and ran the court late in the year, observers no longer wondered if Camby possessed the fire to win games.

With the Raptors' improved-but-still-erratic play on the court and the various ownership wranglings taking place off of it, Isiah remained focused on what he viewed as his number-one directive as the GM of an expansion NBA franchise: to build a team that could one day win a league championship.

In an interview with *HOOP* magazine, the NBA's official publication, Isiah claimed that there were several aspects to succeeding in the playoffs. He emphasized things like team defence, converting free throws in the clutch, a deep bench and mental tenacity, all characteristics that his own Raptors team was developing but hadn't quite mastered.

What was fascinating about the *HOOP* interview, though, was Isiah's steadfast focus on a few keys to post-season success that went beyond the often-stated attributes possessed by winning teams like his own Pistons of the Bad Boys era. One of these was his insistence on a total team commitment to being physically and mentally ready come playoff time. "It might sound a little strange, or simple," he explained, "but the first key to success in the playoffs is to make absolutely certain that nobody on your team has made any plans until after June 30. . . . If you're down 3–2 in a series and a guy on your team has plans to go on a cruise with his wife or friends, then you've got a weak link out there."

Certain Toronto players like Damon Stoudamire even had clauses written into their Raptors contracts that required them to attend playoff games and the NBA finals as spectators, just to give them a taste of what life was like in the toughest of series.

Another ingredient in the recipe of success, continued Isiah, was to "make the microphone your friend." The media pressure surrounding an NBA final or playoff series, he explained, "is intense, and to some extent you need to block out the distractions, but if you're savvy enough, you can use that pressure and place it in the right places on the other team." As an example of a canny team using media scrutiny to their own advantage, Thomas remembered his own days with the Pistons and how "veteran teams that have been around know how to shift that pressure and spotlight and use it to their advantage."

Anyone who'd followed even the barest outline of Isiah's career knew that he was not someone who liked being beaten at anything he attempted, and that his orchestration of a winning team was no different. But those who'd been paying attention during his playing career and beyond into his dealings in the front office knew that he didn't always achieve success by being obvious.

There'd always been something a little sneaky and deceptive about the way he got things done, so it's no surprise that Isiah concluded his list of playoff-success intangibles by referring to a final team characteristic he wouldn't disclose. "The final key" to winning a championship, offered Thomas in his *HOOP* ruminations, "is the most important one. It's the one that gets you over the hump — and it's for that reason that I'll never tell you what it is." Just as he didn't get to be one of the NBA's all-time top point guards by telling the guys he was defending whether he was going to fake left or right, Isiah held back on what he believed was the most significant factor for success in the playoffs.

"One day the Raptors are going to be in the NBA finals," he promised. "I'd rather let some other team get down the path to the finals and not know about this thing I've got up in my head. We're going to use it to beat somebody else."

While Isiah could hint playfully at his "secrets of success" to the NBA's official magazine, he'd long since discovered — beginning ten years earlier with the notorious Larry Bird/Dennis Rodman racial conflict — that the media were always on the lookout for a good story, even if its truth was hard to verify. But nothing could have prepared him for the hurricane of negative press that was about to hit him as the 1996–97 season drew to a close.

In early April, nearing the end of the Raptors sophomore NBA season, a trio of authors led by a former *Sports Illustrated* writer and ABC television correspondent named Armen Keteyian, unleashed a book that would send shock waves throughout the NBA and its fans. The book, entitled *Money Players: Days and Nights Inside the New NBA*, was nothing less than an attempt at an all-out, no-holds-barred, take-no-prisoners exposé of the sordid underside of life in the most hyped professional sports league.

In Toronto, *Money Players* caused a tremendous amount of controversy because of the claims it made about the off-court activities of a certain former All-Star point guard turned NBA executive named Isiah Thomas. The book alleged that Isiah had been involved in high-stakes gambling and had a "problem" with betting, and, most damning of all for a player who had always been seen to be one who'd do anything to help his team win games, accused him of being involved in a point-shaving scheme that affected the outcome of at least two games during the 1989–90 season.

The storm of controversy that broke out across North America and in Toronto in particular was a violent one, as Isiah and others rushed to his defence. "This is a compilation of lies, rumors and innuendoes," he asserted. "It's insulting and it's regrettable that my family has to be put through this . . . but I'll deal with it."

Angered when asked by reporters if it had ever entered his mind to throw a game or to shave points, Isiah responded by invoking his competitive, championship career as a player. "That ain't me. That ain't ever been me," he snapped. "My record speaks for itself and it's insulting that I even have to stand here and answer that question. As I said, put some names on it and stand behind it."

If Thomas was letting the accusations that surfaced in *Money Players* bother him unduly in the days following its publication, he was certainly not letting on. Indeed, less than two weeks after the book came out, Isiah put his signature on a letter of intent that outlined his plans for taking control of the Raptors as the team's majority owner!

To be sure, shortly after Allan Slaight took the reigns of the team from John Bitove, the communications tycoon let it be known that he would be more than willing to sell off some of his huge stake. But it wasn't until Slaight admitted that he'd even consider parting with a majority interest in the franchise that Isiah got interested. At first, Thomas revealed in an interview with David Berman of *Canadian Business* that he "was never really looking to step in and buy or anything, I was kind of on the sidelines watching," but Slaight's interest in selling piqued his curiosity to the point that he began assembling his own group of investors.

Thomas remained absolutely silent on exactly who was joining him in the bid to buy the Raptors, but most sources agreed that it was a mixed bag of U.S. and Canadian investors. The most persistent rumors had Isiah being backed by the Chase Manhattan Bank out of the United States and the Canadian Imperial Bank of Commerce.

Slaight was being somewhat vague telling Mary Ormsby of the *Star* that he was "kind of easy about it" when it came to Isiah's growing interest in the team, stating that "in terms of majority control a lot depends on what Isiah wants, frankly, and I'm just trying to strengthen his own role with the community and with the Raptors." Isiah, on the other hand, was becoming impatient and was hoping that Slaight would give some indication of whether he and his consortium would be considered seriously as potential buyers of the team.

Finally, on April 20, Isiah could wait no longer. In a bold move that easily could have backfired and cost him his entire involvement with the team, Isiah issued this statement: Let me know if my group can buy the Raptors, or I'll walk. "If this thing drags out, I'm going to have to make some tough decisions," Isiah told Ormsby. "But I'll make them quickly because I don't want to hold other people back, making them wait to see what I'm going to do. Nor do I want to hold myself back. By [April 21] the regular season is over and everybody is going to go their own way. If there has to be an exit, I'll make sure it's done properly and professionally and that it doesn't hurt anybody."

Luckily for Isiah, a few unlikely but important figures stepped in to assist him in his bid to take control of the Raptors. A number of key players, including Damon Stoudamire, Carlos Rogers, and Marcus Camby asserted publicly that if Isiah were to leave the team, they would not be far behind him. Stoudamire insisted that he'd demand a trade if Isiah left Toronto.

Confronted with the possibility that he might lose the man who'd come to represent pro basketball for millions of fans in Canada, and for several key components of the Raptors on-court nucleus, Slaight had no choice but to sign a letter of intent indicating his willingness to begin negotiations with Isiah to sell the team, at a price estimated to be $125 million and up.

To each and every observer of the Toronto pro sports scene, it looked as though Thomas would soon own the lion's share of the team he'd done so much to build over the preceding three years. He now had until July 31 — just over three months — to come to an agreement with Slaight on the final price of the team and the terms of the sale.

As he'd done so many times in his 36 years, Isiah had made a daring, heads-up move that looked as if it would pay off handsomely. Front-page headlines across the continent heralded the fact that if the purchase of the Raptors came to fruition, Isiah would become the first African-American to own a pro sports team in North America, a feat that caused a considerable amount of personal stress. "I feel like it's the end of final exams when you've got that last test . . . then you just want to crash," he confessed to Mary Ormsby of the 12-hour conference-call marathon he and Slaight had just completed. And within all of the negotiations surrounding his attempt to buy out Slaight, Thomas promised that he'd remain the GM of the club.

For his part, Allan Slaight did not harbor any ill will towards Isiah, even considering the ultimatum laid on his doorstep at the eleventh hour. But then again, this was the same man who'd introduced John Bitove to the finer points of the shotgun clause a few short months ago. Slaight was no stranger to hard-nosed business dealings. "When I decided to sell down my ownership interest in the team, it was my top priority to try to reach an agreement with my current partner Isiah Thomas," Slaight declared in a press release. "His vision and leadership with our basketball operation has been well-chronicled throughout the NBA, but now the public will have a chance to see that he is a bright, forward-thinking businessman." The agreement-in-principle complete, Isiah could now look forward to the next 100 days as a time for securing his financial backing in the buy-out bid.

Thomas confessed that one of his top priorities would be to take care of the arena debate with the Maple Leafs once and for all. Into the summer of 1997, however, the situation is still as confusing as ever, with both sides seemingly unable to agree with each other and Metro Toronto Council on several key ownership and funding issues.

In the aftermath of the agreement with Slaight, veteran *Globe and Mail* sports scribe Marty York indicated that Thomas even had some interest in extending the boundaries of his sports ownership interests. Thomas, said York, had some serious intentions about participating in the expansion of the National Football League into Canada, if and when it came about. York spoke to Paul Godfrey, CEO of the Sun Media group, a man who had for years been tenaciously pursuing his goal of importing the NFL north of the border, and who'd been successful as Toronto Metro Chairman in the 1970s in bringing pro baseball to the city. "Isiah has expressed interest to me in getting involved with our NFL project," said Godfrey, "and we've agreed to discuss it further in the near future. I have a great deal of respect for Isiah."

Isiah had to keep all of the high-powered wheeling and dealing inherent in the world of pro sports management in perspective. When he talked about it, Thomas sounded more like the top level executive he'd become than a dollar-struck ex-athlete with dreams of grandeur. But then, composure had always been one of his strong suits. "It's glamorous, but it's a business and people who have longevity are people who don't get crazy," he told Diane Francis of the *Financial Post*.

Commenting on the fact that games are played almost entirely in the evenings, and into the early morning hours on the West Coast, Isiah admitted to Francis that "the NBA is nightlife, and I sleep very little. I've seen players get carried away with the nightlife and glamour. But I've seen this happen in business, too — a guy is promoted to vice-president. He has power and he just can't handle it. My business sense comes from the streets. You had to know people and trust your instincts. And your instincts would literally keep you alive or dead."

Many people — from sports sociologists and historians to the average Raptors fan in the streets — were quick to point out that Isiah's rapid ascension through the ranks of the front office to the point that he could realistically expect to become the first black majority owner of a pro sports team in North America happened in Canada and not in the United States. Certainly, the year 1997 had some significance in this scenario, as it was not only the NBA's 50th birthday but the 50th anniversary of Jackie Robinson's first game in pro baseball as well. The first black man to play in the major leagues had arrived in Brooklyn via Montreal, where he'd been a minor league star.

His success within the Canadian context was not lost on Isiah, either. "We were taught in our family that discrimination was not because of color, but because of economics," he asserted in the *Financial Post* interview. "If you think that someone doesn't like you because you're black you will let him beat the hell out of you. That's because once you acknowledge and deal with their racism it becomes your problem." In Canada, though, Isiah felt that because of what he called a "lack of baggage about slavery," it was easier for him to work himself into the position of owner of a major pro team. "Racism exists everywhere; however there are some parts of the world where racism stops you from performing. That's the difference."

No matter how his attempts to purchase a controlling interest in the Raptors were going to be played out, Isiah Thomas was still the General Manager of the Toronto club. And as such, he was responsible for putting the best team available to him on the floor every time the Raptors took to the court. As Isiah suggested to Francis, he wasn't going to overlook talented prospective pro players, no matter where they were. "Anyone who is playing basketball now is logged onto our computer," he pointed out. "We are in the business of buying talent."

Speaking in terms of the straight numbers, the Raptors' 1996–97 season was a considerable improvement on their freshman campaign. In 1995–96 under coach Brendan Malone, Toronto had won 21 games; this time, with Darrell Walker at the helm, the Raptors put 30 contests into the "W" column by the end of the season. It still wasn't good enough to make the playoffs in the Eastern Conference's Central Division, but certainly indicated some progress on the court in that direction. There was definitely reason to imagine the team making a run at the post-season in a few years' time, based on the almost 50 per cent increase of wins in just one year.

Into the summer of 1997, the traditional NBA surge of talent-buying became increasingly frenzied, as both the annual signings of free agents and the yearly draft of college players took place. Raptors Walt Williams and Carlos Rogers were both rewarded for their efforts with lucrative contracts. Around the league, other stars like Michael Jordan (virtually a lock to re-sign with Chicago), Dennis Rodman (almost as sure not to be renewed by the Bulls), and Patrick Ewing (who was re-signed by the Knicks) tested the choppy waters of free agency.

In the Raptors' camp, a couple of key back-court players were also making contract-related headlines because of sign-on-the-dotted-line clauses that enabled them to be inked to Raptors deals one full year before their current contracts expired. One of them, the much-improved Doug Christie, signed a four-year extension deal with the club for about $20 million.

A similar scenario was developing with Damon Stoudamire, the Mighty Mouse around whom so much of the team had been built since Isiah drafted him at the SkyDome in June of 1995. Damon, who'd signed an NBA minimum-length three-year rookie contract with the Raptors, was eligible to re-sign after two seasons if he and Toronto could come to an agreement. Virtually every major newspaper and radio station in Toronto urged Isiah to lock Stoudamire in to some big bucks before he even had a chance to think about going the free-agent route at the end of the 1997–98 season.

In Vancouver, Grizzlies GM and short-time coach Stu Jackson had done exactly that with his team's well-publicized big man, Bryant "Big Country" Reeves. The two posed for publicity photos while Reeves signed a giant mock-up of his six-year, $64.8 million contract extension after his second year of NBA play. At the time of writing, there had been no deal between the Raptors and Damon, but fans who had seen the way he'd carried the team in his first two pro seasons hoped he'd never play anywhere else.

Isiah was publicly cautioning Stoudamire not to become too wrapped up in comparing himself to Reeves and the big fellow's $10-million-per-year deal. He cited his own experiences — and those of some of the game's other superstar players — as proof that making big money and winning NBA titles often did not go hand in hand.

"At some point in your career you have to make a choice," he explained to the Canadian Press from Damon's home town of Portland, Oregon, where he'd flown with Assistant GM Glen Grunwald in hopes of signing Stoudamire again. "You have to ask yourself, 'Am I trying to make as much money as I can, or am I trying to win a championship?' And the irony is, if you take care of winning first, the money comes later anyway. Magic

Johnson, Larry Bird and myself were never the highest-paid players in the NBA. And until recently, [neither was] Michael Jordan. . . . But we're talking about the guys who have won the most championships in the past two decades. We all made certain financial decisions so we could surround ourselves with good players."

With the prevailing salary-cap restrictions in the NBA, a GM like Isiah could sign a high-priced superstar and have very little money left over to pay the supporting cast. Such a move might look good on the surface, but given Isiah's commitment to team basketball, it was easy to see why he did not feel absolutely compelled to match Reeves' salary. "I look at our business plan and certainly Vancouver has a different one. I still believe that to win a title, you need eight or nine players who are contributing and playing well, not two or three," he asserted in the Canadian Press interview. "What Damon is facing is no different than what I faced in Detroit. Teams that want to win have to maintain flexibility under the cap, so Damon has to buy into what I bought into."

Still, it looked as though Isiah had made a tactical blunder by allowing the Grizzlies to set the tone of the summertime contract-negotiation bonanza. Differences in overall salaries between big men and guards aside, it just didn't make sense to allow Stoudamire — who was negotiating on his own without an agent — the leverage of being able to point west and demand similar numbers.

Cynics suggested that Isiah should have done a deal with Damon before embarking on a Hawaiian vacation in early July. At any rate, when he and Grunwald flew back to Toronto in the middle of the month they did not have Stoudamire's signature on a contract extension. In Portland, the Raptors execs had offered Mighty Mouse something like $9 million a year; the little guy said he wanted $15 million. In August, however, Damon admitted that he'd been convinced by Isiah that waiting until the 1998–99 season to renegotiate his contract would be a good idea, thereby allowing the Raptors to sign some new talent with the considerable money that would be freed up by his one-year deferral.

Aside from navigating the often-complicated free-agent pool, where proven NBA talent gets a chance to find out just how much it's worth in cold, hard dollars, pro GMs can bolster their teams with new players through the college draft. Actually, the term "college" has become a bit of a misnomer in recent years, as players from the NCAA ranks have been joined by a handful of high school seniors eager to bypass collegiate ball altogether and take a shot at the pros.

This trend towards the influx of ever more youthful NBA rookies was strengthened by Isiah's pick in the 1997 draft, held in Charlotte, North Carolina. Using the team's ninth pick over-all in the first round, Thomas selected Tracy McGrady, a remarkable 18-year-old guard/small forward from Mount Zion Christian Academy in North Carolina. "If I'd been picking third or fourth I would have taken him," Isiah revealed to John Kernaghan of the *Hamilton Spectator*. "In two or three years of college he probably would have been number 1. I don't deserve this. I don't know why [I was so lucky]. Wow!"

In keeping with his often-stated beliefs that he was building the Raptors towards success in the long run, Isiah noted that McGrady, who'd already signed a $12-million endorsement deal with Adidas, would not be expected to burst into stardom immediately, but would rather be able to hone his skills over time by coming off the bench for the Raptors. And what's more, at only 18, McGrady, already 6–8 and 210 lbs., "would probably grow two inches yet," according to Isiah.

In many ways, the Raptors' first-round selection of Tracy McGrady was emblematic of Isiah Thomas' short but dynamic career as the team's GM and now majority-owner-to-be of the fledgling franchise. Picking an unheralded non-collegian with a big reputation and lots of potential but no game experience outside a high school gym might well have been deemed ludicrous if done by most GMs. But Isiah, who'd been right on the mark in previous drafts with Damon Stoudamire and Marcus Camby, was now seen as a nearly infallible judge of hoops talent.

What's more, the selection of Tracy McGrady seemed to sum up most of Isiah's plans for his team. By picking a guy who, for all intents and purposes, will have his best days two or three years down the road, Thomas was simply confirming that he was looking to gradually build a squad that would one day contend for the NBA crown. In the same way he had believed in guys like Doug Christie, Walt Williams, and Popeye Jones, Isiah put his faith in a raw 18-year-old, confident that Tracy McGrady will add his talents to a well-rounded mix of Raptor players down the road.

While making contract decisions with stars like Damon Stoudamire and ushering in rookie talent like Tracy McGrady is all part of Isiah's job as GM of the Raptors, there was still the major issue of his impending ownership of the club to confront. The July 31 deadline passed without word from Isiah as to whether he'd been successful in securing the necessary financial backing, but Allan Slaight declared in his low-key manner that an extension had been granted.

Then, on August 2 — the Saturday of the Ontario holiday long-weekend — Slaight held a news conference to announce that he'd rejected Isiah's bid to buy a controlling interest in the Raptors. Toronto sports denizens were stunned; the deal had been a sure bet from day one with the only mystery being exactly whom Isiah was bringing into the ownership group with him.

Although Slaight wouldn't say exactly why he'd refused the offer, he did indicate that the team was no longer for sale. "Control is off the table," he told Doug Smith of the *Toronto Star*. "That was only offered to Isiah." Slaight, however, did not completely rule out the possibility of offering up a part of the team again in the future. "Down the road, there are various avenues that can be explored and probably will. I've always maintained I will entertain more partners."

While it wasn't completely clear why Slaight turned Isiah away, two of the most obvious suggestions were that he'd decided that this NBA franchise game was a more lucrative undertaking than he'd imagined, especially if it could be combined with a joint NHL-arena deal, and that Isiah simply couldn't come up with the right kind of cash to satisfy the communications magnate.

For his part, Isiah did not see the second explanation as a realistic one. It became clear that his major backer in the bid was David Thomson, the son of billionaire newspaper and media figure Ken Thomson, and Isiah — who admitted, "I don't know what happened," when it came to his failed bid — called the proposed ownership team he'd assembled "a group second to none in any sport." Some sources speculated that when Slaight found out that Isiah had Thomson money behind him, he'd raised his asking price considerably, but Slaight denied it. Others believed that the $135 million figure that Slaight reportedly wanted for the team was far higher than the $75 million Isiah and his group were said to be willing to pay.

Whatever the reason, Isiah did not manage to buy the Raptors. While his bid to make history as the first African-American pro sports owner was forced onto the back burner, he confessed that the things that had been driving him as team GM would keep him in Toronto. "I'm firmly committed to staying here . . . to taking this team to a championship," he asserted, still seeming a little shell-shocked at Slaight's decision. "Am I going to jump up and go away just because we've gone through this process?" he asked Doug Smith rhetorically. "That would be childish. I don't need a job. I'm doing this because I like it. As we stand here today, there is a commitment to the players and . . . to the organization and the fans of Toronto." It looked as though, in Isiah Thomas' mind at least, he'd be staying with the Raptors for some time.

Still, the thought that he remained on the inside track to an eventual ownership share much larger than his existing 9% may have been keeping Isiah in Toronto. "We're back to where we were a couple of months ago," he told Michael Grange of the *Globe and Mail*, after having had a few days to reflect on Slaight's decision. "Allan has said he [still] wants to sell a portion of his interest, and whoever that partner is going to be I'd like to meet that person and see if we're still on the same page. If you're talking about selling the team, I'm willing to buy it. If you're talking about selling down a portion of the team, then, okay, I'll wait and see who comes in."

Needless to say, a lot happened to Isiah Thomas during the summer of 1996, and on into the NBA campaign of 1996–97 — or perhaps it's more appropriate to say that he's caused a lot of things to happen to him. By patiently steering his club through a second season in which it won 30 games, Isiah put the Raptors in a position to seriously think about a playoff run in the extremely near future.

Perhaps more significantly, by leveraging himself into a position where he had a shot at becoming the first African-American owner of a North American sports franchise, Isiah had made history. It was hard to remember that this was a guy so recently removed from his days as a player, but making things happen quickly had always been one of Thomas' most significant characteristics, whether at the helm of the offence of the Detroit Pistons or in the front office of the Toronto Raptors.

With all due respect to Allan Slaight, the Torontonian's business acumen appeared to be matched by his lack of knowledge about basketball. And that's fair enough, when he was seen as being interested in an NBA team strictly as a business proposition. For all intents and purposes, Isiah Thomas still ran the Raptors' day-in and day-out affairs. Although he fell short in his bid to purchase majority control of the Raptors, Isiah would still be faced with a number of key questions as the 1996–97 season wound down.

Should the team move into a basketball-only facility, or share a stadium with another Toronto team? As GM, what players should he choose to develop the best possible mix of talent, the ultimate team chemistry that will one day launch the Raptors to an NBA Championship? And perhaps most significantly, how could he, as the face of pro basketball in Canada, keep working to ensure that the sport maintains its tremendous popularity here without dissolving to fad status, or falling into the slump experienced by Major League Baseball in recent years?

Certainly, no one could predict whether the Raptors would be best served by playing their home games in their own arena or in a shared one. The NBA, unaccustomed to playing second fiddle to other sports, most notably hockey, has always been unlikely to accept a stadium deal wherein they are not the number-one draw. But realizing that Canada is first and foremost a hockey nation, certain concessions would be needed. What is clear is that average sports fans in Toronto — like those anywhere — would not stand for inflated ticket prices and a scenario in which it appears that high-priced mega-stars and their millionaire team owners are paying little attention to the common spectator and driving ticket prices to unattainable levels.

Especially in a new environment, the last thing the NBA and the Raptors wanted was to alienate a grassroots fan base by appearing to cater excessively to the corporate-box set. And Thomas knew that as the man in charge of running the team, he'd be wise to remember that unlike more established markets like New York, L.A., or Chicago, many young basketball fans in Toronto could still be turned off by the wrong fan/team dynamics.

As far as the Raptors' chances on the court went, it was a little easier to see what had to be done if Isiah was going to build a winning team. Indeed, after the squad's 30-win season in '96–'97, four-fifths of the Raptors' starting lineup could rightly be said to be a possible playoff-level one. With

Stoudamire and Christie in the back court and Camby and Williams up front, Toronto was definitely starting to look like the real deal. Furthermore, with rapidly-improving guys like Carlos Rogers and Popeye Jones coming off the bench, the supporting cast appears sound.

The problem, though — one that's obvious to anyone who's ever heard of the NBA — was that the team still lacked a solid, back-to-the-basket big man at centre. Camby, most experts agreed, had the height but not the girth to do the job; he was really a small forward who just happened to be as tall as a centre. In order to attain the right chemistry, Isiah needed to sign, through free agency, through a trade or even through beating the bushes in some far off land like Croatia or Zaire, a bona fide big guy. Up until that point, all the talk about playoffs and championships would be just hot air. NBA fans in Canada, after all, were only going to listen to the "we're building for the future" spiel for so long before expecting results.

As the face of pro hoops in Toronto, Isiah had one more issue to face: how was he going to keep the fans coming out to games, maintain the interest of young kids and their parents while still garnering corporate support, and ultimately work toward using the Raptors and the NBA to construct a real basketball culture in Canada? As suggested, putting a good product into the stadium and making it an affordable and accessible entertainment package was a fine start.

But what was also needed is really what Thomas had been doing since he came to Toronto. Staying visible, via the media. Running clinics and sponsoring grass-roots youth activity. Keeping the perspective of long-term success in the forefront, while celebrating the small gains. And above all, running an operation that looked as though it was here to stay. With Isiah Thomas as the front man for all of these endeavors, the Raptors certainly looked to be on the right track to building a fan base that can only broaden over the next decade.

All that, though, was about to change.

CHAPTER ELEVEN

Moving On

Hindsight, they say, is 20/20. But looking back on the events of the summer of 1997, it really is easy to see why things turned out the way they did for Isiah and the Raptors — why, ultimately, Isiah resigned as GM of the Raptors and moved on to other basketball-related challenges just a few months  after his August attempt to buy the franchise failed.

The bid to take control of the fledgling franchise had officially come to an end, and despite all the talk by both Isiah and Slaight that there were no hard feelings, and that Isiah would still be around as the key basketball guy in the organization, it was hard not to think that after having been shut out at the 11th hour by Slaight and Co., that Isiah would not at least begin to sniff around at possibilities that did not involve the Raptors. Certainly, for anyone who had followed Isiah's career to this point, his failure to buy the team outright had to be considered just that in the GM's mind — a failure, and a defeat.

This was, after all, not a guy accustomed to losing, and not a guy who when he did lose, was going to take things lightly. As NBA fans had long observed, revenge — or, at the very least, an unwillingness to take defeat lying down — was an Isiah Thomas trademark.

But it was still surprising how quickly the end came for Thomas and Toronto. In mid-November, about seven weeks after the failed buyout and just 10 games into the NBA's 1997–98 season, Thomas announced that he was resigning as the Raps GM, and was moving over to NBC to take a well-paying job as part of the network's team on its NBA broadcasts.

On the court, things were not going well for the Raptors at the time of Isiah's departure, as the squad sat last in the Eastern conference, with a 1–9 record. And on the business side of things, Isiah's decision to leave meant that he would have to sell his 9% share in the team back to Slaight and Co., who, upon Isiah's resignation, promptly announced that they would be replacing him with Glen Grunwald, Isiah's fellow Indiana University alumnus.

At least on the official, for-the-record side of things, the Raptors were certainly sad to see Thomas, whose contract was not going to expire for another 18 months, go. "It is with regret that we say goodbye to Isiah Thomas," said Slaight. "He has made an important contribution to this franchise, and we will miss him. He has laid a solid foundation for the Raptors, one that we will continue to build on for years to come. But what is positive about this team is that one member can move on, and everyone pulls together to ensure that the team continues to build and grow."

That was the official version of things from the Raptors' brass. But many people close to the team noted that after the failed buyout, Isiah had simply had enough of dealing with the franchise's other managers, and that the burdens he was facing as part-owner in attempting to finance the team's new, $200-million-plus arena at the Air Canada Centre, were simply too much to bear. And added to all this was the fact that, from a legal standpoint at least, Isiah had come to the conclusions that his legal dealings with the team were not exactly gentlemanly.

"We got some confidential information which indicated to us that the Raptors did not have intentions of continuing the good-faith negotiations we were conducting," Isiah's lawyer, Frank Vuno, told the media on the day Isiah quit. "We really had no choice but to tender a resignation."

With Isiah gone and heading for the broadcast booth, Toronto seemed to be left with a mixed basketball bag. On the one hand, the team was struggling on the floor, as that 1–9 record early on in 1997–98 indicated. As well, Thomas's departure provoked massive unhappiness in at least one player — team captain Damon Stoudamire, who had long said that Isiah was one of the main reasons for him staying in Toronto. (Ultimately, Stoudamire would return to his hometown team, the Portland Trailblazers.) And many team observers felt that with the current ownership in place, it was going to be tough for the Raptors to get much better, as the team seemed reluctant to spend real money on top talent. Indeed the Toronto payroll — one of the lowest in the NBA — was a source of constant frustration for Isiah and other basketball personnel within the organization.

On the other hand, basketball had become a big draw for fans in the Ontario capital. Despite their first two sub-.500 seasons of 21 and 30 wins respectively, the franchise ranked third in NBA attendance with just over 23,000 fans per home game — and that impressive record was compiled from Toronto's SkyDome, a great place to watch baseball, but far from ideal for hoops.

•   •   •

Without the responsibilities of running a struggling young franchise, Isiah was able to settle into the broadcast job at NBC and do a fine job of it. Combining with other hoops-savvy talent in the game-day studios of the so-called "Peacock Network" such as Bob Costas and Peter Vecsey, Isiah was able to combine his astounding knowledge of the game, along with his articulate and often emphatic point of view, to excellent effect.

But watching those telecasts, on which Isiah played an integral part, one could not help but wonder: how long would this guy be content to put on the suit and the makeup, with time spent on broadcasts being his only involvement in the game he'd loved since he was a little kid? Didn't Isiah always want to coach? And wasn't he able to exercise his ability to control and calculate to great effect as a GM in Toronto? Where were those ambitions?

Well, the hoops world did not have to wait too long for Isiah to supply them with an answer — and an audacious one at that: he decided to buy an entire basketball league.

The Continental Basketball Association bills itself as the "oldest professional basketball league in the world," citing as evidence the fact that it was formed, as the Eastern League, in

April, 1946 — a month and a half before the NBA got started. The CBA has always been a kind of second-tier league — a place where players who did not quite have the A-game needed to crack an NBA roster could go to hone their skills in the hopes of getting the call-up to join a team in the top league. In recent years, several players from the CBA have gone on to star in the NBA, including current talent such as Darrell Armstrong, Moochie Norris, Bo Outlaw, and Rafer Alston.

One of the things that strikes the casual observer of the game, however, when they take a closer look at the CBA, is the out-of-the-way homes of many of the league's teams. Suffice it to say that the CBA does not operate out of the same big-city base that the NBA does, as illustrated by such squads as the Dakota Wizards, Gary Steelheads, Rockford Lightning, Sioux Falls Skyforce, and Yakima Sun Kings. For many players, stints in these cities are simply stops on the way to something bigger and better; for others, these locales represent last-chance attempts to make it in pro basketball before a career fizzles out forever.

The CBA's history, and its existence as a source of potential talent were well known to Isiah when he made the offer to the league's owners to purchase it, as majority owner, for a reported $9 million in October, 1999. Terms of the sale had Isiah, through his company, IT Acquisitions, paying for half of the $9 million up front.

With the Thomas name behind the league, owners of the 10 teams that comprised it were excited about the prospects of the CBA making some serious strides towards better visibility, more fan interest, and, quite likely, increased corporate sponsorship. And for his part, Isiah saw the CBA as a great business opportunity because he envisioned turning it into a quasi-farm system for the NBA, much like the one that exists in pro baseball and hockey. Although he did not have official terms worked out with the NBA by any means, Isiah believed that in concert with the NCAA, the CBA could establish itself as a formal developmental league for the NBA.

"I think there's room for the NBA, NCAA and CBA to work together in a collective effort," he told CNN/*Sports Illustrated.* "What's happening with the guys leaving school early, it's important that we continue to stress that athletics and academics go hand in hand. With the NCAA and CBA players playing against each other, it's a good chance for the [college] players to gauge their skills. And we will continue to stress education in the CBA by teaching life skills to NCAA players in the exhibition competitions."

Early on in his ownership, though — just a few weeks after the purchase of the league was announced, in fact — Thomas began making moves that, to put it mildly, did not draw raves from the CBA's players and fans. He imposed league-wide salary restrictions, dropping the upper limit on rookies' pay to $800 a week, and lowering the average weekly salary from $1,500 to $1,100. As several commentators noted, Thomas was able to do this because the CBA did not have a players' union, and because, as a "single entity" owner, he was more than likely exempt from any anti-trust laws that would normally prevent such a move. (Of course the same critics also noted that there was some irony in the fact that the same guy who was proposing these salary restrictions was, at one time, head of the National Basketball Players Association, the union that, in the NBA, is constantly pushing for the exact opposite type of employer/employee relationship.)

Ultimately, all did not go well with Isiah's attempts to run the CBA — and that's an understatement as far as the league's owners, fans and players are concerned. Unable to secure a commitment from the NBA to work with the CBA as a true developmental league — the NBA had plans of its own to start its own farm organization — and unable to attract any solid sponsorship, the CBA struggled financially until February, 2001, just 16 months after the Thomas purchase, when it suspended play in the midst of Isiah's attempts to sell the teams to local businesspeople. Reports in the Associated Press and the *Indianapolis Star* said that in addition to trying to sell the league back to local owners, Thomas still owed $750,000 from the original sale of the team.

"After a long and exhaustive process," read a press release from CBA headquarters in Phoenix, "the trustee for the Isiah Thomas blind trust has determined it is in the best interest of all parties concerned to return all CBA teams back to local ownership."

And for his part, Isiah sounded disappointed that things did not work out. "My love of the game drove my decision to purchase the CBA. I wanted to give others the chance to pursue their dreams of playing in the NBA," he said in announcing the suspension of play. "It is the decision of the blind trust for the CBA to revert to local ownership. Though disappointing to me personally, the decision allows basketball to continue in the cities that have supported the CBA for many years. This will be good for the players and the communities."

It would be a huge mistake, though, to see Isiah's decision to walk away from CBA ownership as simply an altruistic move towards supporting pro ball in smaller communities. The true fact of the matter is that, in the face of the league not making the kind of sponsorship money and other revenue profits that had been anticipated, and the NBA's unwillingness to play ball, Isiah had received a much better offer, in the summer of 2000, than trying to keep a sinking league afloat — an offer that represented a longtime dream come true for him: after some negotiating with GM Donnie Walsh and other members of the Indiana Pacers' management, Isiah was offered the head coaching job of the perennial Eastern Conference contender, at a reported $20 million over four years.

For anyone who knew Isiah and had followed his career, the chance to coach in the bigs was way too good to be true. Even better, the opportunity came in a basketball-mad state where he'd had a chance to strut his stuff on the college courts a couple of decades earlier, and on a team that had just gone through an excellent, 3-year rebuilding phase behind the coaching of another NBA great (and former Thomas rival) Larry Bird. Too good to pass up, indeed.

There was, however, a snag: The NBA has, understandably, a conflict-of-interest rule that states that their head coaches cannot hold down executive positions — and "owner" would definitely qualify — in other basketball leagues. So the NBA's top brass ordained that Thomas had to get rid of his majority share in the CBA.

"There's a perceived conflict of interest, and, like any other businessman you will resolve that conflict when it's there," he said during the 2000 NBA finals, during which he worked as an NBC analyst. "There are millions of conflicts in businesses, and people sit down at the table and they resolve those conflicts."

At least a few members of Isiah's new Pacers family

supported his decision to sell the CBA — but then again, perhaps they were just glad that he had made the jump from CBA owner to NBA coach. "He did everything he could to make this come out right," said Donnie Walsh. "And he's handled this with the most unbelievable temperament and class of anyone I've ever known in a situation like this."

Of course, it would have been unrealistic for the CBA owners to feel quite the same degree of admiration for the way Thomas had "handled" the situation. "The league has been around for 55 years and it took him 12 months to ruin it," griped Rich Coffey, general manager of the Ft. Wayne (Indiana) Fury. "The responsibility lies with him. He had a lack of understanding for the minor league basketball culture. [It's] like leasing a car, driving it and banging it up for a few weeks and then returning it to the dealer and saying it's his problem now."

Others with an interest in the CBA were a lot more direct. "He can hide behind the corporation, the blind trust or Mother Mary for all I care," said Bill Bosshard, the former owner of the LaCrosse (Wisconsin) Bobcats. "He convinced the owners of his vision. Then he realized he couldn't turn over the profit he envisioned, he couldn't get the corporate sponsors, his business plan was faulty, everything was going bankrupt, so he figured 'I better grab a coaching job' and he abandoned us."

Without the money to pay players, the CBA was in serious trouble. By early February, the CBA had suspended play. And by the end of that month, the league had filed for Chapter 7 bankruptcy. But with Isiah out of the picture in the day-to-day operation of the league, the owners, still seeking to get as much money back from Thomas and IT Acquisitions, decided that the CBA would not die.

Five of the 10 teams were bought back by former owners —
who disavowed themselves of any financial responsibility for
their old teams, saying that was Isiah's problem — and those
teams joined up with the International Basketball League,
another not-quite-NBA caliber group of pro teams. (At the time
of writing, the CBA is still operating as an independent league,
with eight franchises set to start play at the beginning of the
2004–05 season.)

●　●　●

Larry Bird had been an excellent coach for the Indiana Pacers,
taking them all the way to the NBA finals in 1999–2000. Of
course, Bird had always been popular in Indiana, ever since
his college days. And taking the Pacers to the finals was just
another way that the "Hick from French Lick" was able to
cement his legendary status among hoops fans in the Hoosier
state. (The Pacers lost to the Shaq-led Lakers in six games, but
nobody seemed to expect any other result, or to mind all that
much.) What's more, Bird had shown that, far from being a
figurehead who deferred on all important matters to anonymous assistant coaches, a relatively recently retired NBA
legend could command the respect of a pro team, and inspire
them to play well almost every night.

So the pressure was on Isiah to produce for the Pacers, right
away. But, truth to tell, that production, at least in his first season
behind the bench, was not what Indiana fans, who had seen their
squad finish with a 56–26 record the year before, had come to
expect. But then again, the team that Isiah inherited was a much
different — and, most experts agreed, much weaker — team

than the one that had made it to the finals. Gone were point guard and team leader Mark Jackson (via free agency), power forward Antonio Davis (traded), big man Rik Smits (retirement due to injury), Dale Davis (who was traded to Portland for Jermaine O'Neal), and Chris Mullin (also via free agency).

Despite that major change in team chemistry, Isiah managed to rally the Pacers to a .500 season (at 41–41), and the eighth and final spot in the Eastern Conference playoffs. There, they faced the number-one seeded Philadelphia 76ers, stunning them in the first game of the opening-round series before losing three close contests and being eliminated in the best-of-five series. During 2000–01, Thomas worked hard to develop three key young players — O'Neal, Al Harrington, and Jeff Foster — who would contribute mightily in the years to come. In fact, O'Neal, who had entered the NBA as an 18-year-old straight out of high school and struggled in Portland, responded immediately to Isiah's guidance, leading the league in double-doubles (10 or more points and rebounds per game) his first year as a Pacer. As well, Isiah was able to mix these younger players with older, more established guys like veterans Reggie Miller, Sam Perkins, and Jalen Rose.

"I'd say there's a learning curve that every coach goes through — learning your team, learning their tendencies . . . learning what they can and cannot do," Thomas said towards the end of 2000–01. "You know, it's different from watching players play on television, and then actually coaching them and being around them every day for practice situations. There were a lot of different points within the season where our team was right on the brink of playing really bad basketball. Then they'll come back and play good basketball. I think it was all a learning process, a growth process with our young players understanding what it takes to win every single night and going out and trying to apply that."

As well, Thomas knew that he was going to have to make some serious adjustments in his mindset as a he moved from player to coach, especially given the fact that players approached the game — and the salaries they made playing it — a whole lot differently than they did back in his playing days. But at least he was able to draw on some expertise garnered from his business career in dealing with the challenge.

"One of the things that struck me early on was how challenging it can be to manage a group of multi-millionaires," he said. "Imagine what it would be like for a businessman if each of his employees won the lottery but had to keep working for him to get the checks. So, that's what it's like to coach a professional basketball team."

Early on in the 2000–01 season, though, Isiah did get a break from the pressures of NBA coaching, via an event that truly cemented his status as one of the NBA's greatest players. In October, he was inducted into the Naismith Basketball Hall of Fame in Springfield, Mass, an honor that, when combined with his 1996 naming as one of the 50 greatest players all time, certainly established him as one of the sport's greats.

While a .500 record and an opening round knockout might not sound like much for a team that had made the NBA finals the year before, many NBA observers believed that in his first season as coach, Thomas had passed a major test with his much-altered roster. And one of those observers was Donnie Walsh, the Pacers GM who had hired Isiah to helm the team. "I think he accomplished a lot," Walsh told the *Indianapolis Star*.

"He played a lot of younger players and he tried to find a symmetry that could win games, although he sacrificed a lot to do that. I think he showed a lot of sophistication. By the end, I thought his bench coaching was terrific."

And even though the team did go through an up-and-down year, Isiah's players ended up with a playoff season that vindicated the faith their coach had in them — and they in him. "We never discussed the possibility of not being a playoff team," said Rose. "We just always discussed the possibility of how bad we wanted to be one. . . . Obviously there were a lot of people who thought, felt and wondered out loud whether we had what it takes to be a playoff team. Obviously, we silenced them real quick."

With his rookie coaching year in the books, Thomas went to work building an even better team for 2001–02, exhorting the players to push themselves in their summer conditioning programs. What he did not know was that in the following NBA season, he would have yet another challenge — one that is all too common for pro hoops coaches — of managing a constantly shifting roster.

Midway through the season, the Pacers shipped Jalen Rose and point guard Travis Best to the Chicago Bulls. In return, they acquired center Brad Miller — a former Pacer — guard Kevin Ollie and, perhaps most significantly, guard Ron Artest. A college standout at St. John's, Artest had developed a reputation as a skilled defender with a good offensive game to boot — and a nasty, scrappy personality that got him into more than a few scrapes on the court with NBA rivals. In fact, many commentators pointed out that Artest seemed cut from the same cloth as Isiah's Bad Boys of the championship years.

With a late-season surge, Isiah's Pistons made the playoffs for the second straight year, finishing just slightly better than the year before at 42–40, and pushing the Nets to five games in the first round before bowing out. But with new additions Miller and Artest moving into starting roles, the team was starting to gel significantly — a fact that became all too apparent as 2002–03 got underway.

● ● ●

Despite an injury to Reggie Miller, the new-look Pacers came galloping out of the gate in '02–'03, winning 12 of their first 14 games. The led the Eastern Conference at the All-Star break (garnering Isiah the role of the East's coach in the All-Star game), and in the first half of the season had only lost three games at home. Point guard Jamaal Tinsley was one of the NBA's leading assist men, while Miller was starting to remind people of Bill Laimbeer, another Bad Boy, with excellent rebounding, decent scoring and, above, superb defending. Artest continued his stellar ways on "D" while scoring well, and Miller was able to bounce back from his injury with a solid return. And O'Neal was having a breakout year, averaging 19 points and 12 rebounds a game (number three in the league) in the early going.

But in mid-February, following a three-game winning streak, the team seemed to fall apart. They proceeded to drop 12 of their next 13 games, and 19 of their last 30, and ended up finishing third in the East with a 48–34 record — a serious improvement over the previous two years, but far from stellar for a team that had started so well.

At least, thought the Pacers' loyal fans, the squad could regroup for the playoffs, where they would face the under-achieving Boston Celtics, sixth in the East that year. Unfortunately for the Pacers, the Celts chose that series as a good time to start playing like they were supposed to all season and, behind the leadership of their star forward Paul Pierce, beat Isiah's guys on the Pacers' home floor in game one of their first-round series. And although the loss — which effectively forfeited home-court advantage for Indiana — was tough to take, it was the way it came that made things even more galling, since the Pacers had actually led by 17 points, as late as the fourth quarter, no less.

Although Isiah's Pacers fought hard the rest of the way, they were no match for the rejuvenated, Pierce-inspired Celtics, and lost their third consecutive opening-round NBA playoffs series in six games.

No matter how much hoops buffs had admired Isiah's acumen as a player, the trio of early exits raised all sorts of questions about Isiah's ability to coach an NBA team, heading into the summer of 2003.

And, as was so often the case with Thomas, the answer was just around the corner.

CHAPTER TWELVE

Out and Back Again

By many observers' standards, Isiah Thomas was doing a pretty good job coaching the Indiana Pacers. At the end of the 2002–03 season, it was easy to look at his three NBA campaigns calling the shots for the Pacers and see continual improvement. In 2000–01, the Pacers went 41–41, followed by  a 42–40 season the next year, and an impressive 48–34 in 2002–03. That's a 131–115 record overall, and it's worth pointing out that in those three seasons, the Pacers did not fail to make the playoffs.

What's more, Thomas's critics pointed out that although the Pacers did indeed make it three straight post-seasons, they failed to win any of their first round playoff matchups. And even more glaring was the team's apparent choke after the phenomenal start they made in 2002–03. Up to the All-Star break, the Pacers had the best record in the East (which made Isiah the conference's coach in the All Star game) and then proceeded to go 14–19 the rest of the season, ending things by making a pretty unimpressive, six-game exit in the first round of the Eastern Conference playoffs at the hands of the Boston Celtics. (What many people did not know, however, was that the team had been hit by off-court problems beyond anyone's control, affecting the team's play on the court as point guard Jamaal Tinsley's mother was dying of cancer, and Jermaine O'Neal's stepfather attempted suicide during the 2002–03 season.)

There were also some rumors around the league that the Indianapolis-based team occasionally suffered from more than a little bickering and dissent behind the scenes, that Isiah was inconsistent with the way he ran his practices and with his shifting views about whether the Pacers were going to be an offense-first team, or a squad of defensive specialists. And, perhaps most persistent were the rumors that Thomas leaned heavily on the expertise of his assistants — most notably, Brendan Malone, the guy Thomas had fired as Raptors' head man back at the end of the Toronto team's first season — to call the shots when the going got tough.

But, as Thomas knew all too well, the NBA was a league that was fuelled by innuendo and gossip — a place where rumors about grumbling superstars and soon-to-be-canned coaches were reported in the media with as much fervor as game-winning jump shots and three-point percentages. Certainly, at least as far as things looked to any objective observer at the end of the 2002–03 season, Isiah Thomas was in the midst of establishing himself as a true, bona fide NBA coach.

• • •

But the NBA, just like life in the real world, is full of surprises. In the big leagues, there's no truer saying than "what goes around, comes around." And as far as Isiah's coaching career in Indiana was concerned, that maxim was going to hit him square in the face at the end of the 2002–03 season.

Looking at things with the advantage of hindsight, it appeared as though the beginning of the end for Isiah in Indiana really took place in June, as the 2002–03 season wound down. That's when none other than Larry Bird took over from Donnie Walsh, the man who had hired Isiah to coach the Pacers, as the team's president of basketball operations, with Walsh staying on as CEO of the franchise. Of course, Bird was the guy Isiah replaced as Pacer's coach in 2000, after the former Celtic great wound up his own three-year pro coaching career in Indiana with the a trip to the NBA finals.

But, as most NBA fans knew, Bird was also a long-time rival of Isiah's, dating way back to the times when the two battled it out on the court in the 1980s. And, what's more, there was always the persistent rumor that Bird had never really forgiven Isiah for the did-he-or-didn't he part that Thomas was supposed to have played in the "Bird would just be an ordinary player if he were black" debate sparked by Dennis Rodman when Isiah and The Worm were Pistons' teammates.

Whether or nor Bird still bore a grudge — or still harbored any resentments from his playing days — one thing was undisputable: just eight weeks after coming on board as a member of the Pacers' management, Bird fired Isiah as the team's head coach on August 27, 2003 — and almost immediately installed Rick Carlisle as his replacement.

Of course, you didn't have to be much of an NBA insider to know that Carlisle had been a friend of Bird's when the two had been teammates with the Celtics — and, even more significantly, had been the Hall-of-Famer's assistant when Bird had coached the Pacers during his three-year stint behind the bench in Indiana. But Carlisle had also been an increasingly unpopular head coach in Detroit — so unpopular, according to one story making the rounds at the time of his hiring in Indiana, that Piston's star big man Ben Wallace had thrown a going-away party for Carlisle without actually inviting the departing coach.

At any rate, given the fact that some of the more contentious members of the Pacers, including Ron Artest and Jermaine O'Neal, had actually been able to get their heads into basketball and out of squabbling under Isiah's leadership, letting Thomas go was a strange move indeed. O'Neal in particular had signed a seven-year, $126 million contract with the Pacers in early-August, just a few weeks before Thomas's firing, on a promise from the team's top brass that Isiah would be around to coach him in Indiana for a long time to come.

"Without saying too much, bottom line, am I happy about it? No," O'Neal told Ric Bucher of *ESPN.com.* "If it wasn't for Isiah Thomas, I wouldn't be here. He's the reason I'm not only the player I am, but the father I am and the son I am. I don't care who you get to coach the team. If you don't get players who play hard every night, you're not going to win."

Thomas had accompanied the U.S. men's team on a trip to Puerto Rico for a qualifying tournament (where O'Neal was a member of the American squad), and learned of the firing there. Upon his return to the States, he said that he was "taken totally off guard" by the decision. And like most shocking information, there was a good-news/bad-news dynamic for Isiah. The good news was that the Pacers agreed to honor the one remaining year on his coaching contract, which he'd inked in agreeing to helm the team to the end of the 2003–04 season. The bad news was that, with the firing coming so late in the summer, it was going to be difficult — if not impossible — for him to find another coaching gig before the start of the upcoming NBA campaign.

Of course, Bird and the Pacers could always point to the previous season's self-destruction campaign — and the team's failure to get past Round One of the playoffs as justification. "I've known Isiah for a long time. I don't think it was going to work," Bird was quoted as saying, in the *Detroit News*. "I don't want to get into details, but we need a new style. After looking at the film, seeing how things were and evaluating the basketball operations, I detected the chemistry wasn't what it should be."

Donnie Walsh, the Pacers president and CEO, spoke in similar front-office lingo in attempting to explain the decision. "When I hired Isiah [in 2000], I thought he was the right man for the job at the time, and he was," said Walsh. "But as our team has evolved, the decision was made that it's time to go in a different direction. We appreciate what Isiah has done in his three seasons here."

With a bit of time to reflect on the firing, Thomas had to admit that he still could not figure out what had gone wrong. In one of *ESPN.com*'s famous "10 Burning Questions" interviews on its *Page 2* web site, Thomas was asked if the decision by the Pacers' management continued to bother him.

"I haven't found the place to put it yet. It was such a shock and it was so unexpected," Thomas replied. "I'm still trying to deal with it. To me, I can only look at it and say, you know, there was a change in management, and Bird wanted a friend of his to coach the team. He played with Carlisle and coached with Carlisle and basically wanted his friend to coach, and that's the only way I can look at it."

Regardless of how Thomas chose to interpret the Indiana situation in his own mind, one thing rang true: he was out of a job. Of course, as he'd been saying ever since his early days as a Raptors exec., Isiah didn't need a weekly paycheck to put food on the table. He remained in basketball because he loved the game and, after all those years and all those experiences playing, managing and coaching, still found it enjoyable and a field to which he could still contribute. And given the fighting spirit that had characterized his career from the time he was a little kid, Thomas was not about to let a shot from a rival — even if that rival was Larry Bird — keep him down for very long.

As a guy in his early 40s, Thomas still believed he had a lot to offer an NBA team in some capacity, and it was coaching that attracted him the most. "My best personality comes out in the gym," he told *Toronto Sun* basketball reporter Bill Harris a few weeks after the Indiana firing, while watching a Pistons practice as a guest of Detroit coach Larry Brown. "I can wear a suit and tie and handle myself in a boardroom, but the most fun I've ever had in my life has been in the gym. I've been going to the gym ever since I was three years old so if I can make a job out of it, that's great . . . Any time you're in a gym, around basketball, guys sweating, that's what you like."

In fact, Thomas's visit to the Pistons' practice was part of his attempt to visit various NBA teams as they held training camps and practices in the very early days of the 2003–04 season, as they attempted to get ready for the NBA wars ahead. For Isiah, it was a chance to take some notes that he hoped would help him if — and when — he should return to a behind-the-bench position with a pro club. And it was a sign of the high esteem in which Thomas was still held by many NBA coaches that they would allow him to sit in on these sessions.

"It's a great chance for me to learn from some of the best basketball minds," he explained. "It's different than when I was a player. You saw a guy with a good move, you tried to copy that move and put it into your game. But when you are coaching in this league, you're pretty much alone."

Luckily for Isiah and his coaching aspirations, he was not going to be on his own for very much longer.

●   ●   ●

As one of the legendary franchises in the NBA, the New York Knicks have also been the home of some pretty amazing players as well. In recent memory, players such as Dave DeBusschere, Bill Bradley, Earl Monroe, Willis Reed, Walt Frazier, Ernie Grunfeld, and Bernard King have been among the league's most popular players, while Knicks of a more recent vintage such as Patrick Ewing, Larry Johnson, John Starks and Latrell Sprewell have also supplied their fair share of NBA excitement over the last decade or so. Indeed, in 1999, the Knicks shocked everyone by making it all the way to the NBA finals after a fairly lackluster year.

But since then, things hadn't been so rosy in the Big Apple

as far as basketball fans are concerned, with the Knicks missing the playoffs in both 2001–02 and 2002–03. And as the 2003–04 season progressed, it looked as though things were not going to get any better for the Knicks, under coach Don Chaney and a team of journeyman players, with Sprewell having left New York for Minnesota, where he was quickly helping the Timberwolves become a top contender.

New York needed a shakeup, and Thomas was just the guy to do it. Just before Christmas, James Dolan, the chair of the Knicks' corporate owner, Cablevision, announced that the team was terminating Scott Layden as president. And while that firing was no surprise, the announcement of Isiah as Layden's replacement certainly was. Almost everybody around the league had expected Isiah to return to the NBA as a coach, and not a front-office exec, especially given his presence, after he was let go in Indiana, at all those team practices and training camps. But the move did give Isiah the chance to start making an impact on an NBA team right away — and a struggling one at that. While it wasn't a coaching gig, it was certainly one that put his name right back in the sports headlines, in the world capital of hype and media attention.

For his part, Dolan summed up the move as one that was needed from both a basketball perspective, and a business one. "I don't think there is any question that everybody is under-performing. Just look at our record," he told reporters gathered at the press conference where Layden's firing was announced. "This is the thing we could do right now that would most help the team."

Isiah agreed that help was needed, and he knew that the first step in his dealings with his new team was to bring his expertise as a guy who knows the ins and outs of every aspect of a successful team to the struggling franchise. "We've got players and coaches probably a little bit unsure of what's going on," Thomas said at the press conference. "And my job is to come in here and calm the waters."

If anyone wasn't feeling calm upon Isiah's appointment as Knicks' president, it had to be the team's coach, Don Chaney. Not only were the New Yorkers struggling on the court under his guidance, but Isiah's desire to return to coaching was well known. Was it possible that Chaney could find himself being canned, by a Hall-of-Fame player who was then going to turn around and name himself as his replacement? As it turned out, Chaney did not have to wait long at all to find out.

But before addressing the Knicks' coaching needs, Thomas had some even quicker decisions in mind — ones that involved moving players that he believed would be of no help to the flailing franchise, and bringing in those that could contribute right away. For starters, he made a relatively unimportant move, waiving the huge but never-used, 7–5 center Slavko Vranes. And then, on December 30, he made an important one. On that day, Thomas traded forward Clarence Witherspoon to the Houston Rockets for point guard Moochie Norris and forward John Amaechi. Right away, the trade had folks all around the NBA scratching their heads. Certainly Witherspoon was never going to be one of the all-time greats, but he'd always been a rugged, dependable scorer with a solid work ethic. In return, the Knicks were getting Norris, a fair point guard but one with "career backup" written all over him, and Amaechi, another run-of-the-mill player who had looked good early in his career in Orlando, but had not done very much for the

Rockets. (In fact, the Knicks put Amaechi on waivers less than two weeks after he'd arrived in New York.)

So, many skeptical Knicks fans must have thought upon hearing that Witherspoon was no longer on their team, this was the way Isiah Thomas was going to bring salvation to the venerable New York Knicks — by trading for mediocre players?

The following week, Isiah was able to silence those doubters, giving them a New Year's gift for 2004 that suggested that he might actually know what he was doing. On January 5, the Knicks announced that they were making a complicated trade. Thomas sent guards Howard Eisley and Charlie Ward (the one-time Heisman trophy winner), and Antonio McDyess, a former superstar with Denver who had done relatively little with the Knicks, along with Polish big man Maciej Lampe, the rights to guard Milos Vujanic of Serbia and Montenegro, a 2004 first-round draft pick and cash, to the Pheonix Suns. And in return, the Knicks picked up guard Stephon Marbury, an NYC playground product, plus the injury-prone one-time superstar Anfernee Hardaway, and Polish center Cezary Trybanski.

Leaving aside the European players and the draft picks, the trade was, essentially, Eisley, Ward and McDyess for Marbury and Hardaway. And that meant that the Knicks were getting two players who, Isiah hoped, would be able to kick-start their careers in New York — careers that had started promisingly enough but had fizzled somewhat in Phoenix. It was a risky move, especially since the high-pressure crucible of the Big Apple could be a disastrous place for a comeback for any player if things did not go well.

The move to New York was certainly a good one for Marbury — or "Starbury" as he was often called. The point guard, who had grown up in the Coney Island section of NYC before heading off to college at Georgia Tech, had always shown that he had prime offensive skills. But it always looked like he'd never quite hit his stride during his NBA stops in New Jersey and Phoenix. Now, with a chance to play in front of a hometown crowd and with the opportunity to lead a squad that looked to be making all the right moves towards improving its chances and perhaps even qualifying for the Eastern Conference play-offs, Marbury had a chance to really show his stuff.

With the big Phoenix trade, Isiah wasn't done his house-cleaning barrage — not by a long shot. Not surprisingly, it was the Knicks coaching staff that got the broom treatment next. On January 14, the team announced the firing of Chaney, who had amassed a dismal 72–112 record with the Knicks, along with assistant coaches Brendan Malone (the same Brendan Malone who'd coached for Isiah in Toronto and been his assistant in Indiana) and Lon Kruger, and was replacing them with none other than Lenny Wilkens.

The move to hire the 66-year-old Wilkens came as a huge surprise around the NBA, where longtime veteran Mike Fratello had been tapped to move into the Knicks job. A former super-star guard who played for St. Louis, Cleveland, Seattle and Portland during a 15-year NBA career, Wilkens had been inducted into the Hall of Fame in 1989. And as a coach, he was the league's all-time wins leader. But at his most recent coaching stop, Lenny had been, by most people's assessment, far from a raging success. As the head guy in Toronto from 2000 to 2003, Wilkens compiled a 113–133 record over three years, and was at the Raptors' helm for several disappointing seasons, ones in which he was accused of failing to motivate a talented team that included superstar Vince Carter, and ones in which the injury-plagued team never went as far as it should have in the playoffs. In all fairness, though, Wilkens had been constantly faced with a team of players — most notably Carter — that was constantly battling injuries.

The Knicks became Wilkens' sixth NBA coaching stop. Of course, the rumors still persisted that Isiah continued to have coaching aspirations, and that Wilkens was simply being brought in as a temporary gap-filler until the end of 2003–04, at which point Thomas would take over the reigns. Those rumors were unfounded though, and, at the time of writing, Wilkens was all set to lead the team into the 2004–05 season.

Many in the media felt that Isiah had in fact handled the Chaney firing/Wilkens hiring shabbily, giving the outgoing coach very little notice that he was going to be axed. But, clearly, Chaney was not unprepared for the move. Fans had taken to chanting "fire Chaney," and under his guidance the Knicks had fallen to 10th spot in the East. Still, though, it appeared that the coach did not receive the final word of his termination until his final practice, after which Isiah announced that he was gone. "Without hearing anything one way or another is a sign of disrespect to a degree," Chaney said, simply, while Thomas countered, just as simply, that he had never been in the habit of delivering 24-hour status updates to anyone — player or coach.

Despite the messiness that surrounded the coaching switch, many hailed the hiring of Wilkens in New York as a sign that things were going to turn around. By bringing in the winningest coach in NBA history, and a low-key one at that, Thomas was telling the Knicks players and fans that he was looking for results. For Wilkens, the coaching move was a chance to return to his home town, and for players like Marbury, it was a chance to improve their careers by getting close to a proven veteran. "I know he's a winner," said the Knicks new point guard. "I know he's won. Everyone I know who's had contact with him said he's the ultimate players' coach," Marbury said.

Two days after the Wilkens hiring, Thomas also hired his longtime friend and former Bad Boys teammate Mark Aguirre as a Knicks assistant coach.

The following month, Thomas was back at it in the trading department. This time, it was forward Keith Van Horn and center Michael Doleac who were leaving the Knicks, Horn going to the Milwaukee Bucks in exchange for Tim Thomas, and Doleac to the Atlanta Hawks for big man Nazr Mohammed.

Van Horn, a University of Utah grad, had been a solid contributor to the success of the New Jersey Nets and the Philadelphia 76ers at the start of his career, but had never really clicked in New York. Although he was a good outside shooter and had some nice moves around the basket, fans and teammates in both New York and New Jersey sometimes questioned his toughness. As well, in unloading Doleac, Thomas was looking to make the Knicks stronger and quicker at the center position. Although the team still had ace shot-blocker Dikembe Mutumbo, the African star would turn 38 by the end of the 2003–04 season. Adding Mohammed to the roster would give the Knicks a younger center who could score and be active on offence — things neither Doleac or Mutumbo could give the Knicks.

Still, letting go of Van Horn was not easy for Isiah — especially since he'd grown to like the forward's game. "It's probably one of the most difficult trades I've ever had to make, simply because of my fondness for Keith," said Isiah at the press conference that announced the trade. "However, I felt that in getting an additional big man with Nazr Mohammed, it really solidifies our front line. . . . We wanted to get tougher from a rebounding standpoint and a physical standpoint."

Adding Tim Thomas was another plus for the Knicks, especially from the offensive perspective. In his four-plus seasons with the Bucks, Tim (another Thomas for the Knicks, joining Isiah and Kurt) averaged an excellent 14.1 points a game, along with 4.9 rebounds. Although New York would miss Van Horn's scoring touch, they would certainly find that gap made up by Tim Thomas.

Isiah was not quite done with his roster revisions, though. In March, he made two more significant player moves, signing fan favorite Kurt Thomas to a four-year contract extension, and signing the former All-Star Vin Baker to a short-term contract as well.

The two players could not have been more different, but both promised to help the Knicks. Baker had been a standout with the Bucks early in his career, but personal problems off the court had contributed to a rapid slide in his game and his confidence. It looked as though New York was truly going to be last-chance city for the veteran player, and it must have been gratifying for Baker that a veteran talent-spotter like Thomas still saw enough game in him that he was willing to take a chance.

Kurt Thomas was a different story. Never the flashiest player, the "other Thomas" (no relation to Isiah) had spent six seasons — through good times and bad — with the Knicks, making him the player with the second-longest stint on the New York roster, behind Allan Houston. Fans loved his blue-collar work ethic and determination, as well as his involvement in a number of charities and community groups. And Kurt put up good numbers, too, with career stats of 11.2 points per game, and 7.4 rebounds a game, as a Knick.

So when Isiah offered him the four-year extension, it was a move aimed at both keeping a solid team player happy, and telling the fans that a trustworthy, go-to guy would be rewarded on his team. "Rewarding Kurt for his hard work and devotion to the organization, both on and off the court, is the reason we have given him this extension," said Isiah. "His toughness and civic-mindedness epitomizes everything that a Knicks player should be."

As Thomas made his front-office moves in an effort to make the Knicks stronger, something began to happen: the team actually started to win some games. By springtime, there was even talk of the Knicks making a playoff run — something unimaginable back in the pre-Isiah dark days at the start of the 2003–04 season.

Clearly, much of that success could be attributed to the reju-venated play of Stephon Marbury. Perhaps it was the vote of confidence shown in him by one of the all-time greats at his position that spurred him on, or perhaps he just responded well to the directions of the man he called the "ultimate player's coach." Or maybe it was just a chance to be back playing in front of family and friends at Madison Square Garden that resulted in an elevation in Marbury's game. Whatever it was, it's safe to say that Stephon had a career year in 2003–04, and that his stellar year went a long way towards making the Knicks a much better team.

Marbury put up 20 points and 9 assists a game, and led the

Knicks to a 39–43 record, less than stellar in terms of winning percentage, but still good enough for 7th place in the East — and good enough, too, for a playoff spot. Coming down to crunch time in the late spring of 2004, the team, buoyed by Marbury, Houston, Mohammed and Kurt and Tim Thomas, kept its cool and held on for the playoff spot. They were bounced in four physical games by the Nets in the first round, but for die-hard fans of the team, just making it to the post-season was a huge improvement over the way they had started the year with coach Chaney, and the way they'd performed in the past couple of seasons.

• • •

Looking ahead to 2004–05, Isiah and the Knicks had a lot to be confident about. They had signed rookie Mike Sweetney from Georgetown, who looked to be a solid contributor to the future, and had added Jerome "Junkyard Dog" Williams, guard Jamal Crawford and Croatian big man Bruno Sundov to the roster as well. Clearly, with players like Hardaway and Houston eating up lots of space within the NBA's salary-cap rules, the Knicks were going to have to try to build a team of solid players, without signing a huge, bona fide superstar — and that's exactly the kind of challenge Isiah had been facing all his life.

"Anybody who looks at our cap situation, the first thing they say is, 'You can't fix it, you can't do this,'" he told reporters as he was considering player moves in the off-season before 2004–05 got started. "But I was a guy who came into the league at 6–1 and everybody told me I was crazy when I stood up and said the first day of training camp the Detroit Pistons would win the NBA championship."

And entering 2004–05, some experts were even saying that the Knicks had a chance to win the NBA's new Atlantic Division. And what did Isiah have to say about that challenge?

"I'm not going to run away from that," he told reporters at the Knicks' training camp in Greenburgh, NY in early October, just before the 2004–05 campaign got underway. "I like being expected to win. So if you say to me that we can win our Division, I say to you 'thank you.' I like everything that we have. We gave all our guys a mandate to improve themselves over the summer and they all did that. I'm comfortable with our smalls, I'm comfortable with our bigs, I'm comfortable with our interchangeability, I'm comfortable with our depth. We can play fast, slow, we can press, we can shoot from the outside or go with an inside game, we can play at any pace and play well. I think we have a team with an edge. I think we could have a very hot team here. I want the Garden to be a hot place again, with steam coming out of the stands. And I think this team can accomplish that."

That was good news to the ears of the Knicks faithful, and it bodes well for the future of the team. With Thomas leading the New York squad in the NBA wars for many years to come in the foreseeable future, it looked as though his unique brand of leadership would continue to make a real difference in Big Apple basketball.

A Life in Basketball

It's never easy to evaluate the life and career  of a famous sports figure like Isiah Thomas, and to put that life into some kind of perspective in light of larger social trends. There are some — and at times it's difficult not to agree with them — who espouse the "it's just a game" theory, arguing that no matter how much importance one wants to place on sports and their role in society, in the end they are simply hyped-up versions of kids' pastimes and deserve to be treated as such. But while this approach may contain a certain simplistic attraction, it just doesn't take into account the tremendous impact sports have on so many people.

Just take a look at the average Raptors' home game at SkyDome. For one thing, it's usually a pretty good bet that if you go to one, you'll be joined by several thousand other people — in numbers reaching well over 20,000 if one of the bigger draws of the NBA like the Lakers, Spurs or Pistons are in town. Any other event, like a rock concert or a religious revival, that drew those numbers would in most circles be labeled a major event: people coming together around a common interest in big numbers. Added to the concept of sheer human interaction in quantity, though, is the high level of excitement that usually accompanies an NBA game, in whatever league city it's being played. Maybe it's all the result of a big marketing campaign, but you can't deny that there's a tremendous emotional explosion that goes on several times a night during a pro basketball game.

One of the big reasons for all that emotion is that for all of the different people at an NBA game, there's something at stake. For many of the players, this represents their best opportunity to make as much money as possible, perhaps, as was the case with Isiah back in his playing days, to support an entire extended family. For others, the money is secondary to the sense of having "made it" by reaching the big leagues. For fans, the game might have a different importance. Maybe it's the key to securing an important business deal by impressing a client with those $150 seats and an expensive meal in a private box, or maybe it's the chance to see real-life heroes in action. And for those tied up in one of the myriad forms of sports-as-business — concession stands, front-office wrangling, agent-representation, or parking contracts — pro basketball is important because it represents the chance to make a living.

For Isiah Lord Thomas III, all of these elements have been at work as he's taken part in basketball at the highest levels as a player, coach, and executive. And that means that if you're looking for ways to assess his accomplishments as part of the bigger picture of the world around him — either as an armchair sports sociologist or just as a fan interested in more than scores and stats — there are two factors that make the task a little easier.

The first is his age. At only 43 at the time of writing, Isiah is still, by most standards, a relatively young man. Most of today's basketball fans can remember back easily enough to his playing career with the Detroit Pistons, if not his days at Indiana University. In fact, highlight film of Thomas became common in early 2004, as news reports of his being named to the Knicks president of basketball operations post were often accompanied by footage of him in action during his Pistons' days — action that did not look all that different than that being supplied by top point guards in the 2004 version of the game. And in addition to those on-court memories, Isiah's tenure with the Raptors, Pacers, CBA, and now the Knicks have provided even more recent memories. In all, given Thomas' penchant for action, he's managed to cram much more into less than half a century than most people do in an entire life.

The second, and much more significant factor that helps in analyzing Isiah's contributions, is that there are certain fundamental and time-specific divisions in his life that make it easy to split it into handy chunks. Dividing his existence into a basketball-playing part and a non-playing part, for example is helpful. So is using team affiliations as dividers — St. Joe's, IU, Pistons, Raptors, Pacers, and now the Knicks.

However one chooses to divide it up, though, there are certain very definite and enduring character traits that have transcended all the periods of Isiah's life. No matter what he's done — what his "job" has been at any given time or whose colors he's worn while doing it — five major, interrelated elements stand out throughout the short but vibrant existence of Isiah Thomas:

1) **He's a winner:** The first of these qualities is simply the desire to win. As a player, Isiah would do anything it took to win a game of basketball, and ultimately, to win whatever championship represented the ultimate achievement for his team. Playing injured, playing sick, playing tired — these were all part of the normal pattern of behavior for the man who wanted to win. Often, and especially during his career with the Pistons, Isiah would subdue whatever personal goals and aspirations he might have had — scoring titles, assist records, endorsement contracts, whatever — in favor of the greater glory of the team. Given the lucrative possibilities open to the basketball superstar, it must not have been easy to pass up on the chance to get rich based on his own personal achievements. But Isiah did it, convinced that back-to-back NBA titles were worth more than anything else in the long run.

It's the mark of someone who really wants to succeed that he is able to do a number of different things to reach his ultimate goal. When Isiah played, he was constantly changing his game to meet the needs of the situation. When his team needed scoring, he gave it to them. When someone else had the hot hand and needed the ball, he found that player with assists. If tough defence was required, he supplied it, just as he chipped in with the hard foul or sneaky shove when that's what was needed.

It might be argued that Isiah was not able bring that winning approach to his various activities after he'd hung up his sneakers and Pistons jersey. After all, looking at his record as GM of the Raptors, coach of the Pacers, part-owner of the CBA, and now VP of the Knicks, it's impossible to find any league championships. But while that may be a fair assessment in terms of titles won, such an analysis only tells part of the story. During his tenure in Toronto, Isiah's Raptors established themselves as a true presence both in the NBA and on the sporting scene in Canada's largest sports market. There is, after all, certainly no comparison with the way Isiah grew the Raptors in their early years, and the way their expansion counterparts the Grizzlies grew (or didn't) in Vancouver. From the beginning, Isiah stressed that he was willing to build the Raptors slowly, sacrificing a few wins in the early going for a championship down the road. Although he failed in his bid to gain control of the team and ultimately moved out of Toronto, it's tough to argue that Thomas's attempts to build a solid NBA franchise in a new market and a new country were not "wins" as far as long-term development was concerned.

Again, critics will maintain that as a coach of the Pacers, Isiah never won an NBA title. And while that is true as well, anyone with even the barest knowledge of how teams are built and how young players are developed will recognize that in Indiana, Thomas was able to take an extremely young team — and one that had enjoyed extremely limited success before his arrival — and turn it into a perennial playoff contender and regular challenger for the NBA's Eastern Division crown. And even though we'll likely never know what transpired between Thomas and his former on-court rival, Larry Bird, regarding Isiah's firing as Pacer's coach, it's still clear that the former All-Star point guard played a huge role in the development of at least one bona fide superstar in Jermaine O'Neal, who struggled early in his career as a just-out-of high school player in Portland, but really blossomed in Indiana under Isiah's tutelage.

At the time of writing, it was too soon to tell if Isiah Thomas was going to be able to put any kind of magic touch on the New York Knicks. Certainly his arrival in the 2003–04 season — and the trades and coaching shuffle he implemented immediately — did a lot to improve the Knicks' fortunes, turning them from a hopeless bunch to a playoff team. But then again, it would have been tough for New York to have gotten any worse, and most NBA experts were waiting around to see just how the team would fare in 2004–05 before passing judgment on just how well Thomas had done with the Big Apple's venerable Knickerbockers. But at the very least, his short-term rejuvenation of the Knicks into a playoff team, and his seeming resurrection of the team's best player, Stephon Marbury, into an Olympic pick and one of the NBA's top point guards at a relatively late stage in his career, have to be counted as wins.

Likely the one black mark that will count against Thomas, though, in the "winner" department, is his short-term tenure at the head of the CBA. Certainly, there are many former team owners in that league who would brand Isiah as anything but a winner based on his dealings with the league. And that's likely fair criticism. Perhaps the only saving grace, when the basketball historians look back on that one, major fiasco in Thomas's career, will be that, in addition to ending up on his own two feet as Pacers' coach, Isiah's CBA debacle proves that even winners have to lose sometimes.

2) He's tenacious: Closely tied to the concept of winning is that of tenacity. Tenacious people are ones who hold out against tough odds, and don't give up when the going gets really tough. As a player, Isiah fought against a number of very difficult obstacles and came out on top. Given his origins on the West Side, he could hardly have been blamed if he had failed in his quest to support his large family with an NBA paycheck. Indeed, it's unfortunate that a few of his brothers and many of his friends all had similar aspirations but never made it. Winning a scholarship to suburban St. Joseph's and then to IU, Isiah further exhibited the tenacity that more sociological minds might classify as having resulted in "social mobility." And as a player short in stature, Thomas had to be extra tenacious, especially in the NBA where many players would — and often did — just as soon have knocked him to the floor as let him past.

As a basketball executive, Isiah's tenacity has taken on a different form. As a black GM and part-owner of an NBA franchise in Toronto, he was in the minority, and had to constantly fight the stereotype that blacks make good players but should stay out of the boardrooms. Paradoxically, the NBA is a league dominated by black players on the court, and white officials in the front office. Race aside, as a brand new GM of a brand new team, Isiah was constantly facing a barrage of second-guessing and criticism from the media and his peers.

He faced the same dynamics as the Pacers' coach, and will certainly be subjected to the same scrutiny as a hands-on decision-maker in New York, the world's most fiercely competitive and critical sports market. But Isiah has always made the decisions he thinks he should make, shrugging off the criticism because he ultimately believes in his own judgment.

3) He's calculating: While tenacity can be classified as a character trait of the heart and soul, there's another quality that has shaped the life of Isiah Thomas — namely, calculation — that emanates directly from the brain. As a point guard, Isiah occupied the most analytical position on the floor. Like a chess master examining every possible variation in his head, Thomas had to read defences and react to them, all the while making sure that he kept his teammates in synch.

Using the mind's eye to map out events on the court before they happened is not the product of a clairvoyant, it just takes the right kind of intelligence combined with the pattern-recognition that comes from playing thousands of games on playgrounds, in gyms, and in stadiums. And being able to calculate rationally, when those around you are unable to through fatigue or lack of rationality, was what made Isiah such an effective point guard.

It's possible to observe this calculation in action outside the realm of Isiah's on-court activities, too. There's the very real sense that his ascension to the Raptors' front office was part of a very carefully-thought-out master plan that was hatched a long time ago. Indeed, Isiah started planning for a career in business well before retiring as a player, and almost as a reward for this fore-sight, his transition from player to executive was seamless. Indeed, there were very definite family directives that he had to "make it" one day, and Isiah himself decided that this process should involve a profitable life after a career as a basketball player.

In his decision-making with the Raptors, Thomas had to place all the pieces, very carefully and logically, into their proper slots. The fan base, the point guard, the coach, the big men, the merchandising, the marketing, the image — all were part of a carefully thought-out vision. Time and time again, the calculating part of Isiah told fans, reporters, and his coaching staff to look at the "big picture," to keep "the vision" in mind, in terms of winning games immediately versus winning games down the road. Judging that it was better to build a strong base than it is to construct an attractive façade, Thomas's calculating nature stressed his vision of long-term success.

Now, as VP of the Knicks, Thomas is stressing those same goals, attempting to build up a winning franchise by shrewd player moves that keep the realities of the modern NBA and its salary restrictions under consideration while trying to build the best team possible.

4) He's always in control: Directly tied to the theme of calculation in the life of Isiah Thomas is the idea of control. As a player, control meant two things for him. In the first sense of the word, it often fell upon Isiah to "take control" of a game and to do what needed to be done to win. Basketball lore is filled with instances where in a tight game, Thomas poured in an incredible number of points in a short span of time, or was a part of every play — offensive and defensive — in the final minutes of a victory.

Along with the concept of taking control is the idea of being "in control." As a floor leader, it's absolutely essential that a point guard be in control of both himself and of his team. Since almost every team play runs through him somehow, point guards like Isiah have to keep their presence of mind in the tensest of moments or their teams fall apart. Especially in the Pistons' two championship seasons and in IU's NCAA-winning campaign, one can see Isiah steadying his team with clutch jump shots and precision passing, as if he wanted to say "OK, guys, this is how it's done, nice and easy does it!"

In the front office of the Toronto Raptors, Isiah Thomas was all about staying in control. Overseeing each and every aspect of the new team's development, Isiah was the living embodiment of the franchise — the guy people thought of when they thought

"Raptor." Make no mistake, Isiah controlled the Raptors, and as fans noticed during the 1995–96 campaign, this control extended to his ability to pick new players, sign veterans, hire and fire coaches, and generate fan excitement in a new market. The level of control Isiah extended over the Raptors was virtually unprecedented, certainly so for a novice GM.

Clearly, the lessons Isiah learned while holding down the GM post in Toronto served him well when he moved to the coach's seat in Indiana, and are continuing to help him now that he is an exec in New York. It is obvious that, in the same way that the owners of the fledgling Raptors looked to Isiah as a "basketball guy" who would literally and figuratively be the face of basketball in the then-new NBA city of Toronto, the Knicks ownership wants to revitalize a struggling franchise by putting one of the game's legendary players and decision-makers at its helm, and letting him make the moves that will ultimately bring championship basketball back to the Big Apple.

Within the great controlling power he has, though, Isiah always manages to stay in control. Never revealing too much, always telling the media just what he wants them to hear, playing it close to the vest as far as his intentions on drafting, signing, and firing, Isiah exhibits the same coolness under fire as a GM as he did from behind the three-point line.

5) He's a leader: The final big characteristic that comes through constantly in the life Isiah Thomas is also likely the most obvious one. Throughout his entire career as both a basketball player and a basketball businessman, the one, shining trait that Isiah has demonstrated is leadership.

As a player, this leadership exhibited itself in ways that were pretty evident. Of course, the point guard of any team is its nominal leader; the very fact that he gets to handle the ball more than anyone else and usually calls out the pre-set plays designated by the coach means the player at this position has to take on a leadership role to a large extent. But Isiah took this principle much farther than a few hand signals and a lot of assists. In many ways, he was the spiritual and emotional leader of the Bad Boys. His desire to win, his tenacity, his calculation, and his ability to control a game — all rolled into a package that comprised the complete on-court leader. It was Isiah who would kick the coaches out of the locker room for players-only meetings, and who would ride those Pistons he thought were slacking or hot-dogging for personal gain, while praising the guys who were digging deep.

One of the remarkable things about leaders is that they seem to bring out hidden talents and extra efforts in those around them. While certain Pistons were, without a doubt, talented athletes, and good, and perhaps even great, players — guys like Bill Laimbeer, Joe Dumars, Dennis Rodman, or John Salley — playing with Isiah seemed to make them that much better. Perhaps it was the fear of a tongue-lashing from Thomas that kept them going. Indeed, Isiah's old Chicago buddy Mark Aguirre, who'd been known around the NBA and earlier at Dallas as a whiner and a selfish player, completely changed his game around under Isiah's exhortations in Detroit because he was able to internalize his friend's desire to win. It wasn't just that Isiah could make his teammates better by helping them to score more off brilliant passing, although that was certainly part of it. Instead, it was Isiah's example and his straight up, unsolicited advice, criticism, and praise that elevated his teammates to the championship level.

As a GM, coach and exec, Isiah has made those around him better as well. His faith in players like Damon Stoudamire in Toronto, Jermaine O'Neal in Indiana, and Stephon Marbury in New York — all of whom have had their skeptics, critics, and unbelievers — has been repaid by hard effort, determination, and improvement. It's almost as if a light goes off and the player says, "Hey, if one of the all-time greats believes in me, maybe I should, too!"

As GM of the Raptors, Isiah's leadership worked on another level as well. To a great extent, he led professional basketball into Canada. As part owner and GM of the Raptors, he was responsible for the team coming to Toronto, the image they conveyed, the players they presented to fans, the way they played the game, and even the hats and T-shirts people wore on the street. In a market previously dominated by hockey, Isiah managed to serve up the NBA in ways that were most appealing to fans of all ages. Breaking into a new market and a new country wasn't easy, but with a leader like Isiah Thomas at the helm, Canadians had an expert guide to show them the way. (Again, though, it's worth keeping in mind that Thomas's CBA critics would accuse him of leading that league into something altogether different: disaster.)

So what do all these accomplishments represent — the winning attitude, the tenacity, the calculation, the control, the leadership — in the larger context of Isiah Thomas's life, and the role of sports in society as a whole?

Simply put, they signify a brilliant example of someone who's been able to assess "the system," has decided what's required to succeed within that framework, and has accomplished the hardest part of all — actually going out and doing what you dream about. For Isiah Thomas, life has been a series of challenges, and he's met each of them successfully. He's taken the sport of basketball, and used it to take himself places he once could only dream about. And by adopting the leader's role at every turn, he's enriched the lives of many others as well.

In the end, Isiah stands as one person who's gotten the most anyone could possibly hope for out of his chosen sport: enjoyment, reward, victory, and mobility. He's achieved personal gain for himself, and led others to their own achievements and their own enjoyments. He's provided for his family, and in an indirect way, provided for people he'll never know. And as he looks ahead to the challenges that await him in the Big Apple, it seems clear that Thomas will have a lot of past experience — and successes — to draw upon.

Ultimately, then, Isiah Thomas has succeeded. Not bad for a kid from the mean streets of Chicago.

Appendix

Isiah Thomas' Career Highlights

Personal
- Isiah Lord Thomas III
- Born April 30, 1961, Chicago, Illinois
- 6–1, 182 lbs.
- St. Joseph's High School, Westchester, Illinois

College
- Indiana University, Bloomington, Indiana (1979–81).
- Averaged 3.5 rebounds per game, 5.7 assists per game, 15.4 points per game in two years of NCAA competition.
- Member of 1981 NCAA championship team, tournament MVP.
- Member of 1980 U.S. Olympic team.
- Member of 1979 U.S. Pan-Am games team.

Professional

- Detroit Pistons (1981–94).
- Averaged 3.5 rebounds per game, 9.3 assists per game, 19.2 points per game in 13 seasons with the Pistons.
- The Sporting News NBA Rookie of the Year, 1982.
- All-NBA first team, 1984, 1985, 1986.
- Member of NBA Championship team, 1989, 1990.
- Holds NBA Finals record for most points in one quarter (25) and most field goals in one quarter (11).
- Shares NBA Finals record of most field goals in one half (14) and most steals in a single game (6).
- Member of East All-Star Team twelve consecutive years, 1982–93.
- All-Star MVP in 1984 and 1986.
- Holds career All-Star game record for most steals (31).
- Retired on May 2, 1994.
- Named Vice-President, Basketball Operations, Toronto Raptors, May 24, 1994.
- Part owner and Executive Vice President, Toronto Raptors, 1994–98.
- Named to NBA's 50th Anniversary All-Time Team (top 50 players), 1996.
- Majority Owner, Continental Basketball Association, 1998–2000.
- Coach, Indiana Pacers (NBA), 2000–2003.
- Named President, Basketball Operations, New York Knicks, December, 2003.

Compiled with data from *The Sporting News 1995–96 NBA Register* (St. Louis: Sporting News Publishing Company, 1995), the Basketball Hall of Fame, and other sources.

Sources

CHAPTER ONE

Canadian Press. "Abdur-Rahim's Return to Draft Adds to Top Talent." *Hamilton Spectator* June 24, 1996: S9.

"Raptor Rookie Top of His Class." *Toronto Star* May 16, 1996: D1, D16.

Clarkson, Michael. "Raptors Test 'Can't Miss' Allen." *Toronto Star* June 11, 1996: C5.

Goldpaper, Sam. "Isiah's Transition Game." *Toronto Raptors 1995–96 Game Program.* Toronto: St. Clair Group: 40–48.

Hampson, Sarah. "Sizing Up Isiah." *Toronto Life* October 1995: 76–81.

Kernaghan, John. "Bullbleep Fills the Air as Draft Approaches." *Hamilton Spectator* May 24, 1996: C2.

——. "Raptors Give Top Prospects the Once Over." *Hamilton Spectator* June 11, 1996: S4.

——. "Raptors Ponder Their Draft Options." *Hamilton Spectator* May 31, 1996: C2.

——. "Sweet Lottery Draw Could Get Camby for Dinos." *Hamilton Spectator* May 21, 1996: S9.

McCallum, Jack. "Going, Going, Gone." *Sports Illustrated* May 20, 1996: 52–55.

Taylor, Phil. "The Mouse That Soars." *Sports Illustrated* Jan. 15, 1996: 54–57.

Thomas, Isiah. "Early Entry, Tough Calls: In Defense of the Players." *New York Times* May 19, 1996: V III, 9.

Todd, Jack. "Raptors Make Their Point." *Montreal Gazette* June 29, 1995: B5.

Young, Chris. "Crafty Thomas Tosses a Curve, Raptors Get What They Want." *Toronto Star* June 27, 1996: C1.

"Raptors High on 'Real Scorer.'" *Toronto Star* June 25, 1996: C7.

CHAPTER TWO
Berkow, Ira. "Isiah's Mom Still Worried." *Bloomington Herald-Telephone* December 4, 1981: 11.
Cotton, Anthony. "Finding a Profit in Isiah." *Sports Illustrated* November 16, 1981: 75–76.
Gawthrop, Anne. "Isiah Talks About Isiah." *Bloomington Herald-Telephone* April 7, 1981: 12.
Green, Jerry. *The Detroit Pistons: Capturing a Remarkable Era.* Chicago: Bonus, 1991.
Hampson, Sarah. "Sizing Up Isiah." *Toronto Life* October 1995: 76–81.
Howard, Johnette. "The Trials of Isiah." *Sport* June 1992: 66–71.
Kirkpatrick, Curry. "And a Little Child Led Them." *Sports Illustrated* April 6, 1981: 15–17.
Leerhsen, Charles. "Isiah: He Came to Pass." *Newsweek* December 14, 1981: 130.
Nack, William. "I Have Got to Do Right." *Sports Illustrated* January 19, 1987: 60–73.
Smith, Bruce. "Isiah Thomas: Eyes on a Different Kind of Court." *Indianapolis Star Magazine* January 4, 1981: 8–11.
Thomas, Mary, with Roxanne Brown. "How to Save Inner-City Children From Gangs." *Ebony* May, 1990: 29–30, 32.
Young, Chris. "Face to Face with Isiah Thomas." *Toronto Star* May 29, 1994: C12.

CHAPTER THREE
Gawthrop, Anne. "Isiah Talks About Isiah." *Bloomington Herald-Telephone* April 7, 1981: 12.
Kirkpatrick, Curry. "And a Little Child Led Them." *Sports Illustrated* April 6, 1981: 15–17.
Newman, Mark. "IU's Thomas Named All-American." *IDS* (Indiana University) March 10, 1981: 1, 6.
——. "Thomas: A Giver Takes a Giant Step." *IDS* (Indiana University) April 28, 1981: 8, 10.
——. "Thomas 'Feels Good' About NBA Decision." *IDS* (Indiana University) April 27, 1981: 1, 6.
——. "Thomas Still Undecided About Going Pro." *IDS* (Indiana University) April 24, 1981: 17.
Papajohn, George. "IU's Thomas 'Not a Fighter'; Undaunted by Adverse Publicity." *IDS* (Indiana University) February 24, 1981: 9.
Ruffra, Peggy S. "Thomas Deserves the Respect Given to a Professional." *IDS* (Indiana University) April 29, 1981: 4.
Smith, Bruce. "Isiah Thomas: Eyes on a Different Kind of Court." *Indianapolis Star Magazine* January 4, 1981: 8, 10–11.
Stauth, Cameron. *The Franchise: Building a Winner with the World Champion Detroit Pistons, Basketball's Bad Boys.* New York: Morrow, 1990.

CHAPTER FOUR
Alesia, Mark. "Thomas Brings His Magic Back to IU for the Summer." *IDS* (Indiana University) April 29, 1982: 11.
Anonymous. "Mother to Get Isiah's IU Diploma." *Bloomington Herald-Telephone* May 10, 1987: B1.

Benner, David. "Thomas Calls Remarks Joke, Apologizes." *Indianapolis Star* June 5, 1987: 33.

Berkow, Ira. "Isiah's Mom Still Worried." *Bloomington Herald-Telephone* December 4, 1981: 11.

Cotton, Anthony. "Detroit Rolls Out a Hot Model." *Sports Illustrated* November 22, 1982: 73–74.

———. "Finding a Profit in Isiah." *Sports Illustrated* November 16, 1981: 75–76.

Down, Fred. "Mavericks Can't Pass Up Isiah." *Bloomington Herald-Telephone* June 5, 1981: 13.

Gawthrop, Anne. "Isiah Talks About Isiah." *Bloomington Herald-Telephone* April 7, 1981: 12.

Green, Jerry. *The Detroit Pistons: Capturing a Remarkable Era.* Chicago: Bonus, 1991.

Hammel, Bob. "Isiah Opens Pro Career with 31 against Quinn." *Bloomington Herald-Telephone* October 31, 1981: 6.

Kirkpatrick, Curry. "And a Little Child Led Them." *Sports Illustrated* April 6, 1981: 15–18.

Leerhsen, Charles. "Isiah: He Came to Pass." *Newsweek* December 14, 1981: 130.

McCallum, Jack. "There's Just No Doubting Thomas." *Sports Illustrated* May 18, 1987: 30–32, 37.

———. "Tackling a Tough Foe." *Sports Illustrated* June 27, 1988: 22–30.

Nack, William. "'I Have Got to Do Right.'" *Sports Illustrated* January 19, 1987: 60–73.

Newman, Mark. "'Kid Millionaire' Bids Farewell." *IDS* (Indiana University) December 14, 1981: 21.

———. "Thomas: A Giver Takes a Giant Step." *IDS* (Indiana University) April 29, 1981: 8, 10.

———. "Thomas 'Feels Good' About NBA Decision." *IDS* (Indiana University) April 27, 1981: 1, 6.

———. "Thomas Still Undecided About Going Pro." *IDS* (Indiana University) April 24, 1981: 17.

Ruffra, Peggy S. "Thomas Deserves the Respect Given to a Professional." *IDS* (Indiana University) April 29, 1981.

Sakamoto, Bob. *Michael "Air" Jordan.* Lincolnwood, IL: Publications International, 1991.

Stauth, Cameron. *The Franchise: Building a Winner with the Detroit Pistons, Basketball's Bad Boys.* New York: Morrow, 1990.

United Press International. "Aguirre, Isiah Have Lot in Common." *Bloomington Herald-Telephone* June 10, 1981: 11.

———. "An Early Retirement?" *Bloomington Herald-Telephone* January 11, 1986: B1.

———. "Mother Has Heart Attack; Game Goes on for Isiah." *Bloomington Herald-Telephone* November 11, 1982: 15.

———. "Pistons Figure to Get Isiah." *Bloomington Herald-Telephone* June 8, 1981: 12.

———. "Sell-out Crowd Watches Benefit." *Bloomington Herald-Telephone* September 20, 1981: 19.

CHAPTER FIVE

Anonymous. "Mother to Get Isiah's IU Diploma." *Bloomington Herald-Telephone* May 10, 1987: B1.

———. "Zeke and Lamb." *Sports Illustrated* November 29, 1993: 11.

Benner, David. "Thomas Calls Remarks Joke, Apologizes." *Indianapolis Star-Times* June 5, 1987: 33.

Coplon, Jeff. "Motor City Madmen." *Rolling Stone* May 4, 1989: 69–72, 96–98.

Cotton, Anthony. "Detroit Rolls Out a Hot Model." *Sports Illustrated* November 22, 1982: 73–74.

Green, Jerry. *The Detroit Pistons: Capturing a Remarkable Era.* Chicago: Bonus, 1991.

Howard, Johnette. "The Trials of Isiah." *Sport* June, 1992: 66+.

McCallum, Jack. "A World of Their Own." *Sports Illustrated* September 30, 1991: 32–35.

"Inside the NBA: Isiah's Staying." *Sports Illustrated* January 21, 1991: 35.

———. "Inside the NBA: Isiah Is Back — Loudly." *Sports Illustrated* April 22, 1991: 84.

———. "Tackling a Tough Task." *Sports Illustrated* June 27, 1988: 23–31.

———. "There's Just No Doubting Thomas." *Sports Illustrated* May 18, 1987: 30–37.

———. "Thorns in the Roses." *Sports Illustrated* June 25, 1990: 32–36.

———. "Engine Trouble." *Sports Illustrated* December 9, 1991: 52–59.

Newman, Bruce. "Out of Sync." *Sports Illustrated* March 18, 1991: 18–21.

Stauth, Cameron. *The Franchise: Building a Winner with the Detroit Pistons, Basketball's Bad Boys.* New York: Morrow, 1991.

Waitzkin, Fred. "What Drives the Pistons." *New York Times Magazine* January 8, 1989: 30–37, 64.

CHAPTER SIX

Anonymous. "Mother to Get Isiah's IU Diploma." *Bloomington Herald-Telephone* May 10, 1987: B1.

———. "Zeke and Lamb." *Sports Illustrated* November 29, 1993: 11.

Benner, David. "Thomas Calls Remarks Joke, Apologizes." *Indianapolis Star-Times* June 5, 1987: 33.

Coplon, Jeff. "Motor City Madmen." *Rolling Stone* May 4, 1989: 69–72, 96–98.

Cotton, Anthony. "Detroit Rolls Out a Hot Model." *Sports Illustrated* November 22, 1982: 73–74.

Green, Jerry. *The Detroit Pistons: Capturing a Remarkable Era.* Chicago: Bonus, 1991.

Howard, Johnette. "The Trials of Isiah." *Sport* June, 1992: 66+.

McCallum, Jack. "A World of Their Own." *Sports Illustrated* September 30, 1991: 32–35.

———. "Inside the NBA: Isiah's Staying." *Sports Illustrated* January 21, 1991: 35.

———. "Inside the NBA: Isiah Is Back — Loudly." *Sports Illustrated* April 22, 1991: 84.

———. "Tackling a Tough Task." *Sports Illustrated* June 27, 1988: 23–31.

———. "There's Just No Doubting Thomas." Sports Illustrated May 18, 1987: 30–37.

———. "Thorns in the Roses." *Sports Illustrated* June 25, 1990: 32–36.

———. "Engine Trouble." *Sports Illustrated* December 9, 1991: 52–59.

Newman, Bruce. "Out of Sync." *Sports Illustrated* March 18, 1991: 18–21.

Stauth, Cameron. *The Franchise: Building a Winner with the Detroit Pistons, Basketball's Bad Boys.* New York: Morrow, 1991.

Waitzkin, Fred. "What Drives the Pistons." *New York Times Magazine* January 8, 1989: 30–37, 64.

CHAPTER SEVEN

Araton, Harvey. "He Bargains as He Plays: Smartly." *New York Times* January 9, 1994: VIII, 5.

——. "Piston for Life, Thomas Silent on Next Role." *New York Times* January 8, 1994: 32.

——. "Players Man in the Owner' Room." *New York Times* October 24, 1994: C1, C3.

Associated Press. "Isiah Thomas Bids Farewell." *New York Times* May 12, 1994: B19.

Brown, Clifton. "Pistons Give Thomas Money and Power." *New York Times* January 5, 1994: B8.

——. "Thomas to Help Run New Toronto Team." *New York Times* May 24, 1994: B11.

Campbell, Neil A. "Raptors Brandish Their First Basketball Catch." *Globe and Mail* May 25, 1994: C5.

Canadian Press. "Thomas to Run Raptors." *Calgary Herald* May 25, 1994: D9.

Connor, Brendan, and Nancy Russell. *Slam Dunk: The Raptors and the NBA in Canada.* Toronto: Prentice-Hall, 1995.

Daniels, Craig. "Rumors Have Isiah Thomas Coming Here." *Financial Post* May 24, 1994: 31.

Goldpaper, Sam. "Isiah's Transition Game." *Toronto Raptors 1995–96 Season Program.* Toronto: St. Clair Group, 1995: 40–48.

Hampson, Sarah. "Sizing Up Isiah." *Toronto Life* October, 1995: 76–81.

Machan, Dyan, and Vickie Contavespi. "Compounded Interest Are Our Favorite Words." *Forbes* December 19, 1994: 244–258.

Nack, William. "I Have Got to Do Right." *Sports Illustrated* January 19, 1987.

Perkins, Dave. "Isiah Thomas Has Tall Order to Fill For Raptors." *Toronto Star* May 25, 1994: E10.

Smith, Doug. "Hoops and Business: A Perfect Match for Raptor Prez." *Toronto Raptors 1995–96 Game Program.* Toronto: St. Clair Group, 1995: 13–17.

——. "Raptors to Hire Basketball Head." *Globe and Mail* May 24, 1994: D6.

Young, Chris. "Face to Face with Isiah Thomas." *Toronto Star* May 29, 1994: C12.

——. "'Piston for Life' Thomas Named Raptors' GM." *Toronto Star* May 25, 1994: E10.

——. "Few Make Leap from Court to Front Office." *Toronto Star* May 25, 1994: E10.

Young, Chris, and Jim Byers. "Toronto Ready to Jump Through Hoops." *Toronto Star* November 4, 1993: C1, C5.

CHAPTER EIGHT

Araton, Harvey. "Players Man in the Owner's Room." *New York Times* October 24, 1994: C1, C3.

Byers, Jim. "Raptors Ready to Present Malone." *Toronto Star* June 2, 1995: C1.

Daniels, Craig. "Off-Season, Off-Court Turmoil." *Toronto Raptors 1995–96 Game Program.* Toronto: St. Clair Group, 1995: 24–28.

DiManno, Rosie. "Ex-NBA Star Now Great Black Hope." *Toronto Star* February 20, 1995: A1–A7.

Farber, Michael. "A New Ball Game." *Sports Illustrated* November 7, 1994: 114–119.

Friedman, Elliotte. "Four of a Kind." *Toronto Raptors 1995–96 Game Program.* Toronto: St. Clair Group, 1995: 87–93.

Kernaghan, John. "Raptor Mania." *Toronto Raptors 1995–96 Game Program.* Toronto: St. Clair Group, 1995: 95–96.

——. "Raptor Assists." *Toronto Raptors 1995–96 Game Program.* Toronto: St. Clair Group, 1995: 31–32.

McHale, Jack. "Sport Verbatim: Isiah Thomas Talks to Jack McHale." *Globe and Mail* January 3, 1995: C5.

Ormsby, Mary. "Raptors Pounce on Malone." *Toronto Star* June 3, 1995: E1, E5.

Stauth, Cameron. *The Franchise: Building a Winner with the World Champion Detroit Pistons, Basketball's Bad Boys.* New York: Morrow, 1990.

York, Marty. "Laimbeer Rejects Post." *Globe and Mail* May 28, 1994: A17.

———. "Thomas Playing Rookie Ball with Raptors' Future." *Globe and Mail* May 26, 1994: E8.

CHAPTER NINE

Brunt, Stephen. "Another Unforgettable First Time." *Globe and Mail* November 4, 1995: A20.

Campbell, Neil A. "Malone Makes NBA Final without Raptors." *Globe and Mail* June 6, 1996: C16, C15.

Christie, James. "Raptors Muster Up Some Magic." *Globe and Mail* December 18, 1995: D1.

———. "Raptors Streak Past Sonics for Third in a Row." *Globe and Mail* November 22, 1995: C8.

Clarkson, Michael. "Malone's Exit Hit by Parting Shots." *Toronto Star* April 23, 1996: D1, D7.

———. "Malone is Saddened About Lack of Support from Raptors' Brass." *Toronto Star* May 1, 1996: E1, E5.

———. "NBA Lockout Edges Closer." *Toronto Star* June 27, 1996: C4.

———. "Raptor Rookie Top of His Class." *Toronto Star* May 16, 1996: D1, D6.

———. "Raptors Give Camby the Nod." *Toronto Star* June 27, 1996: C1, C4.

———. "Raptors' Progress Pleases Thomas." *Toronto Star* October 26, 1995: D4.

———. "Raptors Ravaged." *Toronto Star* March 30, 1996: F1.

Kernaghan, John. "Bullbleep Fills the Air as Draft Approaches." *Hamilton Spectator* May 24, 1996: C2.

———. "Camby Sees Starting Job as Unlikely with Raptors." *Hamilton Spectator* September 10, 1996: C4.

———. "Damon Is Boss Rookie." *Hamilton Spectator* May 16, 1996: C1.

———. "Decision Day for Raptors." *Hamilton Spectator* June 26, 1996: C1.

———. "Dinos Eye Payback for Grizz Veto." *Hamilton Spectator* June 21, 1996: C3.

———. "Raptors Give Top Prospects the Once Over." *Hamilton Spectator* June 11, 1996: C3.

———. "Raptors Ponder Their Draft Options." *Hamilton Spectator* May 31, 1996: C2

———. "Raptors Reach for Camby, Deft Footwork of Thomas Pays Dividends at Draft." *Hamilton Spectator* June 27, 1996: C1, C5.

———. "Sweet Lottery Draw Could Get Camby for Dinos." *Hamilton Spectator* May 21, 1996: S9.

———. "Time to Share One Facility Raptors GM Says of Leafs." *Hamilton Spectator* June 26, 1996: C2.

Ormsby, Mary. "Camby in High Gear, Ready for Camp." *Toronto Star* September 11, 1996: D7.

———. "Raptor Brass Feud Heating Up." *Toronto Star* March 29, 1996: C1, C4.

———. "Raptors Land Free Agent Murray." *Toronto Star* November 1, 1995: E1.

———. "Raptors' Thomas Airs His Opinions on Team Troubles." *Toronto Star* April 4, 1996: C1–C5.

———. "Walker Takes Everything in Stride: 'I Wouldn't Say I'm a Puppet.'" *Toronto Star* April 23, 1996: D7.

Proudfoot, Jim. "Raptors Sticking with Game Plan that Worked So Well for Blue Jays." *Toronto Star* March 28, 1996: C5.

Smith, Doug. "Piston Tribute to Thomas Family Affair." *Globe and Mail* February 19, 1996: C5.

Taylor, Phil. "The Mouse That Soars." *Sports Illustrated* January 15, 1996: 54–58.

Young, Chris. "Bucks Keeping Malone in Mind for Coaching Job." *Toronto Star* June 11, 1996: C5.

———. "Crafty Thomas Tosses a Curve, Raptors Get What They Want." *Toronto Star* June 27, 1996: C1.

———. "Face to Face with Isiah Thomas." *Toronto Star* May 29, 1994: C12.

———. "NBA Teams in Blocks to Start Free Agent Race." *Toronto Star* July 11, 1996: D5.

———. "Raptors High on 'Real Scorer.'" *Toronto Star* June 25, 1996: C7.

———. "Thomas Has a Lot to Learn; Hornets Eye Malone." *Toronto Star* April 23, 1996: D6.

CHAPTER TEN

Anonymous. "Introducing the Raptors . . ." *Toronto Raptors 1996–97 Game Day Program.* Toronto: St. Clair Group, 1997: 49–76.

———. "Isiah Thomas Set to Buy Toronto Raptors." *Jet* May 12, 1997: 46.

———. "Making a Point." *Sports Illustrated* December 9, 1996: 19, 22.

———. "Slaight Expected to Sell Part of Raptors Team, But Not Immediately." *Financial Post* November 16, 1996: 6.

———. "Smooth Play for Isiah." *Maclean's* May 5, 1997: 51.

Associated Press. "Thomas Denies Book Allegations of Gambling Link." *Toronto Star* April 8, 1997: B5.

Berman, David. "Mr. Big." *Canadian Business* June 1997: 59–70.

Berry, Lee. "It's Only a Game." *XXL Basketball* No. 20 (n.d.): 77.

Brunt, Stephen. "Large Lies Undermined the Dream." *Globe and Mail* November 16, 1996: A22.

Byers, Jim. "Marcus Camby on the Net." *Toronto Raptors 1996–97 Game Day Program.* Toronto: St. Clair Group, 1997: 15–20.

———. "Thomas Believes Long Can Be Raptors Leader." *Toronto Star* November 29, 1996: B5.

Campbell, Neil A. "Local Money Key to Future for Raptors." *Globe and Mail* November 13, 1996: C14.

———. "Toronto's New Arena Three Years Away." *Globe and Mail* November 16, 1996: A22.

Canadian Press. "How Much for Mighty Mouse?" *Hamilton Spectator* July 4, 1997: S13.

Challen, Paul. "Hoops Mania." *Hamilton Spectator* April 24, 1997: D5.

Cheney, Peter. "Raptors Owners Vie for Control of Team." *Toronto Star* October 19, 1996: A1, A28.

Christie, James. "New Raptors Owner Slaight Making Plans." *Globe and Mail* November 16, 1996: A22.

———. "Raptor Ownership Battle Down to the Wire." *Globe and Mail* November 13, 1996: C14, C11.

———. "Slaight Wins Raptor Bidding." *Globe and Mail* November 15, 1996: E1.
Cox, Damien. "It's So Far, So Good, but Now Real Work Starts for Isiah Thomas." *Toronto Star* December 28, 1996: B10.
Daniels, Craig. "Recipe for Success." *HOOP* June 1997: 12–16.
DiManno, Rosie. "Raptors' Slaight Is in over His Head." *Toronto Star* August 3, 1997: C6.
Francis, Diane. "Long Distance From Basketball Court to Executive Suite." *Financial Post* March 22, 1997: 31.
Globe and Mail/Associated Press. "Agent Charged in Camby Affair." *Globe and Mail* December 20, 1996: D1, D5.
Grange, Michael. "Raptors' Future Still Uncertain." *Globe and Mail* August 6, 1997: C11.
———. "Slaight Ends Thomas' Bid for Raptors." *Globe and Mail* August 4, 1997: C7.
Harding, Mark. "Big Turnaround Gives Raptors a Little Revenge." *Toronto Star* April 8, 1997: B1, B4.
———. "Raptors Hope to Improve with Age." *Toronto Star* December 4, 1996: C4.
Kernaghan, John. "Raptors Hope to Unearth Draft Gem." *Hamilton Spectator* June 25, 1997: F5.
———. "Thomas Crows as Raptors Land Their Man." *Hamilton Spectator* June 26, 1997: D1, D5.
———. "Walt Williams Riled by Heat." *Toronto Raptors 1996–97 Game Day Program*. Toronto: St. Clair Group, 1997: 33–41.
Keteyian, Armen, Harvey Araton and Martin F. Dardis. *Money Players: Days and Nights Inside the New NBA*. Toronto: Pocket Books, 1997.
MacMullan, Jackie. "Friendly Rivals." *Sports Illustrated* April 15, 1996: 64.
Millson, Larry. "Raptors Backup Proves He Belongs in NBA." *Globe and Mail* November 5, 1996: D12.
Ormsby, Mary. "Bet Stories in Book 'Lies,' Raptor GM Says." *Toronto Star* April 9, 1997: B1, B8.
———. "'Popeye' Adds Muscle Under Raptor Boards." *Toronto Star* July 24, 1996: D12.
———. "Raptors Give the Big 'O' Another Go-round." *Toronto Star* February 14, 1997: C5.
———. "Thomas Wins Battle to Own the Raptors." *Toronto Star* April 22, 1997: A1, A20.
Smith, Doug. "Raptors Creep Closer to Signing Williams." *Toronto Star* July 2, 1997: B1.
———. "Rogers Walks Away from $11 Million." *Toronto Star* July 1, 1997: B6.
———. "Slaight Could Just Say No." *Toronto Star* April 18, 1997: D4.
———. "Thomas' Raptor Bid Rejected." *Toronto Star* August 3, 1997: C1.
———. "Thomas Sets Deal Deadline." *Toronto Star* April 20, 1997: C1, C10.
———. "Thomas Sets Out on Shopping Trip." *Toronto Star* June 30, 1997: D12.
———. "Walker Earns a New Deal from Raptors." *Toronto Star* April 17, 1997: D4.
Woolsey, Garth. "Fans Taken for Granted in Raps Flap." *Toronto Star* April 22, 1997: B3.
York, Marty. "At Large: Thomas Kicks Around Joining NFL Bid." *Globe and Mail* June 19, 1997: D16.
Young, Chris. "No Looking Back for Isiah Thomas." *Toronto Star* October 19, 1996: C1, C6.
———. "Nothing Solid to Back Rumors About Thomas." *Toronto Star* April 9, 1997: B8.
———. "Raps May Be Swingers at Free Agent Ball." *Toronto Star* July 2, 1997: B4.
———. "Signs Point to Thomas Pulling Up His Stakes." *Toronto Star* April 21, 1997.
———. "Thomas Takes Place as True Pioneer." *Toronto Star* April 22, 1997: B1.
———. "Walker Has Plenty of Assistance with Raptors." *Toronto Star* April 17, 1997: D5.

CHAPTER ELEVEN

Associated Press, "Thomas resigns as GM of the Raptors," November 21, 1997.

——. "CBA suspends league play as teams struggle to meet payrolls," February 9, 2001.

CNN/Sports Illustrated.com "Chat Reel: Isiah Thomas: CBA owner talks expansion, integration with NBA."

Continental Basketball Association official web site: www.cbahoopsonline.com

Herman, Steve, "Thomas seen as frontrunner for new Pacers coach." Associated Press, June 20, 2000.

Martinez, J. "CBA Files for Chapter 7 Bankruptcy", Sportslaw News, February, 2001 (www.sportslawnews.com/archive/Articles%202001/CBABankruptcy.htm)

Montieth, Mark. "Thomas fulfilled by Pacers' growth over season." Indianapolis Star, June 6, 2001.

Walker, Richard, "'He abandoned us,'" Gaston Gazette (Gaston, North Carolina), February 17, 2001

CHAPTER TWELVE

Bucher, Ric, "The real reason why Larry fired Isiah," ESPN.com, August 28, 2003. http://sports.espn.go.com/nba/columns/story/?columnist=bucher_ric&id=1605038

Gerstner, Joanne C, "Pacers give up on Isiah: Former Pistons coach Carlisle seen as likely replacement." Detroit News, August 28, 2003.

Harris, Bill, "There's no doubting Thomas' ability." Toronto Sun, October 16, 2003.

Neel, Eric, "10 Burning Questions For . . . Isiah Thomas" (undated). ESPN.com Page 2 (http://espn.go.com/page2/s/questions/isiahthomas.html.)

Reuters News Agency, "Pacers Fire Coach Isiah Thomas." Toronto Sun, August 27, 2003.

Sandoval, Greg, "Knicks trade Van Horn as part of a 3-team deal." Washington Post, February 16, 2004: D4

Sheridan, Chris, "Knicks hire Isiah as club president" Associated Press, December 24, 2003